Critical Perspectives on Canadian Theatre in English

General Editor Ric Knowles

PLAYWRIGHTS CANADA PRESS

Theatre and Performance in Toronto

Critical Perspectives on Canadian Theatre in English

volume twenty-one

Critical Perspectives on Canadian Theatre in English
volume twenty-one

Theatre and Performance in Toronto

Edited by
Laura Levin

Playwrights Canada Press
Toronto • Canada

Playwrights Canada Press
215 Spadina Avenue, Suite 230, Toronto, Ontario, Canada M5T 2C7
phone 416.703.0013   fax 416.408.3402
info@playwrightscanada.com • www.playwrightscanada.com

Playwrights Canada Press acknowledges the financial support of the Government
of Canada through the Canada Book Fund and the Canada Council for the Arts
and of the Province of Ontario through the Ontario Arts Council and the
Ontario Media Development Corporation for our publishing activities.

Cover image: Jin-me Yoon, between departure and arrival, 1996/1997.
Partial installation view, Art Gallery of Ontario.
Video projection, video montage on monitor, photographic mylar scroll,
clocks with 3-D lettering, audio. Dimensions variable.
Courtesy of the artist and Catriona Jeffries Gallery, Vancouver.
Typesetting/Cover Design: JLArt

Library and Archives Canada Cataloguing in Publication

Theatre and performance in Toronto / edited by Laura Levin.

(Critical perspectives on Canadian theatre in English ; 21)
Includes bibliographical references.
ISBN 978-0-88754-934-2

1. Theater--Ontario--Toronto--History. I. Levin, Laura II. Series:
Critical perspectives on Canadian theatre in English ; 21

PN2306.T6T54 2011   792.09713'541   C2011-901765-2

First edition: May 2011
Printed and bound in Canada by Hignell Book Printing, Winnipeg

To the man who followed me to Toronto

Table of Contents

General Editor's Preface

Canadian Theatre Studies, as a formal discipline, is barely thirty years old, yet already it has moved through empiricist, nationalist, regionalist, particularist, materialist, and postmodernist phases, each of which has made significant contributions to the almost simultaneous construction and deconstruction of the field's histories. This series, *Critical Perspectives on Canadian Theatre in English*, was founded in order to trace these histories in volumes focusing on specific topics of significance to the still emerging discipline.

The series was launched in 2005 with the intention of making the best critical and scholarly work in the field readily available to teachers, students, and scholars of Canadian drama and theatre. It set out, in individual volumes, chronologically to trace the histories of scholarship and criticism on individual playwrights, geographical regions, theatrical genres, themes, and cultural communities. Over its first seven years the series has published twenty-one volumes, collecting work on *Aboriginal Drama and Theatre*; *African-Canadian Theatre*; and *"Ethnic," Multicultural, and Intercultural Theatre*; on playwrights *Sharon Pollock, Judith Thompson*, and *George F. Walker*; on *Feminist Theatre and Performance* and *Queer Theatre in Canada*; on *Theatre in British Columbia, Theatre in Alberta, Theatre in Atlantic Canada*, and *Theatre and Performance in Toronto*; on *Environmental and Site-Specific Theatre*; *Collective Creation, Collaboration, and Devised Theatre*; *Space and the Geographies of Theatre*; *Theatre Histories*; *Design and Scenography, Popular Political Theatre and Performance, Community Engaged Theatre and Performance, Canadian Shakespeare*, and *Solo Performance*. I am very proud of this achievement, proud that these volumes have already been widely cited in subsequent scholarship, and proud that, although this is primarily a reprint series, essays newly commissioned for individual volumes have been nominated for and have won scholarly awards.

The series has had several objectives. Each volume has been edited and introduced by an expert in the field who has selected a representative sampling of the most important critical work on her or his subject since the 1970s, ordered chronologically according to the original dates of publication. Each volume has also included an introduction by the volume editor, surveying the field and its criticism, and a list of suggested further readings which recommends good work that could not otherwise be included. Where appropriate, the volume editors have commissioned new essays on their subjects, particularly when these new essays fill in gaps in representation and attempt to correct historical injustices and imbalances, particularly those concerning marginalized communities. The volume topics have also been chosen to shed light on historically marginalized communities and work, while individual volumes have resisted the ghettoization of such work by relegating it to special topic volumes alone.

Volumes 19 to 21 bring the series to its conclusion. They continue to address specific geographical regions, in this case the "region" of Toronto, and particular genres, including community engaged theatre and the Canadian phenomenon of solo performance. As this series comes to its conclusion with the launch of its final volumes in the spring of 2011, they will be succeeded by a new series, *New Essays on Canadian Theatre*, which will make its own contributions to the development of the discipline. Already in the planning stages are volumes of new essays on Asian Canadian theatre, on new Canadian realisms, on Latino/a Canadian theatre, and on "Affect."

It is my hope that these series, in conjunction with the publications of Playwrights Canada Press, Talonbooks, and other Canadian play publishers, will facilitate the teaching of Canadian drama and theatre in schools and universities for years to come. I hope that, by making available and accessible comprehensive introductions to some of the field's most provocative figures and issues, that they will contribute to the flourishing of courses on a variety of aspects of Canadian drama and theatre in classrooms across the country. And I hope they will honour the work of some of the scholar/pioneers of a field that is still, excitingly, young.

Ric Knowles

Acknowledgements

I would like to thank Ric Knowles for his excellent advice, guidance, and mentorship; Playwrights Canada Press for supporting this project; and York University's Faculty of Fine Arts for providing research funding. A huge thanks goes to Benjamin Gillespie who helped select and prepare articles, compiled bibliographies, and served as a sounding board throughout the process. I also want to thank my other research assistants: Miriam Fernandes, Christine McCleary, Alicia DiStephano, Katie McMillan, Ashley Williamson, and Meg Moran. I am extremely grateful for the intellectual and personal support of my friends and colleagues in Ontario, especially those who offered advice on the book as it came together (Marlis Schweitzer, Kim Solga, Jenn Stephenson, and Natalie Alvarez). Finally, this book would not have been possible without the love, patience, and good humour of my family. Thanks to my parents who took care of my wonderful and precocious son, Jackson, whenever I needed time to work, and to Ren, who offered feedback, encouragement, and perspective as the book came together.

Articles that appear here were originally published in the following books and journals: Sandra Souchotte Ketchum's "Toronto's Baby Building Boom" in *Canadian Theatre Review* 21 (1979): 35–46; Robert Wallace's "Growing Pains: Toronto Theatre in the 1970's" in *Canadian Literature* 85 (1980): 71–85; Renate Usmiani's "In the Beginning Was Toronto: The Emergence of an Alternative Theatre Movement in English Canada" in *Second Stage: The Alternative Theatre Movement in Canada* (© University of British Columbia Press, 1983): 22–42; Amanda Hale's "A Dialectical Drama of Facts and Fictions on the Feminist Fringe" in *Work in Progress: Building Feminist Culture*, ed. Rhea Tregebov (The Women's Press, 1987); Alan Filewod's "Erasing Historical Difference: The Alternative Orthodoxy in Canadian Theatre" in *Theatre Journal* 41.2 (1989): 201–21 (© The John Hopkins University Press); M. NourbeSe Philip's "Six Million Dollars and Still Counting" in *Showing Grit: Showboating North of the 44th Parallel* 2nd Edition (Poui Publications: 1993): 101–30; Michael McKinnie's "Space Administration: Rereading the Material History of Theatre Passe Muraille in Toronto" in *Essays on Canadian Writing* 68 (1999): 19–45; Ric Knowles's "Multicultural Text, Intercultural Performance: The Performance Ecology of Contemporary Toronto" first appeared in *Performance and the City*, ed. D.J. Hopkins, Shelley Orr, and Kim Solga (Palgrave, 2010): 73–91; J. Chris Westgate's "Evicted in—and from—Toronto: Walker's *Beautiful City* at Factory Theatre" in *Comparative Drama* 43.2 (2009): 221–45; Laura Levin and Kim Solga's "Building Utopia: Performance and the Fantasy of Urban Renewal in Contemporary Toronto" in *TDR: The Drama Review* 53.3 (Fall 2009): 37–53. Susan Bennett's "Toronto's Spectacular Stage," was first published in French as "la scène spectaculaire de Toronto" in *Sociologie et sociétés* 37.1 (2005): 109–23. It appears here in English for the first time. Jill Carter's "Decolonizing the *Gathering Place*: *Chocolate Woman* Dreams a *Gathering House* in Toronto" and Moynan King's "The Foster Children of Buddies: Queer Women at 12 Alexander" were commissioned and appear here for the first time. All are published here with permission of the copyright holder. All authors also gave consent.

Introduction

by Laura Levin

It's a Sunday evening in February. I'm planning to take my grad class to the Rhubarb! Festival at Buddies. Normally I might take transit—it's a quick ride from my place to Yonge and Church—but I'm running late so I hop in the car. I take my usual route through Little Portugal, then Little Italy, then past Queen's Park. I am not expecting traffic, so I'm unnerved when the cars in front of me grind to a halt. After several minutes of driving at a snail's pace, I turn on the radio to figure out what's going on. Apparently, Team Canada scored in overtime, beating the US for Olympic gold in hockey, and the city has erupted in mad celebration. Great timing for Team Canada; bad timing for me. Yonge Street, naturally, is almost completely shut down. When I finally make it through the Yonge and College intersection, I park, rush past a group of giddy hockey fans pissing in said parking lot, and make it to the theatre just in time.

My class has come to watch *Everything I've Got*, an autobiographical solo piece by Jess Dobkin about her experiences as a performance artist and her growing apprehensions about her own mortality. As Dobkin takes us into her confidence, sharing deeply personal thoughts and fears, as she takes us even closer by inviting us inside her body, the most personal site of her art, her piece is, quite inadvertently, scored with sounds from the street: the honking of cars, hoots and hollers of fans, and raucous singing of "Oh Canada!" The stark contrast of these environments—one insistently intimate and queer, the other decidedly brash and masculine—heightens the sense of urgency in Dobkin's performance, particularly when she recounts past experiences of gendered violence. At the end of the show, she tells the story of a unicorn who fails to board Noah's ark during the flood, perhaps a metaphor for the historical positioning of queer bodies. As the story is told, the sound of nationalist pride echoes in our ears. We hear the mighty triumph, their place in the ark of history secure.

This collision of theatrical and urban space is, of course, hardly unique. The act of viewing theatre is always haunted by "the urban repressed" (Garner 96), by spatial and temporal aspects of performance that are rendered effectively invisible by the traditional conventions of theatrical practice. Stanton Garner notes that "playwatching today forms part of a wide network of social practices, and these practices—purchasing tickets, traveling through the city, approaching the theater façade and marquee, milling about the sidewalks and streets during intermission, eating out—negotiate the urban landscape in a number of ways" (96). In effect, the whole experience that I've recounted—the time it took to travel to the theatre, its location downtown, the positioning of queer theatre relative to the apparently more popular "show" on that night—illustrates the experiential density of theatre-going in the Toronto landscape.

This volume, as my opening paragraphs suggest, is not a book of criticism about Toronto plays and playwrights. It is not an attempt to define a canon of important playmakers and the critics who influence their reception. As Toronto is the largest theatre city in Canada, such a project would require many volumes and would, I think, quickly become unwieldy. Yet while much has been said about theatre that has been "made in Toronto"—some say too much—there are far fewer articles that actively reflect on the "Toronto-ness" of these productions, on the interdependent relationship between theatre and its urban location.

Theatre and Performance in Toronto argues for the importance of this kind of analysis by exploring critical works that situate theatre *within* the Toronto context. As Garner argues, when writing about theatre we need to work against the "occlusion of the cityscape, in order to understand the place(s) of theatre within the city's material and cultural environment" (96). The essays gathered here remind us that cultural economies and ecologies of Toronto are instrumental in shaping the identity of theatre in this city. So, too, theatre and theatricality shape the way in which Toronto's civic and global identity is performed. In what follows, I will outline some methodologies for urban analysis that yield rich readings of Toronto theatre and explain how they can be used to think through the intersections of "performance" and "city." These strategies are not "new," nor are they an outgrowth of the "urban turn" of the early twenty-first century. Rather, as I hope to demonstrate through these essays, those strategies have been central to the history of Toronto theatre criticism since the 1970s.

Historiographical Interventions

The first set of articles in this book explores the history of Toronto's "alternative" or "alternate" theatre of the late 1960s and 1970s, an origin story that continues to dominate Canadian theatre history. Renate Usmiani's book, *Second Stage: The Alternative Theatre Movement in Canada* (1983), epitomizes key features of this type of historical analysis. First, she cites Toronto as the mythical origin of Canadian theatre, as illustrated by the title of her chapter, "In the beginning was Toronto," an excerpt of which is included here. Second, she seeks to define theatre's alternative stance through three familiar tropes: its rejection of Canada's colonial identity and nationalist embrace of "indigenous" drama; its rebellion against an "elitist theatre establishment" embodied by regional theatres like Stratford; and its adoption of an experimental and counter-cultural orientation. Third, she identifies a set of influential figures and companies to anchor this history: George Luscombe of Toronto Workshop Productions; Ken Gass of Factory Theatre Lab; Martin Kinch and John Palmer at Toronto Free Theatre; and Paul Thompson at Theatre Passe Muraille. While one or two additional theatres like the Tarragon might show up on the short list, criticism on Toronto alternates in the 1970s is generally preoccupied with this precise cast of characters and follows a similar narrative structure.

The story usually ends with the "mainstreaming" of alternative thea... eventual coming of age (through owning property). This process is described by Robert Wallace in his article, included here, "Growing Pains: Toronto Theatre in 1970's." "For better or for worse," he muses, "theatre has become business in Toronto, the inevitable result of an artistic evolution in which success is equated with an ever-widening audience." For some, these changes meant the end of an era of experimentation and a confirmation of the essential conservatism of the Toronto theatre industry (Gass); for others such as Wallace, they suggested the encouraging prospect of striking a balance between theatrical innovation and financial viability.

While this critical narrative fostered many emerging Toronto theatre artists, and is still taught at many universities today, this collection offers alternatives to the "alternative story" by putting it into dialogue with other historiographies that expose its blindspots. By the end of the 1980s, this story comes under fire from a number of directions. Alan Filewod was one of the first critics to challenge what he called "the alternative orthodoxy," arguing that the term "alternative theatre" raised more questions than it answered. While it might tell us something about a play's aesthetic content and/or the "nationality of [a company's] repertoire," he argued, its use was rarely accompanied by a rigorous class analysis. Such an analysis would instantly trouble the conflation of radical politics with cultural nationalism, the description of all regional and commercial theatres as Euro-American-centric and politically conservative (when some are left-leaning and champion Canadian content), and the insistence upon the 1970s as the starting point of a political alternative theatre when its roots can actually be traced to the workers' theatre of the 1930s. [1]

This collection takes up Filewod's challenge to consider how the alternative/mainstream binary represses other forms of difference that structure Toronto theatre. For example, it is worth noting that the alternative theatre's appeal to an "indigenous" and "post-colonial theatre"—one that would free Canadians from the tyranny of Euro-American culture—often effects a troubling erasure of the Toronto's *other* Indigenous past. As Jill Carter reminds us in "Decolonizing the *Gathering Place*," published here for the first time, a vibrant Toronto theatre did not begin in Toronto in the 1970s; Toronto has been a site of Aboriginal performance for many thousands of years. Acknowledging this *other* history of Toronto performance, as well as the contributions of Indigenous and non-white artists for the past few decades, reveals the persistent neocolonialism of many Canadianist proponents of alternate theatre as well as their failure to recognize Toronto as itself an extension of urban settler-colonialism. "Because cities have been hubs of broader networks of power, engines driving regional economies, and places where settler populations and resources were concentrated," Victoria Freeman explains, "cities have been important sites where colonial relations were enacted and have played a major role in the development and diffusion of national, colonial, and imperial ideas and practices" (22).

Further, Toronto's alternative theatre did not translate into radical alternatives for women. The official history of alternates is a story of young rebellious men, of heroic male playwrights and directors who banded together to buck the establishment. Not

to be found in these origin stories, but the anti-
...rratives is often thoroughly masculinist. Its heroes
...Burgess 36)—framed in opposition to effeminate
... Sallies" (Bryden 8). The mainstream St. Lawrence
...d Bryden, is "a rich but insecure Toronto hostess, forever
...suitable dresses" (9). More importantly, as Amanda Hale
...icle in this volume, the political change sought by alternative
theatr.... ...to do with gender inequality. She explains: "[T]he great male revolution of the ...ties and Seventies did not improve the status of women in theatre."

This collection is thus part of a growing body of literature that seeks to highlight genealogies and contexts of artistic production that are routinely marginalized within Toronto theatre criticism. This includes recent criticism on popular theatre (Filewod), intercultural theatre (Ric Knowles), Native theatre (Jill Scott), feminist theatre (Dorothy Hadfield, Shelley Scott), queer theatre (Wallace, Paul Halferty), disability theatre (Kirsty Johnston), and, most recently, non-professional theatre (Robin Whittaker).[2] Hale offers an early example of this approach in her discussion of women's performance in the 1970s and 1980s, including Toronto companies like Nightwood Theatre, Red Light Theatre, and Company of Sirens, and performance art groups like the Clichettes (a satirical drag king band) and the Hummer Sisters (who ran for mayor of Toronto in 1982). Hale's article reminds us that women's performance often fails to register in theatre histories because of its location outside of traditional theatre settings. It is frequently staged as "community event," and can take place in urban locales like coffee houses, galleries, and union halls. This physical context is essential to understanding the political efficacy and popular appeal of the work. At the end of this volume, Moynan King returns to the question of "women's place" in an urban historiography in her essay on women at Buddies in Bad Times, North America's largest queer theatre. Echoing Hale, King locates queer women's performance in cabarets, festivals, and street interventions, sites that tend to attract less media attention than shows in Buddies's mainstage season. She also offers a close analysis of the kinds of season slots and development resources often accorded to women and argues that, if we want a full picture of the status of women in Toronto theatre, we need to go beyond the fact of a woman's play having been staged and examine the material conditions of that staging.

Materialist Critique

The historiographical interventions discussed above signal important shifts in critical methodology since the late 1980s. Filewod and King's histories, in particular, attest to the importance of cultural materialism for reading Toronto theatre in context, as a product of socio-political and cultural forces rather than merely as a literary text or as a text to be interpreted theatrically. This methodology draws on the work of Raymond Williams, who sought to interrogate the relationship between what Marx called the base (the economic relations of a given society) and the superstructure (its cultural, legal, ideological, and political structures). Materiality, for Williams, referred to more than economics; it saw culture as a crucial part of the means of production.

Ric Knowles has been a driving force in reading Toronto theatre through a materialist lens. In his many essays and books outlining this methodology, Knowles encourages us to consider not only the cultural conditions that shape performance, but the *"theatrical* conditions through which it has been produced by theatre works, and through which its meaning is produced by theatre audiences" (Knowles and Fletcher 207). These conditions include things like theatre architecture, training of practitioners, rehearsal and production processes, funding structures, programs, playbills, and publicity materials. In his 1993 article "Reading Material: Transfers, Remounts, and the Production of Meaning in Contemporary Toronto," Knowles interrogates the practice of remounting or transferring successful small theatre productions to larger venues. He argues, for example, that a play like Ann-Marie MacDonald's *Goodnight Desdemona (Good Morning Juliet)*, when originally presented by the feminist company Nightwood, read as a subversive, queer work; when transferred to the mainstream Canadian Stage Company, it was received as a universal romantic comedy. Knowles explains: "something changed after the moves to more opulent surroundings. Apparently containment occurred in the new settings: what had been empowerment devices in the first productions became ways of constructing a kind of unity and universality that effaced difference" (74).

If materialist analysis has been central to Toronto theatre criticism since the 1990s, a major theme within this work is theatre's imbrication with the free market. Mira Friedlander described the recession of the 1990s as a time when "[t]he economic sands [were] shifting below our feet with the ferocity of a desert sandstorm" (14). Government subsidies had been shrinking for years, and neoliberal capitalism exerted pressure on companies "not built for profit margins" (14). How, she asked, would small theatres survive when forced to compete with the rising mega-musical—a magnet for large-scale corporate investment—that was quickly reshaping not only audience tastes but Toronto's cultural economy?

M. NourbeSe Philip's contribution here brilliantly interrogates the power of corporate capital in the context of the *Show Boat* controversy of the early 1990s, which surrounded the use of the racially frought American musical *Show Boat* to open the publicly-funded North York Centre for the Performing Arts. Philip situates the staging of *Show Boat* in relation to the city's attempts to boost the local economy, as well as the opening of the US-Canadian border with the pre-NAFTA Free Trade Agreement. She describes the actions of producer Garth Drabinsky and North York mayor Mel Lastman as a grand performative misfire: by using an overtly racist play to launch a new Broadway North, it privileged a profit-driven model of arts and culture over a deeper, community-based understanding of culture. Weaving a metaphor of accounting throughout her critique, she writes: "The black of six million dollars does not appear on the only relevant balance sheet—the one that tallies relations between whites and African Canadians. By my reckoning, this balance sheet remains deeply in the red to Black and African Canadians." Later in the collection, Jill Carter continues this conversation by exploring the pressure on Native artists to create theatrical works that are intelligible to—and easily consumable by—mainstream non-Native audiences, and how this impacts the dramaturgical forms that Native artists use to tell their own stories and to speak to their own communities.

While it is tempting to locate materialist criticism in the 1990s and beyond, it is important to note that many in-depth analyses of the economic basis of theatre can be found in earlier critical works. Don Rubin and Robert Wallace, for example, frequently offered close examinations of funding structures and cultural policy and their impact on artistic work. When looking back at the "Toronto Movement" of the 1970s, Don Rubin reflected on the particular material context that gave rise to alternative theatre: the availability of subsidies and their use by theatre-makers; the growth of professional associations that lent community support; and the creation of publishing opportunities for practitioners and critics (11). So too, this collection begins with a painstaking cost analysis of Toronto theatre by Sandra Souchotte Ketchum, published in one of the earliest issues of *Canadian Theatre Review* (1979), which seeks to understand the artistic and financial impact of the high costs of property ownership on Toronto theatres seeking the stability of permanent real estate.

The City from Above: Urban Geography

I have chosen to begin with Souchotte Ketchum's article on Toronto theatre's "Building Boom" in the 1970s—rather than one of the more familiar manifestos on alternative theatre—to foreground the importance of urban geography within Toronto theatre criticism. An analysis of space is central to materialist critiques of urban theatre, leading us to ask important questions about theatre's location (proximity to specific neighborhoods, areas of commerce, etc.); its relation to private and public space; the costs of property ownership and rental; and its relation to urban development (see Harvie 24–32).

Michael McKinnie's book *City Stages: Theatre and Urban Space in a Global City* (2007) extends earlier materialist analyses by drawing upon methods of cultural geographers to come to terms with Toronto's theatrical past and present. How, he asks, "[did] the particular urban geography of Toronto itself play a part in theatrical production in the city? And inversely, did theatre play a part in the urban development of Toronto?" (4). In his essay included here, first published in 1999, and revised for *City Stages*, McKinnie takes up what historians have called Toronto's "edifice complex," a term originally used to describe regional theatres that became associated with permanent buildings and grand facades. Towards the end of 1970s, this becomes the "alternate edifice complex" (Souchotte Ketchum) as Toronto's alternative theatre companies acquire permanent theatre structures. McKinnie reads this shift from theatre as "event" to theatre as "architecture" (Wallace) by situating it in relation to Toronto's urban political economy. For example, he claims that the factory spaces that were converted into theatres were available because of the suburbanization of manufacturing, and that the "massive property-value inflation that came to characterize the downtown real estate market in the 1980s had not yet occurred" (*City Stages* 74–75). McKinnie explores how Passe Muraille negotiated its relationship to the challenges of property ownership and architectural permanence at different moments in its history, using its home—and its status as heritage building—to assure audiences and funders of its stability and legacy.

Later in the collection, J. Chris Westgate acknowledges the influence of McKinnie's work and the methods of urban geography on his analysis of George F. Walker's *East End Plays*. Unlike many critics who read in Walker's plays a generalized sense of anxiety about modern life, Westgate locates in them a specific critique of gentrification in Toronto, which, in the 1980s, was replacing historic neighbourhoods with luxury condos and shopping complexes, and displacing working-class families. The context of gentrification would have been especially resonant at Factory Theatre, which produced the plays, and which had been evicted from its previous space. In its new Bathurst location, it anxiously defended itself against the "clamour" of developers.

An analysis rooted in urban geography also draws our attention to Toronto's performance as "global city." Susan Bennett's contribution to this volume examines how theatre is used to attract transnational capital within a larger economy of inter-urban competition. She explains that "large-scale spectacles" like mega-musicals and international arts festivals have become important vehicles through which Toronto brands itself; because they attract Canadian and international tourists, they support its performance as a world-class theatre city or, as it frequently boasts, the third-largest theatre centre in the English-speaking world. This marketing strategy is summed up in Toronto's ten-year Culture Plan, published by the Culture Division in 2003, which tells artists that they have important roles to play in the global economy by turning their work into "amenities that everyone wants to see" (18). "We have two tough audiences to entice," the Culture Plan states, "Torontonians, and those who might want to come and visit if they knew about what we have to show. How can we talk to both groups best?" (16). In my collaborative article with Kim Solga, also included here, these trends are linked to the influence of Richard Florida's model of the creative city on urban development in Toronto, a model that encourages cities to move towards an economy driven by "knowledge workers" like artists, engineers, and scientists who will bring "urban cool" to a city and create hip neighborhoods and cultural activities that attract tourists, investors, and more "creative types."

Certainly, as Jamie Peck warns, we need to recognize how these creativity-driven branding strategies and cultural policies "work quietly with extant 'neoliberal' development agendas, framed around interurban competition, gentrification, middle-class consumption and place-marketing" (Peck 741). At the same time, an awareness of this neoliberal context, as well as the role played by the arts in Toronto's performance of self, can allow artists to play with and push at—if even in a limited way—the terms of their inscription within it.

The City from Below: Other Spatialities

In her book *Theatre and the City* Jen Harvie reflects on a potential shortcoming of certain applications of cultural materialist analysis. Because it presents a view of social life as disciplined by larger institutional structures and dominant ideologies, "[it] can paint a picture of the role of theatre in the city where citizens and audiences seem to be inevitably caught in an oppressive, exploitative, uncreative culture with no opportunity to escape its hold" (43). This image of an immobilizing city recalls the model of the city-from-above described by Michel de Certeau, as seen from the 110th floor of the World Trade Center. Looking down, one sees a stationary mass of buildings and a sea of vertical lines—the "*universal* and anonymous *subject* which is the city itself" (94). De Certeau contrasts this vision with the city "down below," where the ordinary practitioners of space carry out their daily lives. In this lived space, "one can analyze the microbe-like, singular and plural practices which an urbanistic system was supposed to administer or suppress" (96), and which contain the possibility of challenging the animating conditions of that system. There too, I would argue, we can see the fulfillment of the cultural materialist project that marshals a critique of hegemonic social structures precisely for the purpose of changing them.

These practices might include utopian performance interventions in Toronto—such as guerilla gardening, subway parties, flash mobs, and other practices discussed by Levin and Solga here—which attempt to transform the city from a place of alienation to a meaningful place of connection. A more overtly political image of performative dissent can be found in Phlip's description of public protests by African Canadians responding to *Show Boat*, as well as less visible "individual and collective acts of resistance and courage" like the mass resignation of individuals working for the United Way, an organization supporting the production.

Knowles offers a final model for imagining the alternative spatiality and political promise of the "practiced" city. In his contribution to this volume, he maps a vibrant ecology that connects intercultural practitioners and companies in Toronto such as Native Earth, fu-GEN, Obsidian, and Cahoots, among many others. This "complex web of interconnections," which operates across urban cultural communities, includes the close proximity of company offices to one another in downtown Toronto, sharing of staff, and collaboration on each other's productions. Knowles describes this ecology, following Mayte Gómez's work, as "a kind of co-operative intraculturalism-from-below," a form of intraculturalism based on everyday lived realities, accumulated alliances, and co-habitations of communities. This shared, "heterotopic space" contests official multiculturalism—what Philip calls "an impoverished definition of culture"—which market cultural difference in the service of Toronto's global city brand.

Finally, although it is not explicitly articulated in these terms, we can read the Native performance work of the *Chocolate Woman* Collective, described by Carter, as a subtle, resistant form of transnationalism that contests not only dominant narratives of multicultural difference, but also Western models of transnational urbanism. As Knowles comments in his previous writings on Native performance work in Toronto, while companies like Native Earth focus on building "intra-national solidarities across cultures, and employ Native and other performers, writers, directors and dramaturges from across the country," Monique Mojica's work has been more insistently "hemispheric" ("Red" 127). So too her project, *Chocolate Woman Dreams the Milky Way*, described by Carter, involves not only Canadian and Toronto-based artists but artists from across the Americas. The Native performance methodology adopted by this group has necessitated a re-gathering of nations within Toronto, the Gathering Place, to access a continental, but ultimately very personal, understanding of cultural tradition and history. The process also required Mojica to travel extensively outside of Toronto, and thus we could say that to find oneself *in* Toronto may require searching outside of it. In this way, the book ends by challenging us to rethink the very idea of "city" as a useful category for writing about Toronto performance. This organizing concept, as the *Chocolate Woman* Collective suggests, threatens to reify geopolitical boundaries that otherwise are made irrelevant by pan-American ancestry, hybrid cultural identities, and translocal experiences of Indigeneity.

Notes

¹ It is worth noting that Usmiani rarely receives credit for beginning her narrative in 1959 with the politically-oriented work of Toronto Workshop Productions, and for discussing the influences of some of the forerunners of alternate theatre—Herman Voaden, Roy Mitchell, etc.—even if she is unconvinced of their direct impact on Toronto's alternative theatre.

² For bibliographical listings (except Whittaker) see Suggested Further Reading in this volume. For Whittaker's unpublished essay on Toronto's Alumnae Theatre Company see Works Cited.

Works Cited

Bryden, Ronald. "Toronto Theatre: *Mademoiselle* est Partie." *Canadian Forum* (August 1978): 7–11.

Burgess, David. "When Cowboys are Ranchers." *Canadian Theatre Review* 51 (1987): 36–43.

Certeau, Michel de. *The Practice of Everyday Life*. Berkeley: U of California P, 1984.

"Culture Plan for the Creative City." *Official Website of the City of Toronto*. 2003. Toronto Culture Division. 26 October 2006 http://www.toronto.ca/culture/brochures/2003_cultureplan.pdf.

Filewod, Alan. "The Spectacular Nation of Garth Drabinsky." *Performing Canada: The Nation Enacted in the Imagined Theatre*. Kamloops: U College of the Cariboo, 2002. 83–100.

Freeman, Victoria. "'Toronto has no history!' Indigeneity, Settler Colonialism, and Historical Memory in Canada's Largest City." *Urban History Review* 38 (2010): 21–35.

Friedlander, Mira. "Growing Pains: The Changing Face of Toronto Theatre." *Theatrum Magazine* (February/March 1995): 14–17.

Garner, Stanton B., Jr. "Urban Landscapes, Theatrical Encounters: Staging the City." *Land/Scape/Theater*. Ed. Elinor Fuchs and Una Chaudhuri. Ann Arbor: U of Michigan P, 2002. 94–118.

Gass, Ken. "Toronto's Alternates: Changing Realities." *Canadian Theatre Review* 21 (1979): 127–35.

Harvie, Jen. *Theatre and the City*. Basingstoke: Palgrave, 2009.

Knowles, Ric. "Reading Material: Transfers, Remounts, and the Production of Meaning in Contemporary Toronto Drama and Theatre." *Essays on Canadian Writing* 51–52 (1993–94): 258–95.

———. "Red Sky, Native Earth: Performing Toronto's 'Indian diaspora.'" *Essays in Theatre* 21.1 & 2 (2002): 119–40.

Knowles, Ric and Jennifer Fletcher. "Towards a Materialist Performance Analysis: The Case of Tarragon Theatre." *The Performance Text*. Ed. Domenico Pietropaolo. Toronto: Legas, 1999. 205–26.

McKinnie, Michael. *City Stages: Theatre and Urban Space in a Global City*. U of Toronto P, 2007.

Peck, Jamie. "Struggling with the Creative Class." *International Journal of Urban and Regional Research*. 29.4 (2005): 740–70.

Rubin, Don. "The Toronto Movement." *Canadian Thetatre Review* 38 (1983): 8–17.

Whittaker, Robin. "Intellectual and Un/Disciplined: Relocating Toronto's Alumnae Theatre Company, from Philanthropic Theatre to the Original 'Alternative.'" Conference Presentation. *Canadian Association for Theatre Research/L'association canadienne de la recherche théâtrale*. May 2010.

Toronto's Baby Building Boom

by Sandra Souchotte Ketchum

In the fall of 1976, just at the beginning of a new theatre season, Toronto's alternate theatres were pulling out of the previous year's tailspin of energy which had signalled the end of a five-year period of intense development and creative experimentation. A re-charging was taking place based primarily on the need for new survival tactics in the theatre and the concurrent availability of a new source of financial assistance from Ontario's lucrative lottery Wintario, which was making so much money that it finally started to give some of it away to non-profit theatre organizations.

This secondary phase, forming a kind of coda to alternate theatre's introductory and formative movement, demonstrated a strong orientation to place instead of just artistic product. Bigger and better theatrical structures it seemed would revivify a stagecraft, especially a Canadian stagecraft, which was petering out of new plays and fresh approaches. Alternate theatres which had moved into old warehouses, firehalls, churches and various holes-in-the-wall were sprucing themselves up and going commercial—though not without an ironic appreciation of the fact that it was an opposition to capitalist/commercial theatrical enterprises that had been the impetus for their formation in the first place. By September 1976 over three million dollars of federal, provincial and private funds had already been allotted to several Toronto theatre companies embarking on renovation projects which would provide them with more professional-looking structures and the security of a place to call home. It was the beginning of what Walter Learning, as theatre director of the Canada Council, was later to call the "alternate edifice complex." [1]

The two biggest projects were the $1.18 million proposal of Toronto's Young People's Theatre which planned to transform a 19th century warehouse into a theatre centre and the $1.4 million Adelaide Court/Cour Adelaide venture which proposed to turn an old York County courthouse, dating back to 1852, into a restaurant/theatre complex to be shared jointly by three small theatre companies, Open Circle Theatre, New Theatre and Théâtre du P'tit Bonheur. As it turned out these figures were early estimates for both projects. The Young People's Theatre Centre expenditures eventually escalated to $2.2 million and the actual cost of Adelaide Court is about $2.4 million (final cost estimates currently vary from $2.3 to $2.5 million).

Accompanying these projects was the $300,000 expansion of Toronto Free Theatre (a figure eventually increased to $500,000) which was raising funds to remodel and enlarge its own historic warehouse and the $150,000 interior facelift (larger auditorium, redesigned lobby and improved technical facilities) of the Tarragon Theatre which also operated out of a warehouse but one lacking historical distinction.

All of these projects were slated for completion by the fall of 1977. The less ambitious efforts proceeded more or less according to schedule but the larger renovations experienced unforeseen structural problems and gruelling fundraising tasks which played havoc with anticipated expenditures and projected completion dates. Even so, the Young People's Theatre Centre had a gala opening in December 1977 and Adelaide Court was tentatively open for business by November 1978, with an official opening delayed until January 1979 when minor interior touch-ups and exterior embellishments would finally be finished.

By October 1978 Theatre Passe Muraille, Toronto's most populist alternate theatre, had also joined the ranks of experienced renovators and fundraisers though somewhat unwillingly. In December 1975 Theatre Passe Muraille had purchased an old factory building at 16 Ryerson Avenue for $100,000. A down payment of $30,000 had come from the large box office proceeds from a satirical show-and-tell sex show *I Love You, Baby Blue* which attracted enormous crowds and a major censorship battle. Passe Muraille ran into immediate zoning problems and quickly discovered that the surrounding residential neighbourhood equated theatre with hooliganism and not culture. After months of solving the zoning issue, making peace with its neighbours and completing basic renovations, the theatre was again closed down by building inspectors just days before the scheduled opening of *I Love You, Baby Blue Part II* in March 1977.

By the time the theatre was back in business, renovations had cost $250,000 and as Artistic Director Paul Thompson tells it, two and a half years of hassles that were so exhausting that by the time the theatre was finally done he just wanted to hand it over to someone else. "We spent three months trying to save the beams while the city people just wanted to cover everything up with drywall." He acknowledges though that the Passe Muraille house style, which seems superficially casual and loose, just didn't work well with the formal levels of bureaucracy; the spirit dynamics were in opposition. Even so he maintains that real estate was an absolute necessity. At the time when the building was purchased more and more theatres were vying for the same rented spaces, budgeting 25 per cent of box office revenues for rent money was becoming prohibitive and Theatre Passe Muraille's roving phase (during which it staged plays all over the city, including on a streetcar) meant losing audiences who couldn't be bothered trying to find some of the theatre's obscure locations. "We're like a home farm now," says Thompson. "Farmers know that the only way to keep in business is to own land. They live cheaply but they're property rich."

The Theatre Passe Muraille building now houses three self-contained theatres on two levels. A small backspace (704 sq. ft.) is the only one with fixed seating. The additional upstairs and downstairs spaces are each 56 ft. wide by 70 ft. long though part of the downstairs area is occupied by washrooms and offices, making it somewhat less flexible than the versatile upstairs theatre which can seat about 250 in almost any configuration. Apart from box office proceeds and grants, the theatre relies on a minimum of $2,500 in rental fees per year. Like all theatres which now own their own real estate or have long-term leases, rental income is a vital part of the budget—those who formerly paid are now paid to. But with more and more theatres or arts-related groups acquiring their own buildings, there may be fewer and fewer companies in need of temporary occupancy and the managing theatres obviously tend to occupy their own spaces at prime-times meaning that they have to rely largely on their own box office success and not that of others.

With the exception of the Tarragon Theatre, all of the renovations in question involved buildings which had been or would eventually be declared historic sites and it was only by appealing to a preservation and conservation ethic that small theatre companies were able to win government and community support for their goals and solicit helpful funding from the Ontario Heritage Foundation. But when the buildings were first discovered by budget-conscious theatre people, they were without exception so neglected and run-down that only those who were desperate or idealistic could possibly have had the least interest in them. When Tom Hendry, Martin Kinch and John Palmer (who founded Toronto Free Theatre in 1972) first looked at the 1890's building which had been the old Consumers Gas Works:

> There wasn't an unbroken window in the place and the grounds upon which it stood looked like a miniature garbage dump. The place was in a hell of a mess, but after we climbed over a wall, waded through broken glass up to our ankles and took a look at the inside we figured it would be ideal.

Today, Toronto Free Theatre is a model example of historic architectural restoration and contemporary design. A two-storey steel and glass addition joins two previously separate old brick buildings providing a large lobby, box office space and a staircase to a second 100 seat theatre which now operates in tandem with the main 250 seat down-stairs theatre. Though the building is actually owned by Greenspoon Brothers Limited, Toronto Free Theatre has a 10-year lease with a renewable option and a good relationship with its preservation conscious landlord.

When Susan Rubes, Artistic Director and Administrator of Young People's Theatre (YPT), first investigated a living tomb of a warehouse on the southeast cor-ner of Frederick and Front Streets in the oldest section of Toronto, it lacked floors, heat and any of the rudiments for human occupation. It did have mice, pigeons and a huge overhead crane which, in a moment of inspiration, was retained and later used to hold up the main stage curtains which slide along the crane's runway shrinking or enlarging the stage area with magical ease. Built in the 1880s and used until 1929 to store Toronto Transit Commission (TTC) generators, the building had been empty for years. It really had nothing but possibilities and Young People's Theatre, which had been touring schools and operating out of borrowed spaces for 10 years, was desper-ate for "a home to come home to."

When Susan Rubes first incorporated YPT in 1966 she was not so much seeking an alternative as filling a void. But her attempts to discover and encourage Canadian actors, directors and playwrights and her interest in documentary-style plays dealing with Canadian politics, sports and colourful personalities gave YPT an operational philosophy in tune with adult alternate theatre. Susan Rubes was also acknowledged to be a determined and dynamic fighter for what she wanted and every ounce of that energy was needed to make the YPT Centre become a reality.

Though Rubes initially wanted to buy the building, that was not possible once it was declared an historic site. A final agreement resulted in the city leasing the building from the TTC for 30 years (with a renewable option) and passing on the lease to YPT for a yearly rent of $15,000 (though most metro-owned buildings catering to the arts [Massey Hall, the O'Keefe Centre, Adelaide Court] pay only a token rent of $1 a year). The centre is also faced with an annual realty tax of $25,000, a load that adds injury to insult because the TTC which formerly owned the building had not been paying taxes to either the province or the city. Susan Rubes is still battling these issues but in the best of agitprop tradition her defensive stance is dramatically simple: "Do people think that the city is justified in charging such rent and tax to a non-profit organization on a building that had not been used for years and that was full of mice?" Aside from tax and rent problems, the budget squeeze, program cuts and the current government policy of austerity towards the arts, Rubes is delighted with her theatre centre. "Physically the building is divine."

The controlling premise of the YPT renovation is of multiple-use space and the Bauhaus design precept of form following function. Visually, the dominating look is of sandblasted bricks, colour-toned scaffolding balconies and railings, high open spaces, a spacious lobby, wide curved steps on which youngsters can sit and a fascinating basement, with storytelling nooks and crannies, that looks like a remodeled catacomb. The 8,000 sq. ft. of usable space in the basement contains work areas for props and costumes, dressing rooms, storage areas, facilities for theatre classes and a small snack bar. The upstairs lobby, with space for art shows and small performances, leads into the main 350 seat theatre. The slope and general arrangement of seating is variable allowing for a total flexibility of audience/stage configurations. Upstairs the second floor contains a projection booth, board room and offices. A third floor houses the main control room, a small space for a marionette theatre (holding about 20) and the Nathan Cohen Studio Theatre with room for about 80 sitting on benches or the floor.

Although YPT is an ideal realization of what it was intended to be, Rubes points out that a centre that performs for children, teenagers and primarily the family has special problems. Children and teenagers are not interested in plays with two people. They go to the theatre in hopes that they will see something really theatrical which means more actors, more extravagant production values and, of course, more expense. On the other hand, a theatre catering to family-oriented entertainment (an average of five tickets per family) must keep its prices low. In addition, she stresses, it's very important that children and teenagers have eyeball to eyeball contact with live actors—that's really what it's all about—but this means an ideal seating arrangement of about 300 seats. Even if the theatre is sold out, with 300 to 350 seats and reasonable family-priced tickets it's impossible to break even.

YPT has only $65,900.49 still to be raised for the building fund. But even with the healthy box office which it has so far sustained, the theatre will probably show an operating cost deficit of $200,000 this season or about $40,000 per show. A Young People's Centre is, by its nature, antithetical to profit or even a costs/revenue equilibrium, explains Susan Rubes, though she can articulate a profit-making situation.

> If we'd had 50,000 sq. ft. of space to work with (about four times what YPT does have) and maybe a budget of $5 million instead of $2.5 million then I would have put in a restaurant/bar complex and a cabaret theatre and it would have been a much larger, more diversified centre. Basically you have to have subsidiary operations. You can't function anymore without those commercial ventures.

Susan Rubes has recently been approached by people from Vancouver and Calgary where major new arts complexes are planned. She advises combination planning; a theatre for children which also has a cabaret space or a large centre which can accommodate theatre, opera, symphony, an art gallery and the real money-makers, a restaurant and bar. The minimum house space for a profit-making theatre, she feels, is 600 seats. "If you're not going to have a large enough theatre (600 seats), then you must have a restaurant and bar because you will be making money from operating the restaurant and bar against what you're losing in the theatre."

The ambitious Adelaide Court project, on the other hand, does utilize some of the business savvy advocated by Susan Rubes. Three theatre companies will occupy the two-theatre building on a co-operative basis sharing a small production staff (a general manager and his assistant, box office person, carpenter, two technicians, a house manager and costume co-ordinator) and general operating costs of about $8,000 a month. The property's atmospheric basement bistro and main floor Victorian bar are being rented to Triomph Restaurants for $3,000 per month plus a percentage of the gross; so that for example if the restaurant grosses $800,000 in a year Adelaide Court will receive $101,000 plus $36,000 rent. The big unknown of course is how popular the complex will be.

In a complicated contractual agreement, each of the three theatres is liable for one-third of the operating costs of Adelaide Court and is entitled to one-third of surplus revenues. Each theatre is also responsible for filling the theatres for one-third of the year. But since the individual theatres retain complete artistic autonomy, their biggest financial commitment is still to their own staff and production costs. An early brief detailing expenditures and revenues suggested that the three theatres would pay a fixed rent of $35,000 per year to Adelaide Court and that with income from all sources (restaurant, box office and theatre rentals) this unique theatre co-op would show a bottom-line profit of $44,000 with a reasonable expectation of $88,000 a year. These are all paper figures, however, and as General Manager Robert Hanforth points out, there are no real figures for Adelaide Court yet because the building has only just opened and final building costs, running costs and even theatre programs are still being worked out.

The problem is that when Adelaide Court was first proposed it looked like a wonderful way of combining historic restoration and theatre consolidation in one multi-use, revenue-producing place. But in the current frigid climate of grant cutbacks to theatres, of budget nightmares, programming uncertainty and box office desperation, Adelaide Court is being viewed with a certain degree of skepticism; suddenly 2.5 million dollars has to be justified and the spotlight is on three theatre companies who have not yet had a chance to prove themselves in a very expensive new location.

Physically the 126-year old structure exemplifies a painstaking mid-Victorian restoration. Doorknobs and windowpanes, mouldings, staircase trim and carpets are all faithful to period and a few structural gems, like an original spiral staircase, have been salvaged after prolonged diplomatic negotiations with building inspectors. The building is also amply supplied with attractive dressing rooms as well as offices, lobbies, an intercom system and its own scene and costume shop. And only about 16 percent of the total square footage is occupied by the restaurant and bar operations.

The upstairs Adelaide Theatre with 1,800 sq. ft. of space seats up to 280 with four possible audience/stage relationships: a proscenium set-up, theatre-in-the-round and corner or thrust stage configurations. There's also a semi-permanent balcony supplying one row of seating which can be extended all around the theatre. Downstairs the 1,224 sq. ft. Court Theatre can also be adapted to four stage configurations providing 86 to 140 seats. Original courtroom fittings, the judge's bench, dock and witness stand, are now removable and will be used for one of the centre's supplementary educational activities *Issues on Trial*, a special lunchtime drama series during which well-known people will be placed on trial with real-life lawyers acting as judge, prosecution and defence while the audience serves as jury. The Adelaide Court enterprise, consisting of a board of directors representing the three resident theatre companies, has a 10-year renewable lease on the building for which it pays the city rent of $1 a year.

The big question is whether the theatres can now supply programming to match the elegance and the aspiration of their surroundings. Jonathan Stanley, artistic director of New Theatre, says he's still in the same old survival game. Though the building itself has received over $1.5 million in grants, his particular theatre has so far only received $60,000 from the arts councils for the 1978/79 season—a situation which he is appealing.

The trouble is that there's an underlying credibility gap between what Adelaide Court represents and what alternate theatre represents. Open Circle Theatre has always specialized in social action, anti-bureaucracy plays in sympathy with the have-nots, not the haves; New Theatre has consistently produced experimental new plays from a variety of international sources and though it has done some quality productions, the theatre is also known for its erratic program scheduling. Théâtre du P'tit

Bonheur, Toronto's only French-language theatre, has a loyal following but has never attracted large segments of an English-speaking public. The present public image of the three companies is fundamentally incongruous to the decorous Victorian building which once again looks like a bastion of the conservative establishment.

On the other hand there is something to be said for commercial success, and Artistic Directors Sylvia Tucker, Ray Whelan, Jonathan Stanley and Eugene Gallant have now learned valuable entrepreneurial skills which may make them the survivors in an increasingly precarious theatrical environment. They've been guided by John Fisher, the managing director and founder of Adelaide Court, who has become a specialist in audience development and fundraising for non-profit groups. The theatre companies are still committed to a non-profit premise. Surplus revenues will be ploughed back to play production and building expenses and as Jonathan Stanley defines it, a theatre with a profitable restaurant business is "like the Red Cross having a cafeteria in their building."

Paul Thompson worries that the big danger of the "edifice complex" is that the building can start ruling you. "What do big fancy buildings do but reassure people that all is right with the world." They destroy the adventure mythology of theatre, he says, and admits that his theatre can get money to sandblast the outside of its building more easily than for artistic purposes.

In defence of the "edifice complex," Thompson acknowledges that if you don't go to the arts councils and funding bodies with a big splash and large concepts and ask for a lot of money you probably won't get anything. You've got to think big. The paradox is that in finally learning to think big Toronto's alternate theatres may also have to sacrifice everything they once stood for.

(1979)

Notes

[1] The sources of the quotations in this essay are unrecoverable—ed.

Growing Pains: Toronto Theatre in the 1970's

by Robert Wallace

> *The geography of the situation becomes so dense, so rich with possible paths, that the instinctive sense of direction fails; and questions of destination are rapidly replaced by the concerns of survival.*
>
> —Martin Kinch (4)

> *In this country there's an appetite to put buildings up, to equate culture with cupolas and glass palaces.*
>
> —Paul Bettis (qtd. in Conlogue, "Little" 7)

In an article published in *Canadian Theatre Review*, no. 21, in 1979, Ken Gass, founder of Toronto's Factory Theatre Lab, concludes:

> Toronto may be a bustling, chic metropolis with abundant resources and an active theatre industry, but it is also thoroughly conservative and not the most conducive environment for serious theatre work. (127)

Gass's opinion of Toronto theatre at the end of the seventies is not as important as the fact he takes for granted: in just ten years, an "active theatre industry" has emerged where little was before. The 1979/80 edition of the *Canadian Theatre Checklist* contains over fifty listings of theatre buildings and companies in the Toronto area, few of which existed in 1969 (Rubin and Mekler). *City Nights*, a weekly entertainment guide circulated throughout the city, offers a constantly changing roster of theatrical events. At least one review of a new play, cabaret act, or theatre piece can be found in the entertainment sections of Toronto's daily newspapers. Commercial ticket agencies with offices in the suburbs are thriving while pre-curtain box-office queues are customary at many downtown theatres. Dinner theatres, cabarets and revue houses flourish across the city, not to mention the taverns, bars, and pubs featuring a wide variety of acts and complementing the legitimate theatres. For better or for worse, theatre has become business in Toronto, the inevitable result of an artistic evolution in which success is equated with an ever-widening audience.

Toronto theatre has also become real estate. Theatre Passe Muraille, Tarragon Theatre, The Factory Theatre Lab, and Toronto Free Theatre—the cornerstones of new theatre in the city over the last decade—have all acquired buildings, mortgages and renovation bills. Modest beginnings such as Theatre Passe Muraille's basement workshop in Rochdale College in 1969 have grown to two- and three-stage enterprises—the theatre "complex" replete with bar, restaurant, and office space, projected if not already built. The "two-stage" season of the regional theatre is now an accepted feature of many Toronto theatres, as are subscription series, preview performances, press kits and, in the case of Adelaide Court, the highly successful home of Open Circle Theatre, Théâtre du P'tit Bonheur and New Theatre, dinner packages and twelve-dollar seats. That a dissatisfaction with the regional theatre's "balanced" seasons of proven plays was a major impetus to the rise of theatres such as these seems to have been forgotten. And the premise that "theatre is event, not architecture" [1] (Press Release, Theatre Passe Muraille, 1969), an attitude which united artists as diverse as Passe Muraille's Paul Thompson and Tarragon's Bill Glassco in the early seventies, appears to have been definitely revised.

The changes—some would say compromises—that have accompanied the phenomenal growth of Toronto theatre during the seventies have elicited considerable criticism from outside the theatre community as well as substantial self-analysis from within. [2] Central to most of the criticism is a disillusionment with the various theatres' acknowledged shift from "alternate" to "establishment" status. The reasons for this shift are both artistic and financial, and worth considering as many Toronto theatres begin to pursue commercial independence. The results of the shift are less clear, being part of the transition which is still going on. That the shift is well developed needs little debate. Gass in his article in *CTR* suggests that the term "alternate" is already archaic and can only be appreciated in its historical context ("Toronto's Alternates"). A legitimate discussion of Toronto theatre demands "removing the label of Alternate from what is now clearly the mainstream" (134). Gass's idea echoes a statement by Martin Kinch who, as artistic director of Toronto Free Theatre, said two years earlier, "[t]here's a need for us to become an institution. At least then people will get out of the habit of calling us a small theatre or alternate theatre or any of those condescending terms" (qtd. in Conlogue, "Little" 7). Bill Glassco, a pioneer of Toronto's "all-Canadian" theatrical stance, presumably agrees: an article in the *Toronto Star*, March 1979, begins with his statement, "[w]e're trying to create a Broadway," and concludes with "I know down to my toes that I want to do a Rogers and Hart Musical, but I don't know when the time is right" (qtd. in Mallet).

Clearly, the time is fast approaching. January 1980 saw six musicals premiere in Toronto's "new" theatres. Although two of these—George F. Walker's *Rumours of Our Death* at the Factory Theatre Lab and Michael Ondaatje's *Coming Through Slaughter* at Theatre Passe Muraille—continue the "serious theatre work" traditional to their respective theatres, the others amount to entertaining diversions of little challenge or consequence. Their emergence and, more importantly, their success, suggests that a major cause of the shift from an "alternate" aesthetic that typified Toronto theatre during the late seventies will continue to affect it during the eighties. Discussion of this cause is best begun by considering Bill Glassco, who as early as 1974 recognized the need to re-evaluate his theatre's artistic policy in light of financial pressure and audience response. After four short seasons, Tarragon Theatre had been acclaimed "the most alert and influential in Canada" (Kareda, "Alternative" 63), "the brightest and most professional showcase for new Canadian plays" (Kareda, "Tarragon"). Such acceptance had its negative effects, however, as Glassco explained when he decided to close the theatre temporarily in 1975:

> Suddenly, you see, we had four box-office winners: French, Freeman,
> Reaney and Tremblay. We had won this special reputation for delivering
> a first-rate show and the more we used our increasingly successful play-
> wright, the more intolerant we all—the audience and the theatre—
> became of experiment and failure. (qtd. in Fraser, "Tarragon")

The freedom to experiment and to fail had been central to the development of
new Canadian plays and to the search for Canadian themes and talents that
contributed to the alternate aesthetic. Gass, in fact, cites "the development of new theatrical experiences, particularly in terms of new Canadian plays, which the regional
theatre system had markedly discouraged" ("Toronto's Alternates" 127) as the prime
artistic aim of the alternate movement. That "new experiences" should become intol-
erable so quickly says less about the power of the new plays than the immensity of the
need that they filled. David French's *Leaving Home* was hailed as a minor masterpiece
not because of its theatrical daring, which is all but non-existent, but because of the
identification it allowed the audience with its characters. It, like David Freeman's
Creeps, Michel Tremblay's *Forever Yours, Marie-Lou*, and James Reaney's trilogy about
the Donnellys, more than fulfilled Tarragon's original intention "to produce new plays
of our own culture as well as possible, to nurture Canadian playwriting talent, to act
as a testing ground and as a source of new plays from which other Canadian theatres
could draw" (Press Release, Tarragon Theatre, 1972); but that it should be viewed as
the prototype for new Canadian drama was more than unfortunate—it was debilitat-
ing, given the demand it created in the audience. The problem, quickly labelled "the
hit syndrome," would have long-lasting effects, the nature of which Jane Glassco,
Tarragon's publicist, suggested in December 1974:

> We've been programmed into becoming an institution. You don't gam-
> ble anymore when you're programmed… If a new David Freeman came
> along with a play that called for a cast of eight or nine, we couldn't do it.
> We couldn't take the risk on a new play, but we'd have to wait until his
> second or third… (qtd. in Adelman)

As Glassco was to acknowledge in 1977, this problem didn't go away:

> In season one I did Canadian plays, because we had to do Canadian; and
> I wasn't thinking of a big audience then because there wasn't any audi-
> ence at all; and when I didn't have that many dollars, I wasn't risking
> losing many dollars. It all made sense then, but it would be folly now.
> (qtd. in Conlogue, "Little")

Tarragon's 1977 season suggested the sobering effects of Glassco's new pragmatism
and marked a significant change in the theatre's artistic direction. Stating "we're at a
stage where it's important that we test ourselves against established work from the rest
of the world" (qtd. in Bale), Glassco included in his lineup three adaptations of world
classics, Chekhov's *The Seagull*, Frank Wedekind's *Lulu*, and Strindberg's *A Dream
Play*. This trend continued the next year with productions of Lillian Hellman's *Toys in
the Attic* and Racine's *Bajazet*. The 1978/79 season also introduced another departure

from Tarragon's original artistic policy: the inclusion of plays, productions, and directors from other Canadian theatres—in this case, John Gray's *18 Wheels*, which had
premiered at Passe Muraille the previous year.[3] Explaining this development, Glassco
might have been summarizing what appears to be his present attitude: "I realize now
the object is to fill your season with the best possible shows" (qtd. in Johnson). These,
of course, are not necessarily Canadian nor are they likely to be untried scripts by
unknown authors—at least not very often. Although both the 1978/79 and the current seasons contain new works by Canadian playwrights, these "risks" are balanced
by shows that have proven themselves elsewhere. In short, the Tarragon season now
resembles that of Toronto Arts Productions, the regional theatre whose consistently
formulaic offerings at the St. Lawrence Centre invariably include a modern classic, a
contemporary British or American play, a period drama in modern dress and a
Canadian play, rarely new.

***

Charting the chances that Tarragon has made during its rise to national acclaim is
useful only insofar as it establishes a historical context from which to view the current
situation of Toronto theatre. Although Bill Glassco is no longer fostering new
Canadian plays and developing new playwrights to the degree he once did, his commitment to Canadian drama, like his contributions, remains integral to his work.
"What's at stake now is how can our theatre remain unique and grow at the same
time" (qtd. in Mallet). His question is crucial and indicates the very real dilemma of
Toronto theatres much more vulnerable than Tarragon to the vagaries of commercial
expediency. Discussing Tarragon's problems with success does little to explain the
financial crisis that all these theatres must continue to face; indeed, a full understanding of Tarragon's policy changes demands the recognition that its funding structure
has also altered drastically during the last decade. Mallory Gilbert, Tarragon's administrator in 1977, explained that "cost per production is two or three times higher now
than it was when we began six years ago" (qtd. in Conlogue, "Little"). Ironically, this
is partly a result of Tarragon's success as well. In October 1974, for example, Actors
Equity found it necessary to reclassify the theatre from a studio operation because it
had grossed more than $3,200 a week. This reclassification required the theatre to
raise actors' salaries to $130 a week; this, in turn, broke the projected budget and
necessitated corporate fundraising when the Canada Council refused to enlarge its
grant to compensate for the unexpected deficit. The scaling of Equity rates to the size
and solvency of a theatre is now common practice and has resulted in higher costs for
Toronto theatres above and beyond ordinary inflation. Government grants, on the
other hand, have not risen comparatively; rather, the theatres have been pressured by
subsidizing bodies to increase their box office and pursue private grants. Although the
arts councils correctly maintain that this allows them to adjudicate theatres according
to their community support, it also makes the theatres dependent on their community appeal. Marketing a theatrical product that attracts the widest possible audience is
more appropriate to television than indigenous theatre; yet this is what the councils
demand. In such a situation, the freedom to experiment and develop new talent
becomes increasingly restricted.

Given such a climate, the increased commercialization of Toronto theatre is hardly as surprising as the fact that experimentation continues to exist to a fairly healthy degree. And that most theatre being produced in Toronto at the beginning of the eighties continues to be Canadian, albeit "safe," suggests the inestimable impact of the alternate movement. Although Ken Gass feels he must plan his future theatre work elsewhere, many other artists are now able to plan their careers at home ("Toronto's Alternates" 134). As Glassco says: "There's so much work for the better actors in this country. You can't hold on to them even for a tour.... They're already in the situation of picking and choosing what they want to do. And it is on them that the new Canadian theatre is focusing.... When I talk of making our theatre strong, I mean making actors survive and grow" (qtd. in Mallet). Although Glassco's remarks are overly optimistic—many young actors still move south in search of more regular work—they reflect a real increase in opportunities for actors, directors, playwrights, and designers who have developed reputations within the city. Actors such as R.H. Thomson, Fiona Reid, Clare Coulter, and Brent Carver now receive "star billing" in production publicity. Plays by local playwrights as diverse as Larry Fineberg, Erika Ritter, and George F. Walker do healthy business regardless of reviews. Innovative directors the like of Paul Bettis, Pam Brighton, and Eric Steiner often attract more publicity than their productions. And designers such as Michael Eagen and Mary Kerr need to travel less to win contracts and recognition. What has yet to emerge is a transfer house that will allow popular productions by such artists to move from their original theatres for a longer run. The emergence of commercial producers like Marlene Smith and David Pacquet, however, suggests that one might soon be found; Smith's successful run of Tarragon's production of David French's *Jitters* at Toronto Workshop Productions in 1979 augurs well for the future. And as extensions of popular plays such as Pam Gems's *Dusa, Fish, Stas and Vi,* or the Miller/Witkin musical *Eight to the Bar* become more common, Glassco's pursuit of "Broadway North" proves more feasible.

Given the current situation, Glassco's switch in focus from the playwright to the actor is also understandable: traditionally, the theatre audience is most interested in the performer. Ironically, this switch is consistent with one of the avowed principles of the alternate aesthetic, at least as it was defined by Theatre Passe Muraille, the other Toronto theatre that has captured the most national interest besides Tarragon. Jim Garrard, founder of Passe Muraille, outlined this principle in one of the theatre's first manifestos in 1969:

> The renaissance of the theatre as experience, as event, demands that contact be made (i) among the actors, who must work together as a continuing ensemble; (ii) between the actors and those individuals termed "the audience"; and (iii), because theatre is a human event, between people and people. (Press Release, Theatre Passe Muraille, 1969)

The most appropriate name for such a theatre, Garrard explained, would be "theatre without walls"—hence Theatre Passe Muraille. Although Passe Muraille acquired its own theatre in 1976, its interest in "a theatre free of distinctions between actor and spectator, between 'inside' and 'outside,' between drama as one art form, music as another and dancing as yet another," survived the move; indeed, Garrard's demand for a theatre without walls should be regarded as a figurative, not a literal, direction. A theatre "whose main reason for being is the link between it and its audience" can exist anywhere, as Passe Muraille's utilization of playing spaces as unconventional as haylofts, auction rings, church basements, and union halls makes clear. What is important is that the theatre "find new ways to reach people and use people… that every project must be approached freshly and that the methods must be rediscovered." Passe Muraille's constant search for the "authentic" and "alive" experience for both audience and performers is responsible for its unique position in Toronto theatre today; of all the Canadian theatre groups that participated in the Festival of Underground Theatre in August 1970—an event which is often cited as the beginning of the Toronto alternate theatre (see Mays)—only Passe Muraille has been able to integrate its alternate aesthetic with a viable commercial policy. Although this has not been achieved without compromise, the theatre still maintains many of its original aims; doing so, it persists as a nucleus for much of the city's experimental theatre.

Most of the credit for this must go to Paul Thompson who, as Artistic Director, assumed Garrard's position in 1971 after it had fallen briefly to Martin Kinch. Although Thompson has allowed the theatre to develop in the multi-directional ways appropriate to its compass-like logo, he has persistently influenced his co-workers with an anti-establishment approach to both the making and marketing of theatre that is still remarkably consistent with Garrard's original intentions. In an interview with the now-defunct *Toronto Telegram* in 1969, Garrard made these abundantly clear: he is worth quoting at length both to recognize the manner in which Toronto theatre has altered in ten years and to realize the ways in which Theatre Passe Muraille has not:

> Theatre must be indigenous. It must be organic… The professional artist is ruining theatre. They think theatre takes place in glass cages. They think theatre is real estate so they build big amphitheatres but they have no one to fill them. We don't need a St. Lawrence Centre. Not if George Luscombe [of Toronto Workshop Productions] can't pay his mortgage. It's important to get out of the theatre. Out into the streets, into schools and parks, into prisons, and apartment buildings… We need a guerilla theatre front, to involve people in real warm confrontations. Theatre in the subways, get a truck and do theatre in small towns, real circusy, grab people in the streets… I'd like to make theatre as popular as bowling. People say theatre is dead but in Nathan Phillips Square we had an audience of 300 standing around on those ramps watching while we did exercises. If we could build fourteen to fifteen people who work well together, who have a dialogue, we could probably turn a lot of people on to theatre. The ensemble becomes the resource. (qtd. in Shain)

Although Garrard's "living theatre" rhetoric now may seem embarrassing to some, its relevance to Theatre Passe Muraille's success can't be ignored. The basis of Passe Muraille's reputation is its use and refinement of "collective creation," the process by which a group of people—usually the cast—collaborates to develop a play through research and improvisation. The development of an ensemble that could "dialogue" about their experience of an event, place, or person was central to such early Passe Muraille hits as *Doukhobors, The Farm Show, 1837: The Farmer's Revolt,* and *I Love You, Baby Blue*; here, actors such as Miles Potter, Janet Amos, David Fox, and Anne Anglin were allowed (required?) to transform personal experience into scenes that were then juxtaposed to become an episodic play. In an interview with *Open Letter* in 1973, Thompson explained his use of the actor as resource in such productions:

> Part of the concept of doing "collective" plays is saying that the actor has more to give than often is required or demanded of him in traditional plays. I think, you know, he should be more than a puppet. He's got a head, he's got his observations and he's quite as capable as anybody else of making a statement or passing on observations. In the kind of work we're doing, we like the actor to really put some of himself in the play. We also work through the skills an actor has. If an actor could yodel, for example, then I'd really like to put his yodel into a play. (Wallace 54)

The discovery and utilization of the actor's skills within the creative process continues to result in some of Passe Muraille's best productions and to make Paul Thompson a magnet for actors from all across the country. That some of these, like Ted Johns or Linda Griffiths, unearth a genuine talent for writing while working with him, is an added dividend. Although Thompson dismisses his function in the collective process as that of "gluepot," both his critics and collaborators are quick to proclaim his centrality. Reviewing Griffiths's *Maggie and Pierre,* for example, one Toronto critic wrote, "[m]uch of the show's charm comes from the stagecraft [Linda Griffiths] has developed with director Paul Thompson, her long-time mentor" (Conlogue, "Maggie"). That Thompson's contribution has been prolific as well as consistent can be recognized by glancing at the *Members Catalogue* of the Canadian Guild of Playwrights: twenty-two collective creations are attributed to Passe Muraille up to 1979 and, as the editor states, "Paul Thompson, as scenarist and director, centralized the shaping of the Collective Creation into a staged play production, by himself where no playwright or other name is mentioned, and as a shared function where a name is mentioned other than the collective" (Mallgren 38–39).

***

Although it would be presumptuous to trace the national interest in collective creation[4] to Passe Muraille, the theatre's popularizing of the form within Ontario can't be denied. In all fairness, George Luscombe at Toronto Workshop Productions had been preparing Toronto audiences for the revue form most typical of the collective product throughout the sixties: but Luscombe's development of productions like *Hey Rube!* and *Chicago Seventy*, heavily influenced by his apprenticeship at Joan

Littlewood's Theatre Workshop in England, always bore the imprint of Luscombe's own particular vision and style. Thompson's work is more varied, marked more by its eclecticism than by any consistent visual or presentational form. This is partly due to the fact that he, more than Luscombe, allows his actors free reign and that he works with writers the strength of Carol Bolt, Rudy Wiebe, Rick Salutin, and Betty Jane Wylie. The Passe Muraille collective creation, rather than becoming predictably stylized, changes according to the interests and energies of its various creators. As a result, the shows continue to attract both old and new patrons, assisted by Thompson's aggressive attempts to reach people for whom theatre is a new experience. Passe Muraille's decision to decline an offer to take *The Farm Show* to New York in 1974 in favour of touring Ontario farm communities suggests the degree to which Thompson was adhering to one of Garrard's original demands, namely that the theatre "get a truck and do theatre in small towns." Thompson's subsequent use of various spaces throughout the city for the staging of plays—most notable in *The Immigrants*, a play devised for Italian, Greek, and Portuguese community clubs—although not always successful, reveals another, namely that "the theatre find new ways to reach people." As Thompson said in 1973, "I'm interested in discovering the audience. I think the really interesting people are the ones who don't go to theatres" (Wallace 64).

Thompson's fear of becoming "locked in" or creatively restricted by any one dramatic form or theatrical style was well developed as early as 1972. A statement he made that year, as well as being prophetic of the current situation, reveals his awareness of "the hit syndrome" and suggests that an adherence to social and artistic integrity is still commercially viable:

> Once you have one show that works you start looking for another. The Factory has had three light comedies in a row. Within a year four or five *Brussels Sprouts* will be offered to it. Canada's answer to Neil Simon! Tarragon Theatre and Factory are going to have to turn somewhere. If you become dependent on a box office you become dependent on the success of your shows. Or dependent on subsidization. That's not the point of Passe Muraille... If you're going to work that way, you work towards acceptance. The Passe Muraille is like an art gallery—it changes with each exhibition. (qtd. in Whittaker)

Although Passe Muraille's production history is not without shows that pander to commercial tastes and expectations (as, for example, *I Love You, Baby Blue 2*—a blatantly empty attempt to exploit the name and publicity of their earlier success), it demonstrates a consistent avoidance of revivals and extensions that suggests the theatre's adherence to more than commercial aims. Money, of course, has always been as much a problem in Toronto as anywhere else. Indeed, *I Love You, Baby Blue* was allowed to run for months to capitalize on its attempted closure by the Toronto morality squad and the interest that ensued. The show was accused of "sexploitation" and, because of its extended run, is sometimes used to argue that Passe Muraille would "go commercial" if it only could. Such arguments usually fail to recall that *Futz*, Passe Muraille's very first production in 1969, also was invaded by the Toronto Morality

Squad: "daring" and "controversial" are consistently applicable to this theatre even as "obscene" is not. And, as Thompson explained in an interview with the *Canadian Theatre Review*, *Baby Blue* was quite in keeping with the theatre's policy:

> Much of the work at Passe Muraille is built upon a kind of idealism. What ties people together is the exploration of a theme and the challenge of exploring that theme in a theatrical way. For *I Love You, Baby Blue* we took the techniques of *The Farm Show* and tried to apply them to the sexual fascination of a big city. We had a feeling that if it worked it would be a hit and a lot of people would come and see it—but *our* definition of a hit did not remotely anticipate the potential of *Baby Blue*. As an intense theatrical experience *1837: The Farmer's Revolt* was just as important, perhaps more important in political terms. But in *Baby Blue*, because of the taboos and the unavoidable personal nature of one's own sexuality, the doors were really opened. I don't think there was any attempt to see what we could do with the morality squad... (Thompson 8)

That the proceeds from *I Love You, Baby Blue* were used for the down payment on Passe Muraille's permanent home might seem less than idealistic if it were not for what the theatre has been able to accomplish because of the acquisition of a permanent space. Thompson's organization of Passe Muraille's warehouse into different types and sizes of performing areas has allowed him to expand experimentation and pay for it at the same time. Playing commercial successes like *Les Maudit Anglais* and *Billy Bishop Goes to War* on the main stage has financed an ambitious programme of new works on the two smaller stages that facilitates Passe Muraille's support of new talent and maintains its interest in "theatre as experience."

In a time typified by the depletion of investment funds, Theatre Passe Muraille's research and development function becomes increasingly important. The theatre's original seed programme, by which unknown artists were given minimal budgets and rehearsal space with which to develop a show, resulted in a series of readings, workshops and showcases throughout the city, twenty-one of which are described under Theatre Passe Muraille in the 1977 and 1978 editions of *Canada on Stage*; at least three of these went on to main-stage productions. More importantly, they provided a focus for what might be termed Toronto's "new alternative," a community of artists and spaces still available to experimentation and failure who attract an audience interested in less mainstream work. That some of these artists, notably Cheryl Cashman, Michael Hollingsworth, and Margaret Dragu, have already gained more "establishment" reputations is an inevitable progression; that others such as Marien Lewis and David Type fight such mainstream co-option is just as worthwhile. The success of the seed programme has resulted in its expansion into Passe Muraille's New Works programme which, under the directorship of Clarke Rogers, has seen workshops of twenty to thirty productions over the last year; the arts councils' enthusiasm for the project is evident in their increased subsidization, with funds specifically ear-marked for new works. Clearly, they recognize that Passe Muraille's discovery of such innovative artists as John Palmer and Hrant Alianak in the early seventies and its introduction of groups like Newfoundland's Codco and Saskatoon's Twenty-fifth Street House to Toronto audiences throughout the decade is a tradition that must be supported if the city's theatre is to creatively continue.

Passe Muraille's ability to simultaneously finance experimentation and attract a popular audience is its major accomplishment and what distinguishes it from the Factory Theatre Lab, the other Toronto theatre actively involved in the development of new plays and playwrights. The Factory's reputation as "the home of the Canadian playwright" has declined in recent years from its ascendancy during the early seventies when it staged such highly-acclaimed productions as Herschel Hardin's *Esker Mike and His Wife, Agiluk* and Larry Kardish's *Brussels Sprouts* to the point where recent productions like Ken Gass's *Winter Offensive* and George F. Walker's *Rumours of Our Death* have been reviewed as "trash." Such irresponsible "criticism" fails to suggest, let alone support, the valuable contribution of this theatre's artistic policy which, by nurturing new work regardless of audience expectations and critical response, continues to challenge and enrich Toronto theatre. The Factory's refusal to bow to commercial expediency following its early string of hits is well maintained by its current workshop programme which, under the industrious guidance of Bob White, remains adamantly "fringe." The ideal that the Factory should "pursue unconventional programming and [a] restless search for something indigenous and unique" (Gass, "Perspective") has plagued the theatre since Ken Gass founded it in May 1970. Rather than change his intentions when the going became rough, Gass insisted that the Factory "remain eclectic and not settle into formula programming" ("Perspective"). Writing in 1975 about his difficulties with this approach, Gass could be summarizing what is still the Factory's predicament:

> there has always been a discrepancy between what the public (including the critics and funding agencies) recognized about the Factory and what we considered our most important accomplishments. The public has wanted recognizable products, more hits, and a clearly defined policy. They can't pin us down. The Factory has been preoccupied with the search itself, with the process, with experimentation, yet with an outward energy that often borders on proselytism. Somehow in the midst of financial turmoils, bureaucratic battles with government councils, the unions, city inspectors, the powerful pigeon-hole mentality of critics, we have tried not to compromise our ideals. ("Perspective")

The Factory Theatre Lab's inability to find "the Canadian middle road [between] meaningful experimentation on one hand [and] public acceptability on the other" (Gass, "Toronto's Alternates" 127) has resulted in its loss of profile in the daily press but not its status in the theatre community. Nor has it disappointed a consistently loyal audience eager to participate in the theatre's experiments despite negative reviews. One of the most positive signs that Toronto theatre is surviving commercialization in early 1980 is that *Rumours of Our Death* has been so popular.[5] Although it relies on music and a popular rock performer for its appeal, the play is by no means "safe"; publishing the script as a "work-in-progress," *Canadian Theatre Review* terms it "a Jarry-esque allegory of man's incoherence towards man, of a mythical country's incoherence towards its mythical people, of a not-so-exotic world's incoherence towards itself. An allegory of national diseases…" (Rubin, "Epigraph"). That such a play could develop a following attests to the Factory's continued viability and suggests that "pioneering" principles are never obsolete.

***

That they are demanding, however, is a fact that even such a brief look at Toronto theatres in the seventies makes clear. By 1975 most of the theatres that had emerged during the first half of the decade were suffering not only financial problems but also artistic uncertainty and creative fatigue. As Martin Kinch, co-founder with John Palmer and Tom Hendry of the Toronto Free Theatre in 1972, put it: "There seemed to be creative exhaustion everywhere. We had filled the first promise and many of us simply didn't know where to go… There were other attendant problems too. The arrival of CBC drama attracted a lot of actors and scripts away from the live theatre and for the first time we were having to scrounge" (qtd. in Fraser, "Revolution's Over"). This latter problem was particularly detrimental to Toronto Free Theatre, which saw as its mandate the development of a permanent company of actors who could work with a small core of writers and directors "to build a repertoire of representative Canadian work" (qtd. in Hendry). In 1972, Kinch suggested, "These days, almost any given Canadian play can get a production. But there is no process of development. The Factory Theatre Lab develops playwrights, Theatre Passe Muraille develops directors and we wanted to develop a relationship between actor, director and playwright in a residence sense" (qtd. in Kareda, "Alternative"). Within three years, Free Theatre had achieved its goal, gathering a marvellous pool of actors— including Saul Rubinek, Chapelle Jaffe, Brenda Donohue, Booth Savage, Nick Mancuso, David Bolt, and R.H. Thomson—who contributed to a succession of hits such as John Palmer's *The End*, Kinch's *Me?*, Carol Bolt's *Gabe* and *Red Emma*, and Michael Ondaatje's *The Collected Works of Billy the Kid*. But by 1975, these actors and, to a lesser degree, Palmer and Kinch, were receiving attractive offers elsewhere. Recognizing how the new theatres were affecting the mainstream, Kinch began a reevaluation of Free Theatre's aims, concurrent with Glassco's sabbatical at Tarragon, Thompson's move to a permanent home, and Gass's period of redefinition. His conclusion made as much sense then as it does now; it also foreshadowed the creative conundrum which continues to inhibit Free Theatre's realization of its potential:

> What should be happening now, and is to a small extent, is that the people—the writers and actors and directors—who have worked their way up in the Toronto theatres, be allowed into the major theatrical institutions of the country. That will make room for the new ideas coming up here, which is what will keep our particular perspective alive and help renew the larger institutions. If this process doesn't happen, I don't really like to think of what will become of places like the Free Theatre… (qtd. in Fraser, "Revolution's Over")

Within two years, many of Kinch's actors were working elsewhere. Palmer had moved to New York. Kinch, in his own evaluation of the Toronto theatre climate published in *This Magazine*, revealed his growing despair about the situation. Although his words address the plight of many Toronto theatres in the late seventies, they are most applicable to his own experience at Free Theatre:

> Theatres allowed themselves to announce entire seasons long before the announced plays were actually in existence. Panic-decisions were made to fill the holes when the promised works failed to appear. In the rush, and the acceptance of rigid opening-night dates, supposedly dictated by audience needs, many plays opened in the second draft which should have opened in the fifth. For the playwrights, on whose output the growth of the theatres depended, the pressures resulted in quick debilitation. Some developed blocks. Some moved rapidly towards formulaic repetition. Very few were able to develop and mature in this atmosphere. Fewer could produce the deep and resonant images needed for the creation of strong dramatic experience. (Kinch 6)

Although Free Theatre offered some exciting fare during the second half of the seventies—notably the collective creation *The Fits* and George F. Walker's *Zastrozzi*—its focus became increasingly diffuse. In 1978, artistic direction fell to William Lane, whose productions of new British and American playwrights such as William Hauptman and Sam Shepard caused more interest than those of new Canadian writers like Tom Walmsley or curiosities such as Brecht's *Baal* and Somerset Maugham's *Rain*. Guest productions such as Centaur Theatre's *Nothing to Lose* by David Fennario and touring shows like *Paper Wheat* or the Newfoundland Mummers's *Some Slick* were used to round out subscription seasons. 1980 began with a transfer from Adelaide Court of Erika Ritter's hit comedy, *Automatic Pilot*, in a production directed by Lane for New Theatre. Not only has the creation of "a repertoire of representative Canadian work" apparently been abandoned, but the development of a "small flexible group of artists and other theatre workers who are united by a sense of mutual respect, faith and belief" (qtd. in Hendry) seems, temporarily at least, to have been dropped. Although there is considerable validity to Kinch's notion that "the Canadian play and a commitment to its production will mean increasingly less if its mere presence is considered a success," its mere absence does not insure the theatre's return to "its initially serious purposes" (8). Free Theatre's current situation, in fact, hints at the opposite effect: that the theatre, "in its desire for a short term hit, abnegates its more serious function—the imaginative exploration of our life and our reality." As Free Theatre's actors, directors, and writers become interchangeable with companies as expert as New Theatre, Open Circle Theatre, The Phoenix Theatre, Young People's Theatre, and Theatre Plus, as well as Toronto Workshop Productions, Toronto Arts Productions and the other once "alternate" theatres with which it has shared the limelight, it loses the unique approach and perspective that was its raison d'être. That Toronto's burgeoning theatre market may support such a change is probably true; that it should require it would mean an unfortunate loss for Canadian drama.

It is just such a loss that makes the shift from an alternate aesthetic problematic. With financial considerations increasingly controlling the size, nature, and appearance of new plays, enthusiasm for the possibility that Toronto theatres may achieve commercial independence in the eighties is half-hearted. Kinch's fear in 1976 that "the audience has stopped growing and is diminishing" (3) appears to have been unwarranted; its corollary, that the audience is expanding, can be seen as equally disturbing. Although Bill Glassco is probably correct when he asserts that "the days of the production company are passing" (qtd. in Mallet), the possibility that Free Theatre might become merely a transfer house for productions such as Tarragon's is disturbing. Certainly such a space would contribute to the greater solvency of some Toronto theatres; but that it "would also clear the already available spaces for a wider range of new works" (8), as Kinch hoped in 1976, is unlikely. What is a surety, however, is the increased co-operation amongst all the Toronto theatres. A grouping of various theatres to protest the *Toronto Star's* hiring of Gina Mallet as drama critic in 1976 achieved self-recognition of communal strength, if nothing else. The cost sharing of co-productions has now become a reality that may mean survival for Toronto's smallest theatres. Unless they cynically pursue commercial status in the manner of the phenomenally successful Toronto Truck Theatre by mounting plays like Agatha Christie's *The Mousetrap*, or attach themselves to a sponsoring "institution" like Passe Muraille for the duration of a production, there are few alternatives to amalgamation. The possibility that a new, small, and experimental theatre could now emerge and survive becomes increasingly slight. Paul Bettis, Artistic Director of Theatre Second Floor, one of the most original theatres to develop in Toronto during the seventies, closed his theatre in 1979, explaining "I don't want to get bigger and I don't want to charge more at the door" (qtd. in Conlogue, "Little"). As Bettis's attitude becomes a rarity, the complexion of Toronto theatre in 1990 grows indeterminable. That it will survive is indisputable; how is another matter.

(1980)

Notes

[1] Press release available through the Theatre Department, Metro Toronto Public Library, whose "vertical files" of press clippings and information on Canadian theatre history and criticism are an invaluable resource for the student of Canadian theatre.

[2] For an example of the former, see Rubin, "Sleepy"; of the latter, see Kinch.

[3] This trend has also been continued with, for example, Jack Blum's production of Joe Wiesenfeld's *Spratt* (April 1978) and Guy Sprung's productions of Tom Walmsley's *Something Red* (February 1980).

[4] This is now so developed that two festivals by Canadian theatre groups involved with collective creation have been held. See Zientara.

[5] This was accomplished by the ten-member company taking over co-operative responsibility for the extension [of the run], working without pay and sharing the profits. See "People" for a report.

Works Cited

Adelman, Sid. "Eye on Entertainment." *Toronto Star* 9 December 1974: D4.

Bale, Doug. "Toronto's Tarragon Theatre Faces Challenging Dilemma." *London Free Press* 12 February 1977: 30.

Conlogue, Ray. "Little Theatres Try to Get Out of the Wilderness." *The Globe and Mail* 15 August 1977: 7.

———. "Maggie and Pierre Shows Power, Finesse and Insight." *The Globe and Mail* 15 February 1980: 17.

Fraser, John. "The Revolution's Over in Underground Theatre." *The Globe and Mail* 27 August 1975: 29.

———. "Tarragon, Glassco Back in Business." *The Globe and Mail* 3 June 1976: 29.

Gass, Ken. "Perspective." *Theatre Notebook* 1.1 (1975): 3.

———. "Toronto's Alternates: Changing Realities." *Canadian Theatre Review* 21 (1979): 127–35.

Hendry, Tom. "The Stage." *Toronto Citizen* 27 January 1972: 13.

Johnson, Bryan. "Glassco's Mission a Matter of Trust." *The Globe and Mail* 16 September 1978: 33.

Kareda, Urjo. "Alternative Theatre Offers Hope For the Future." *Toronto Star* 16 September 1972: 63.

———. "Tarragon's Short History Buoyant with Success." *Toronto Star* 8 September 1973: E3.

Kinch, Martin. "Canadian Theatre: In For the Long Haul." *This Magazine* 10.5–6 (November-December 1976): 3–8.

Mallet, Gina. "Tarragon Theatre Boss Rolls Up String of Hits." *Toronto Star* 17 March 1979: D1.

Mallgren, Chris, ed. *Members Catalogue: Canadian Guild of Playwrights* 1 (1979): 38–39.

Mays, John Bentley. "Taking it on the Road." *Maclean's* 92 (June 1979): 60.

"People." *Maclean's* 93 (25 February 1980): 27.

Rubin, Don. Epigraph preceding *Rumours of Our Death. Canadian Theatre Review* 25 (1980): 43.

———. "Sleepy Tunes in Toronto." *Canadian Theatre Review* 20 (1978): 93–95.

Rubin, Don and Mimi Mekler, eds. *Canadian Theatre Checklist.* Toronto: CTR Publications, 1979. 11–24.

Press Release. Tarragon Theatre, 1972.

Press Release. Theatre Passe Muraille, 1969.

Shain, Merle. "Pursuing the Need for a Guerilla Theatre." *Toronto Telegram* 1 March 1969: Sec. 3, 2.

"Tarragon Will Take Time Off." *Toronto Sun* 13 March 1975: 19.

Thompson, Paul. "The Trial of Baby Blue." Interview with Ted Johns. *Canadian Theatre Review* 13 (1977): 7–17.

Wallace, Bob. "Paul Thompson at Theatre Passe Muraille: Bits and Pieces." *Open Letter* 2.7 (1974): 49–71.

Whittaker, Herbert. "Artist's Sets Give Play Unique Look." *The Globe and Mail* 22 May 1972: 20.

Zientara, Jerry. "Theatre Synergy: A Collective Festival." *Canadian Theatre Review* 24 (1979): 114–21.

from **In the Beginning was Toronto:**
The Emergence of an Alternative
Theatre Movement in English Canada

by Renate Usmiani

Canadian theatre history offers evidence for the existence of antecedents to the alternative theatre movement, along the lines of both introspective/poetic and committed/political theatre; however, there is as yet no demonstrable influence of these developments, which mostly took place in the 1930s, upon the new wave. Only now, at a time when the alternative theatre movement itself is already on the decline, are these antecedents being discovered by historians of the theatre. And there is no evidence that the leaders of the movement were aware of these antecedents at all. Nevertheless, it is interesting to glance briefly at just what sort of a Canadian background there was for alternative theatre, even if a definite hiatus separates the past from the more recent developments.

On the side of political theatre, a militant workers' theatre existed in French Canada as early as the nineteenth century, and in English Canada, from the 1930s on. The French Canadian workers' theatre operated in conjunction with the Typographical Association of Quebec City, Canada's first labour organization, from the 1830s on. These labour union plays were either contemporary satires and plays of social criticism or classical plays which carried a subversive message: for example, a production of Voltaire's *The Death of Caesar* in 1839, which led to violent audience reaction and the arrest of the man responsible for the production, a newspaper editor by the name of Napoléon Aubain.

In English Canada, workers' theatre began with the rise of the Progressive Arts Clubs in the major cities; the first such club was founded in Toronto in 1931. From 1932 on, the Workers' Experimental Theatre (later known simply as The Workers' Theatre) set itself up as a deliberate antithesis to bourgeois theatre. Its slogan was "Art is a weapon," and its goal, as described in the socialist newspaper, *Masses*, was to produce "[p]lays that would fill a deep need in the hearts of a working class audience, and etch there the fundamental ideas of a revolutionary philosophy of life" (qtd. in Souchotte, "Canada's Workers" 170). The plays themselves followed the pattern of agitprop everywhere, ranging from mass recitation to socialist realism. Rehearsal and performance took place wherever a space could be found—in parks, labour halls, on the backs of trucks, or even on street corners. A minimum of props and costumes was used, a frequent uniform being a black sateen shirt with a red kerchief. The most ambitious of these productions was a six-act play collectively produced by four

authors and entitled *Eight Men Speak.*[1] Besides its social and political goals, the
Workers' Theatre also served as a form of protest against the regular fare of British
West End comedies served up by the mainstream Canadian theatres—the same
protest that was repeated forty years later with the members of alternative theatre
groups.

On the side of introspective, or poetic theatre, two pioneers deserve mention: Roy
Mitchell, whose almost unknown theories proved truly prophetic; and Herman
Voaden's plays of symphonic expressionism. Voaden, playwright and visionary, fought
a losing battle throughout the 1930s to make his Canadian contemporaries aware of
the backward state of theatre in this country. A violent opponent of naturalism,
Voaden developed a highly poetic style which he termed "symphonic expressionism"
and which incorporated choral recitation, music, and choreography into the drama.
His principles of total theatre were close to Wagner's. As he wrote in a manifesto of
1929, "If our stage is to save itself, it must no longer be the scene for the actor and the
producer in the narrow sense… it must… embrace the playwright, the student, the
thinker, the poet, the musician, the designer and the artist" (Voaden). Voaden, it
turned out, was a prophet who was sadly ahead of his time; in response to his manifesto, the British dramatist Harold Brighouse published a note, which appeared in the
Toronto Globe, in which he suggested Canadians would do better to stick to a volume
of plays for amateurs, rather than follow Voaden's ambitious theories. Roy Mitchell
did not fare much better. In 1929, he published a book entitled *Creative Theatre*, in
which he developed his ideas of theatre as a mystical experience. Although much of
his work sounds excessively romantic and somewhat naive to a contemporary reader,
his basic ideas are surprisingly modern. He realized the deadly effect of American
commercialism upon the theatre, and he insisted that another way must be found if
theatre was to fulfill its essential function. He saw the importance of the link between
a theatre and the community within which it operates and he realized the significant
part played by the audience within the total theatre experience. His evocation of the
ideal theatre of the future sounds exactly like the goals described by alternative theatre
leaders forty years later:

> Not a state theatre with its burden of high-salaried incompetents… not
> a civic theatre to be tossed about by politicians. Not a coterie theatre to
> be the vehicle of literati and esthetes. Just a forthright, ingenious, native,
> friendly theatre, living for and by a wide enough circle of friends to sup-
> port it, rather as a church lives, or a club… Such a house, then, will be
> built in the expectation that people may come to the theatre to spend the
> evening, may possibly arrive early, may stay late, may like to eat or per-
> haps dance after the play. (Mitchell 124)

From the vantage point of the 1980s, the prophetic character of Mitchell's work
is indeed striking; and it is a sad comment on the cultural scene of Canada that the
importance of his ideas was never realized, not even by the proponents of alternative
theatre some forty years later, who followed in his footsteps without being aware of
the fact. Alternative theatre in Canada is definitely a phenomenon of the 1970s, a

movement of protest and rebellion against th[...]
emergence reflects the development of a new [...]
influenced by the European and American preced[...]
in the text of an anonymous manifesto, passionate [...]
was read on the occasion of the premiere performanc[...]
revue *Wouf wouf* at the Gesù theatre in Montreal on Nove[...]

> Le fait d'être assis sur un siège de théâtre numérot[...]
> intégrante d'un jeu, d'un divertissement, d'un hasard [...]
> snobisme, mais… plutôt, partie d'un acte social, politique, [...]
> uel et magique, posé en toute conscience et en toute acce[...]
> [Sitting on a numbered seat in a theatre is not part of a game, a[...]
> tainment, an accidental occurrence or a certain snobbishness, b[...]
> rather it means taking part in a social, political, spiritual and magical a[...]
> performed with full consciousness and fully accepted.] (qtd. in David [...]
> 109).

Somewhat ironically, the rise of an alternative movement confirms beyond a doubt that Canada had indeed developed both a theatrical tradition and a theatre establishment strong enough to bring about a vigorous opposition movement. The period between 1950 and 1970 had been one of enormously accelerated development, in dramaturgy as well as in the setting up of theatre centres; this was largely the result of a newly arisen sense of nationalism, spurred on even more by the centennial celebration of 1967. By 1970, Canada could boast a national theatre of its own, Stratford; a National Art Centre; and a series of regional theatre and art centres across the nation. Canadian theatre, finally, had arrived.

However, for the young artists who grew up during this period of cultural progress, the ultimate results seemed anything but satisfying. They attributed the emergence of art centres from coast to coast to a kind of collective "edifice complex" (Rubin 152), rather than to a genuine understanding of the cultural needs of the country, and they soon rose up in rebellion against this newly created "concrete establishment" and the social and cultural value system which it represented. The main accusation was that cultural colonialism not only persisted, but was even being reinforced, by these new developments. Nationalists pointed out the irony of placing Canada's "national theatre" in a town named Stratford, rather than in the nation's capital, and of running that theatre as a Shakespearean company, rather than as a showcase for Canadian playwrights, directors, and actors. Regional theatres were accused of being unduly under foreign influence and totally unreceptive to Canadian work. In 1970, Jean-Claude Germain created the following witty satire of the typical theatre establishment director:

> Les gens de théâtre tolèrent les auteurs dramatiques québécois comme
> un mal nécessaire, tout en se gardant bien de faire quoi que ce soit pour
> que la maladie se propage… Molière dans une main et Beckett dans
> l'autre, le cul posé sur une pile de Shakespeare et la tête appuyée sur
> Brecht ou Tchekov ou Pirandello ou Sacha Guitry ou Anouilh ou Pinter

: citation de Racine à la
ez, repus de culture uni-
;stie, l'homme de théâtre
attendant, il se fait la main
people tolerate Quebecois
, great care the evil should
kett in the other, his behind
ead on Brecht or Chekhov or
r Pinter or Albee or I don't
his buttonhole and his nose
al culture, farting with good
ois theatre director waits for
keeps in practice by putting on

26

: views. Ken Gass, founder of Factory
ly Canadian works as follows: "I do not
.... simply trying to relate to the world around me… The
major theatres of the country have reneged on their commitment to Canadian plays"
(Gass, "Prelude"). Jim Garrard, who started Theatre Passe Muraille, also emphasized
the need for an approach more clearly directed at the Canadian people than that of
the elitist theatre establishment and its classically educated leaders: "Theatre must be
indigenous. It must be organic… The professional artist is ruining the theatre. It's
important to get out… into the streets, into schools and parks, into prisons and apartment buildings. We need a guerilla theatre front" (qtd. in Wallace 77).

Ironically, if not entirely surprisingly, the anti-Stratford movement was partly
started in Stratford itself: Jean Gascon, artistic director of the festival, brought in a
number of young, aspiring directors to assist him (John Juliani, Paul Thompson);
instead of falling into the pattern of Stratford as expected, these young rebels took the
festival as a negative role model and went off to found companies of their own in
protest. Some of these emphasized the need to provide a workshop and showcase for
local artists; others stressed a socio-political or aesthetic and experimental orientation; but all were based on the premise that their work must be original, national, and
popular. In John Juliani's words, to the "exorbitance, elitism and museum theatre" of
the establishment they opposed an alternative of "poverty, democratization, contem-
poraneity."

In 1976, the grievances of young Canadian theatre artists were summed up in the
form of a brief play—the satirical monologue *Henrik Ibsen: On the Necessity of
Producing Norwegian Theatre*, written by John Palmer as a curtain raiser for Factory
Theatre Lab. This witty speech, delivered by "Ibsen" dressed in period costume ca.
1900, deserves to be quoted at length, since it exposes all the flaws and inadequacies
of the Canadian cultural scene as they are viewed by the young generation of frustrated artists:

> I... find myself in the untenable position of trying to address something vital to a gathering of no one, for no equitable reward, to no apparent purpose... It seems to me that we in Norway are having difficulty with the definition of a nation. This is not surprising, as we have been part of first Denmark, then Sweden, up until the present year... [W]hile art in general is an international commodity, it is produced by an artist of a particular culture and there is, in fact, no such thing as an international work of art... A nation that emulates all but itself is the true homeland of decadence and dictatorship. (Palmer 1–5)

At this point in the lecture, the actor produces a national flag from behind his pulpit and waves it tauntingly at the audience; he then folds it up again, with a reassuring "[T]hat wasn't so bad now, was it?" (6).

He then goes on to discuss the problems of native dramaturgy, specifically, the arguments that there are no Norwegian plays in the first place and that producing new plays would cause the demise of the classics, a cultural catastrophe. Countering these arguments which he considers patently false, he launches into a vigorous attack on the theatre establishment and the state of theatre criticism:

> Why is our largest theatre controlled by a foreigner? Why are many regional theatres, all subsidized as well by Norwegian tax payers, equally manacled? Why do these aliens overwhelmingly produce drama originating in any nation other than Norway? ... Why is government condoning this state of affairs with subsidy and indifference? What is suicide? (8).

And he goes on to denounce the offerings of the concrete establishment as:

> this eternal soiree given by an obsequious Norwegian government and Boards of Governors as culturally lobotomized as they are impressed and grovelling at the sound of a foreign title... [T]he state of criticism here is even more unhealthy than that of the theatre to which it owes its keep. It is a sad fact that Norwegian criticism is irrelevant to Norwegian theatre because the critics themselves are yearning after something they will inevitably not see on the Norwegian stage since it is not the English stage or the German stage... Why this tautology should cause them so much anguish and confusion is beyond my modest powers of comprehension... the criteria these critics use in diagnosing our indigenous drama are from other times and other places. You cannot find a liver ailment if you are looking for a broken heart... Norwegian art is abundant, and at this very moment, it is clearly defining Norwegian existence... We have embarked on nothing less than a fight for our own culture. I can think of nothing sadder than inaction now... We will produce well and badly but we must produce" (Palmer 9–13).

It has sometimes been said that unlike the American alternative groups who had the passion-rousing cause of the Vietnam war, the Canadian alternative theatre did not have a real "cause" to rally around, and that because of this difference, Canadian productions lack both dynamism and originality. It is true that the Canadian alternative phenomenon followed a decade after the American and was obviously heavily influenced by this precedent, becoming at times exceedingly imitative. Nevertheless, the distinguishing mark of Canadian theatre, and the feature which gives it a certain uniqueness in spirit if not necessarily in style, remains its nationalistic commitment. If there is a "cause" common to Canadian alternative theatre groups from coast to coast, it is this commitment to indigenous talent. A cultural and local cause, as opposed to the social, political, and universal implications of the Vietnam war, it obviously could not arouse the same tempestuous feelings. However, within the context of Canadian theatrical revolution, it served as a significant catalyst to bring about new and original productions.

Three different dates could be given to indicate the formal beginning of an alternative theatre movement in English Canada: 1959, the founding of Toronto Workshop Productions by George Luscombe; 1970, the year of the first Underground Theatre Festival and also the year when the term "alternate theatre" was first used; 1971, the year of the Gaspé and Niagara-on-the-Lake Playwrights Conference.

The founding of Toronto Workshop Productions by George Luscombe meant the creation of a model for much of the "underground" or "off-Yonge Street" theatre which was soon to follow, as small, unsubsidized companies set up highly idealistic, if shoestring, operations in warehouses, basements, and lofts (John Herbert's Garret Theatre was one of these).

The Toronto Underground Theatre Festival of 1970 led to a greater sense of cohesion and common purpose among the participating groups; with the adoption of the term "alternate theatre" reputedly coined by Tom Hendry, the underground or "off-off-Yonge" theatre groups proclaimed themselves, in an indirect manner, a "movement" within the Canadian theatre scene. "Alternate" remained the Toronto expression; however, I shall continue to use the wider term "alternative" to designate the movement in general and in the international sense.

The Playwrights' Conferences of 1971 were instrumental in instilling a sense of urgency about the need for greater support for Canadian dramatists in Canadian theatre. As has been noted earlier, a concern for the development of a genuine native dramaturgy became one of the major features of Canadian alternative theatres; this concern was the result, in a large part, of the growing discontent of Canadian playwrights which was expressed at the Gaspé and Niagara-on-the-Lake conferences. The Gaspé conference, sponsored by the Canada Council, resulted in a manifesto by the playwrights in which they demanded that the Council provide a 50 percent Canadian content requirement for all subsidized theatres; the second conference repeated the demand. The playwrights' requests met with violent protest from the directors of the traditional theatres, most of whom felt that such a policy was highly unrealistic in terms of audience demands. They did not consider the support of Canadian writers an important priority within their mandate. Alternative theatre companies stepped into the breach. With the creation of the LIP (Local Initiative Projects) and OFY

(Opportunity for Youth) grants by the federal government, these small companies became viable, and local playwrights turned to them to have their work workshopped or performed, on a small scale at least.

Not all playwrights looked upon this development favourably, of course. George Ryga, for example, expressed his dismay at the rise of what he termed a "beggars' theatre," and he refused to have anything to do with it, suggesting that Canadian dramatists should attempt to take over the administration of the state-funded theatres themselves rather than accept the humiliations perpetrated upon them by the regional theatres (28). Nevertheless, the movement gained momentum rapidly: by 1975, *Canada on Stage* lists no less than twenty alternate theatres in Toronto alone;[2] and similar movements occurred, on a smaller scale, all across the country. With the government money freeze of 1978, a gradual decline set in, as well as a noticeable change in attitude: companies had to adopt a more commercial viewpoint in order to survive. Also, by the end of the decade, several of the "alternative" theatres had become successful enough to attract a "mainstream" audience and thus lost some of their rebellious and experimental thrust. Many did not survive. Others, like the Tarragon Theatre in Toronto, became fully mainstream: the Tarragon now presents only the works of well-established Canadian writers, such as James Reaney, Michel Tremblay, David Freeman, and David French. Ken Gass is probably correct when he suggests that "alternate" (with reference to Toronto, anyway) should now be considered a historical term, applicable essentially to the decade 1969–1979. He himself resigned from the Factory Theatre Lab in 1979, declaring that (at that point), "Toronto… is simply not a conducive environment for serious theatrical experimentation" (Gass, "Toronto's Alternates" 130). He suggests that the avant-garde of the future is to be found in the cabaret scene, rather than in theatre.

If the alternative theatre movement in Canada had run its course by the end of the decade, it is justifiable to look upon it from a historical point of view, even if the vantage point of the 1980s does not afford much distance. Going back to the beginnings of alternate theatre in Toronto, then, I will discuss here Toronto Workshop Productions, as the earliest example and model for future developments; the Factory Theatre Lab, as a prime example of concern with native dramaturgy; and, briefly, Toronto Free Theatre, as an example of extreme attitudes, both in its popular approach and shock tactics. Together with Theatre Passe Muraille, these provide a representative cross-section of the alternate theatre scene in Toronto. Because of its enormous impact across the country, and the overall success of its operations, Theatre Passe Muraille will be dealt with in detail in the following chapter [of *Second Stage: The Alternative Theatre Movement in Canada* ("A Success Story: Theatre Passe Muraille")].

Toronto Workshop Productions set the pattern for alternative theatre groups in both its political orientation and its experimentation with new performance styles. Definitely leftist from the start, the company aimed at producing social drama for a "popular" audience; to this end, it evolved a documentary style of performance, often based on collective creation, which incorporated such traditional techniques of popular theatre as improvisation, mime, and puppets. This approach was partly influenced by George Luscombe's apprenticeship years in England from 1952 to 1957, when he was exposed to Brechtian techniques through his work with Joan Littlewood.

Toronto Workshop Productions was the result of an amalgamation of two groups, both of which started out in 1959: the Arts Theatre Club, founded by Basaya Hunter, which had an ambitious programme calling for the development of a professional company, a theatre school, and workshops; and Workshop Productions, founded by George Luscombe. In 1961, Luscombe was appointed permanent director of the combined operation. Although still on the amateur level, the first show, *Hey Rube!*, a collective creation, proved a great success. From 1963 on, Toronto Workshop Productions became a professional company: actors were now able to work eight hours a day and submit to the rigid standards set by the director. To build his company, Luscombe auditioned some ninety aspiring actors and actresses, from whose number he selected twenty for further training without pay during a two-month period. At the end of that time, he chose nine promising candidates to form a high-powered ensemble. By 1976, some fifty original works had been produced in three different genres: collective creation; free adaptation of classics; and original scripted plays. For the first eight years, the company performed in the basement of an old factory in Toronto's West End, with a seating capacity of 100 on bleachers around an open stage. In 1967, the company moved to a permanent home at 12 Alexander Street, in downtown Toronto; the new house could seat 300 and still kept the open stage arrangement.

A disciple of Brecht, Luscombe feels that the theatre's most important function is to "say something" (Personal interview), to make a social statement. He defines the purpose of the company as "popular theatre":

> Popular theatre... means bypassing existing audiences, going into areas where people are totally unconverted and thereby creating new awareness... The aim of popular theatre is not only to entertain, but to show that entertainment is, above all, saying something worthwhile, and saying it well. (Luscombe, "European")

In order to achieve the high standard he aimed for, Luscombe emphasized actor training and the ensemble idea. He developed a special approach to prepare his actors for working in the collective creation genre which, he realized, made greater demands than the more traditional approach on both actors and director. His workshops aimed at developing actors along three major lines, all calculated to achieve maximum expressiveness: to be "witty in mind and body," to "achieve voice," and to be "wise enough to be alert to poetry" (Luscombe, Personal interview). Luscombe also felt that the presence of a director "strong in knowledge and discipline" was essential for the new genre, both to give a sense of cohesion and direction to the group and to assure a proper balance between the more timid actors and those aggressive enough to take over in that particular setting. His "group theatre" workshops for actors soon became known beyond the confines of the theatrical world, and he had to turn away candidates sent to him by well-meaning physicians, eager to use the works. groups for their patients.

Toronto Workshop Productions performed on the basis of all three ech-niques adopted by alternative theatre: collective creation; free use and adaptation of classics; and original scripted plays, with variants and combinations of these techniques. The collective creations were usually built around a current social or political problem. *Hey, Rube,* for example, dealt with the immediate urban problem of people (in this case, the artists themselves) being evicted from the building they occupy; it was given the framework of a circus setting. More wide-ranging political themes were carefully researched and documented, and the documentary style Luscombe used for these productions came close to the Living Newspaper technique used by the American workers' theatre in the thirties. These included productions such as *Chicago '70,* a comment on the Chicago crisis of that year, and *You Can't Get Here from There,* on the Allende crisis in Chile. Another typical production was *Mister Bones,* a play based on writing contributions by five members of the company and performed by a cast of nine. These nine actors divided all the parts among themselves, with as many as nine parts being played by one actor—the aim here being broadly sketched outlines rather than in-depth characterization, since the emphasis is on the social message of the play, rather than psychological analysis. Although the practice of having each actor take on a number of different parts is obviously based on simple economics (large casts are expensive), it also serves a definite aesthetic purpose: because the audience is unable to identify an actor with any one character, an alienation occurs which draws the attention of the audience away from the character to the overall message of the play as a whole. *Mister Bones* dealt with the race problem in America and used the framework of a mock minstrel show, with satirical scenes ranging from a parody of Abraham Lincoln to one of contemporary Harlem. Although the play exhibits many of the weaknesses inherent in political theatre, such as too much undisguised propaganda and excesses in language, it also contains a number of lively theatrical scenes which help to make its statement both forceful and enjoyable.

Toronto Workshop Productions also pioneered the utilization of classical works for what Brecht calls their "Materialwert," or raw material, for contemporary, original productions. Their adaptation of Büchner's *Woyzek,* an early production, used about 50 percent original material and 50 percent of Büchner's play to create a freely adapted version. A variant of this technique is the montage: a combination of texts from various authors are combined to form a new work. A brilliant example of that genre was exemplified in the satirical *King Richard Third-String* (1973), which was advertised as "A Tragical-Comical-Historical Theatre Thing, lifted from Shakespeare, Machiavelli and others." Brecht himself felt no compunction about "lifting" texts from appropriate sources and incorporating them into his own work; he did not feel that such a use of a canonized text as a building block within a new script took away from the originality of his own work.[3] *King Richard Third-String* was a violent satire on Richard Nixon and the Watergate scandal. The montage, created by Steven Bush and Richard McKenna, owed much of its satirical punch to the wide range of texts (from

Renaissance to contemporary) it employed and to its stylistic alternation of blank verse and contemporary idiomatic speech.

Original scripts came mostly from Jack Winter, writer-in-residence at Toronto Workshop Productions for most of the period between 1961 and 1976; occasionally, the company and the resident playwright worked on a production together, as they did for *Summer of '76*, a history of the Olympics. Some plays resulted from co-operation between the director and a writer, such as *Ain't Lookin'* (1980), another treatment of the racial problem in the US. This play is particularly effective because of its simple, straightforward story line and characterization. It presents the case of a white man who, having disguised himself with the use of shoe polish, joins a black baseball team and finds out for himself the difficulties, restrictions, and humiliations which black athletes have to accept in order to survive. Occasionally, Toronto Workshop Productions also commissioned scripts from, and produced the work of, better known Canadian dramatists such as Len Petersen or Rick Salutin (their production of Rick Salutin's *Les Canadiens* won the 1977 Chalmers Playwriting Award).

While Toronto Workshop Productions emphasized its political and social commitment and pioneered in the area of collective creation, Factory Theatre Lab was dedicated from its inception to supporting the new Canadian playwright. We have seen its basic philosophy illustrated in John Palmer's satire *Henrik Ibsen: On the Necessity of Producing Norwegian Drama*. This monologue expressed exactly the attitude of Ken Gass, founder of Factory Theatre Lab, who wanted to provide a training ground for actors, directors, and most especially, writers who, he felt, had no chance of gaining access to the regional theatre establishment. In this way, the Factory Theatre Lab functioned as an essential catalyst within the alternative theatre movement.

The theatre began in 1970, through the efforts of Ken Gass, assisted by Frank Trotz. It originally opened in a makeshift complex on top of a garage on Dupont Street in Toronto, but eventually it found more suitable quarters downtown on Adelaide Street. Its youthful founders proclaimed their enthusiastic creed with a sign over the door which read "Don't wait for the Yanks to discover Canada." Gass and Trotz realized the urgent need for a laboratory set-up in which new, original material could be given a first chance at discussion, criticism, and development; and they saw the need for a showcase in which to present the eventual products of these efforts. In keeping with these ideas, they began operations with a series of playwriting contests, followed by workshops. The result was that within a year, eight full-length plays and nine one-acters were produced. Among the new authors discovered were David Freeman, with *Creeps*, and George Walker, with *The Prince of Naples*. Freeman very quickly moved on to the wider recognition of Tarragon Theatre; Walker, whose ironic/absurdist plays carried less appeal for the mainstream audience, remained the unofficial house writer for Factory Theatre Lab for many years to come. Soon many of the other small theatres were putting on plays by new Canadian authors. Gass's policy proved highly successful: within four years, in 1974, an anthology of representative Factory Lab Productions came out in print (see Brissenden); by 1979, Factory Theatre Lab had premiered fifty new Canadian plays. Gass's introduction to the anthology reiterated the rationale and philosophy of Factory Theatre Lab:

> [The founding of the theatre] was a simple and arbitrary way of escaping the Canadian theatrical rut of following fashion. Regional playhouses were (and largely still are) shaping their seasons to reflect fashions of Broadway and the West End, and young directors like myself in Studio or University companies were modelling our work after the *Tulane Drama Review* descriptions of Off-Off-Broadway and Eastern Europe. By limiting the Factory to only new Canadian plays, we were forced to abandon the security blanket of our colonial upbringing. We found ourselves in a vacuum without roots and, indeed, without play-wrights. The plays soon surfaced. ("Introduction" 7)

It is interesting to note that while Gass's remarks were quite correct with regard to English Canada, by 1971 French Canada had developed a flourishing dramaturgy, and major writers such as Gratien Gélinas, Marcel Dubé, and Michel Tremblay were well established. By 1980, of course, the same is true for English Canada, and Factory Theatre Lab now continues as a training ground for the second generation of young Canadian playwrights.

Probably the two most successful productions at Factory Theatre Lab during the period of Ken Gass's administration were Herschel Hardin's *Esker Mike and His Wife Agiluk* and Gass's own *The Boy Bishop*. These two plays will be examined here, as well as some of the early work of other important Factory Lab writers, especially George Walker and Hrant Alianak.

The production and publishing history of *Esker Mike* provides a good illustration of the reasons for the disillusionment of many young Canadian dramatists and their subsequent demand for an alternative theatre outlet. In his introduction to the published version of the play, Peter Hay describes Hardin as one of Canada's "lost playwrights," unable to find an audience in spite of their talent "because they were or are not British, American, French, or anything—except what they are, Canadian" (Hay 5). Hardin wrote *Esker Mike and His Wife Agiluk* in 1967. The play was published in the prestigious *Drama Review* of New York in 1969, but it was not brought before a Canadian public until Factory Theatre Lab premiered it in 1971; it was not published here until 1973. According to Hay, the reason given for its rejection by establishment theatre directors was its "epic scope" and "large cast of characters," which made it expensive to perform. These features, typical of Hardin's plays generally, are a result of his themes—he gives a social panorama rather than focusing in on the psychology of one central character—and a strong Brechtian influence. However, the cast of *Esker Mike* numbers only fifteen—certainly not an excessive demand for a reasonably well-funded theatre.

Esker Mike and His Wife Agiluk is subtitled "Scenes from Life in the Mackenzie River Delta"; it attempts to provide the audience or reader with some insight into the atmosphere and specific problems of life in a small community of the Northwest

Territories, ca. 1960. It is a short play (some seventy-five printed pages), structured along epic lines in a sequence of fourteen scenes. The three central characters, Esker Mike, a white Northerner, Agiluk, his native wife, and William, his best friend, also an Eskimo, provide unity and a central axis for the plot. Although the play contains no overt social criticism or propaganda, it is an inflammatory work, revealing the depth of degradation and despair of native people, especially the women, in the face of a well-meaning, but totally ineffectual white administration.

The play centres upon Agiluk, who, after "[f]our men and ten children" (18), none of whom she is able to provide for, decides she will have no more babies and refuses to have any further sexual relations with Esker Mike. When she eventually gives in to a visiting friend, the mate off the boat, she knows that not only will she have conceived again, but that she will also be duty bound to give yet one more child to her husband to restore a proper balance. Her solution to the problem reflects the pitiless and uncompromising logic of the far North: she decides to kill two of her already living children to make up for the impending arrival of the next two.

While *Esker Mike and His Wife Agiluk* is a play in the rather straightforward tradition of Brechtian political theatre, Ken Gass's *The Boy Bishop* of 1976[4] is a much more complex work. Set in 17th-century New France, this historical play on a Canadian theme operates on a number of levels simultaneously, some obvious, others exceedingly subtle. The structure is epic, with many scenes grouped into three acts. *The Boy Bishop* is a combination of historical play and medieval pageant, but it also contains some rather acidic comments on the English-Canadian situation under the guise of French-Canadian history. It provides a personal catharsis for the author and enables him to voice his disillusionment with the Canadian theatre scene. In an interview which accompanies the version of the play published by *Canadian Theatre Review,* the author explains his social and artistic goals in this particular production:

> [I]t's a history play about English Canada—not about New France... the history of my perceptions of living in the Canadian reality... [a metaphor for] the malaise of here and now in English Canada. (Gass, Interview 123)

The character of the Boy Bishop becomes a metaphor for the frustrations of the pioneer theatre in Canada: "He struggles to create a world which he doesn't understand," and, expressing his own pessimism, "he has learned that the art of effecting change is futile" (124). Gass's description of the production itself reveals an experimental and environmentalist approach:

> The key to the production, although it was big and spectacular, was its immediacy—the very close personal contact with the audience. At times the audience members were face to face with the actors, and at other times were watching it from further away, at oblique angles. Integral to the play is the feeling that something is being created, something is happening right then and there... We worked with the idea of creating a spontaneous event. (125)

The action is set in 17th-century Quebec. Governor Montcalm, Intendant Bigot, and Bishop Laval, all three corrupt to the core, represent authority and the establishment. Aware that they might have gone too far in their oppression and exploitation of the people, they decide to give the populace a Boy Bishop ceremony to prevent a revolution. The masses are represented by a crowd of teenagers, beggars, and half-wits, among whom a few special characters stand out.

The third act describes the eventual demise of the Boy, who had managed to seize power, and the final take-over by the "legitimate" reactionary authorities. In his disillusionment, the Boy becomes exceedingly bitter. His speech at this point obviously reflects the views of the author on his own society, both general and theatrical:

> The people of this colony don't need liberation. They liberated themselves long ago. Their freedom is not in the mastery of their destiny, however. They have willed themselves into perpetual serfdom, where there is no need for thinking, no need for moral consideration. Reaction, menial reaction, has become a way of life. (Gass, *The Boy Bishop* 85)

The pessimism of this play, and its claim that it is the people themselves who are to blame for their wretched condition because of their inability to achieve inner liberation, strongly echoes earlier and contemporary French-Canadian drama, especially the views expressed in the plays of Marcel Dubé.

Probably the most interesting work produced at Factory Theatre Lab came from George [F.] Walker, who experiments with grotesque and absurdist techniques in his heavily satirical plays. As Gass points out, Walker has been widely misunderstood in Canada:

> Even English-speaking audiences have no difficulty translating Michel Tremblay's kitchen-sink squabbles into political realities. But when George Walker writes about living in a cultural desert and banging one's head against an increasingly grotesque wall, English Canada thinks he's writing a fantasy. ("Introduction" 8)

In his first play, produced at Factory Theatre Lab, *The Prince of Naples,*[5] Walker deals with the theme of re-education to the real needs and facts of life through the characters of Oak, a fifty-two-year-old student, and his instructor, Sayer, a man in his twenties. Among other things, the play comments on the conflict between different generations, pointing out both the arrogance of the young (Oak is referred to as "the old man" throughout) and the need for the old to continually review and readapt their understanding of the world. Through the dialogue between pupil and teacher, and particularly in the long monologues of the instructor, Walker brings out the young generation's enthusiasm for new learning and new approaches, as well as the eventual futility of it all. In the process, specific contemporary issues, such as the excessive optimism of the hippie period in the 1960s and the state of contemporary theatre, come in for some scathing criticism. Sayer's instruction begins with an admonition to the old man to discard all of his traditional knowledge, especially the classics: "Forget Thackeray. Forget Henry James. Forget them all… empty your mind and follow me"

(Walker 5). The goal, of course, is "to bridge the gap from then to now" (Walker 11). The impact of the play comes mainly from Walker's dynamic use of language in the long monologues; words pour out in torrential fashion, carrying the listener along. The development of the speeches is based, not on logic, but on the association of ideas or sounds; words are often used for their rhyme and rhythmic effects, rather than their meaning. Definitely, Walker is using language here in the manner suggested by Artaud; there are also echoes of music-hall dialogue and an alternation between brief exchanges and long monologues, both of which are typical of the Theatre of the Absurd. Here is an example of a typical "torrential" monologue, which is recited at an accelerating tempo and eventually emphasized by the sound of foot stomping:

> **Sayer:** We've got a lot of ground to cover. Psychic resources, surrealistic caus-
> es, social corpses… the casting out of demons, the enticement of the
> truth.
>
> Conventions and pretensions, contemplation and deviation,
> humanity, divinity, and human and divine proclivity… casual percep-
> tion… political perception… the new left, the new right… walking in
> the rain at night. Sensuality, logicality… art without form, the form in
> the formlessness. Reason, chaos, order, dissemination, impregnation.
>
> Understanding Mohammed, selling Jesus, sympathizing with
> Judas… We've got to blend optimism with pessimism, overestimate the
> occult, utilize apathy, serenade the young and pacify the old… We have
> to pierce the great minds in our history and then discard them in favor
> of the great minds of the present. (Walker 37)

The absurdity of the proposed programme, greater in scope than the giant-scale edu-cational system devised for Gargantua by his tutor Ponocrates, becomes apparent instantly in spite of the hypnotic effect of the flow of words. Also in the tradition of Artaud, Walker builds into his plays exorcism through religious ritual. Thus, a long monologue on the glories of the "sixth decade" is followed by an admonition to his student to rise and "praise the sixth decade"; when the endless, litany-like list of prais-es produces fatigue and chest pains rather than enthusiasm in the reluctant Oak, Sayers bites his arm fiercely to bring him back to alertness.

Eventually the old man is promoted to "teacher and lecturer" himself, but he pan-ics at the sound of thousands of students flocking to his door—only to be informed by Sayer that it was all a hoax, the noise having been produced by a record player to test the old man's reaction. Obviously, he has failed the test and must return for a fur-ther course of study. Sayer offers philosophical comfort: "Don't be disheartened, old fellow. It's not unusual to have to go through the whole process three or four times. Remember, this was just your second time around" (Walker 48). Like absurdist plays in general, *The Prince of Naples* makes a negative statement about the human condi-tion and it also comments on a specific local and contemporary issue. *The Prince of Naples* set the tone for Walker's subsequent and more ambitious plays, such as

Zastrozzi or *Bagdad Saloon*. Although still not a mainstream author, George Walker is probably English Canada's most innovative and controversial playwright at this time.

[In the section omitted here for space reasons, Usmiani discusses the work of several other playwrights at Factory like Hrant Alianak and Michael Hollingsworth—ed.]

The efforts of Factory Theatre Lab to create a home and showcase for new Canadian playwrights in the 1970s thus made it possible for young dramatists to experiment widely, to learn the potential of the instrument which is the stage, and to see their work exposed to audiences, occasionally even published. The existence of Factory Lab and other alternative theatres also enabled Canadian dramatists to break with the realistic tradition—fail-safe from the commercial point of view—and finally to join the modern avant-garde in all its theatrical manifestations.

Of all the alternate groups that arose in Toronto in the seventies, the Toronto Free Theatre was perhaps the one most openly dedicated to avant-garde productions—like Dada earlier in the century enjoying nothing more than a good chance to "épater les bourgeois." Toronto Free Theatre deserves brief mention here also because its founders, playwright/directors Tom Hendry, Martin Kinch, and John Palmer, attempted to take seriously the concept of the popular theatre in the sense of theatre for the masses: they started out operations on the basis of free admission. This system had to be changed when their original LIP grant ran out, and "Free" theatre now refers more to artistic freedom than financial. Toronto Free Theatre occupies a renovated Victorian building on Berkeley Street, combining the preservation of a historical site with theatrical performance.

The theatre has aroused a great deal of controversy because of the kind of productions it presents. Some are simply bold statements, such as Carol Bolt's *Red Emma*, or Michael Ondaatje's *The Collected Works of Billy the Kid*. But when the theatre staged *Clear Light* by Michael Hollingsworth in 1973, it was closed down by the police morality squad. The founding playwrights have all been accused of sensationalism; their plays do indeed exhibit such controversial themes as incest, homosexuality, lesbianism, nymphomania, and alcoholism, alone and in various combinations. Their rationale for such controversial fare is the theatre's dedication to "psychodynamics," that is, "dramas of psyche and mind in which passions and neurotic conflicts have been given an intensely physical and sometimes surrealistic expression" (Souchotte, "Toronto Free" 36). Again, this seems to be a rather primitive and unsophisticated realization of the principles enunciated earlier by Artaud; the arguments in defence of the company's often excessive shock tactics do not appear entirely convincing:

> Martin Kinch has described this as "narcissistic" theatre, confronting the audience with familiar personal obsessions and strong visual images that carry ambiguous messages of danger and eroticism. Sex, violence, blood or guts… have often helped form the scenario but as a realization of our darker selves rather than as unmotivated sensationalism. (Souchotte, "Toronto Free" 36)

A wide range in style, theme, and technique evolved on the Toronto alternate the-atre scene during the 1970s. While all of the theatres discussed here remained within the local sphere of influence, Theatre Passe Muraille exerted its impact on communities and new, small groups across the nation.

(1983)

Notes

[1] The authors were Oscar Ryan, E. Cecil-Smith, H. Francis, and Mildred Goldberg.

[2] Black Theatre Canada, Creation 2, Factory Theatre Lab, Global Village Theatre, Homemade Theatre Company, The NDWT Company, New Theatre, Open Circle Theatre, The Performing Theatre Company, Redlight Theatre (Women's Theatre), Smile Company, Theatre Fountainhead, Theatre in the Dell, Theatre Passe Muraille, Theatre Plus, Theatre Second Floor, Toronto Free Theatre, Toronto Workshop Productions, Upstairs at Old Angelo's.

[3] For example, his use of the famous Goethe lyrics "Über allen Gipfeln ist Ruh" in his poem "Das Lied vom Hauch."

[4] Produced at Factory Theatre Lab April–May 1976.

[5] First produced at the Factory Theatre Lab July 1971.

Works Cited

Brighouse, Harold. "What Is Wrong With the Canadian Theatre?: Harold Brighouse, Noted British Dramatist, Writes a Supplement to H.A. Voaden's Article, Published June 22 on This Page." *Globe* (Toronto). 16 November 1929.

Brissenden, Connie, ed. *The Factory Lab Anthology.* Vancouver: Talonbooks, 1974.

David, Gilbert. "Notes dures sur un théâtre mou." *Etudes Françaises* 11.2 (1975): 95–109.

Gass, Ken. *The Boy Bishop. Canadian Theatre Review* 12 (1976): 42–122.

———. Interview with Roy Keizer. *Canadian Theatre Review* 12 (1976): 123–26.

———. "Introduction." *The Factory Lab Anthology.* Brissenden 7–10.

———. "Prelude." *Factory Theatre Lab Programme.* 1971/72.

———. "Toronto's Alternates: Changing Realities." *Canadian Theatre Review* 21 (1979): 127–35.

Germain, Jean-Claude. "C'est pas Mozart, c'est le Shakespeare québeçois qu'on assassine." *Jeu* 7 (1978): 9–20.

Hardin, Herschel. *Esker Mike and His Wife Agiluk.* Vancouver: Talonbooks, 1973.

Hay, Peter. Introduction. Hardin 5–8.

Juliani, John. "The Free Theatre." Unpublished. 1972.

Luscombe, George. European Tour Folder. Toronto Workshop Productions. 1976.

———. Personal Interview. 19 November 1980.

Mitchell, Roy. *Creative Theatre.* New York: Kindle, 1969.

Palmer, John. *Henrik Ibsen: On the Necessity of Producing Norwegian Theatre.* Toronto: Playwrights Co-op, 1976.

Rubin, Don. "John Juliani's Savage God." *Theatre Quarterly* 5 (1975–76): 151–63.

Ryga, George. "Theatre in Canada: A Viewpoint on Its Development and Future," *Canadian Theatre Review* 1 (1974): 28–32.

Souchotte, Sandra. "Canada's Workers' Theatre." *Canadian Theatre Review* 9 (1976): 169–72.

———. "Toronto Free Theatre." *Canadian Theatre Review* 14 (1977): 33–38.

Voaden, Herman. "What is Wrong with Canadian Theatre?" *The Globe and Mail* 22 June 1929: 22.

Walker, George F. *The Prince of Naples.* Toronto: Playwrights Co-op, 1971.

Wallace, Robert. "Growing Pains: Toronto Theatre in the 1970s." *Canadian Literature* 85 (1980): 71–85.

from A Dialectical Drama of Facts and Fictions on the Feminist Fringe

by Amanda Hale [1]

The last fifteen years have witnessed the international emergence of feminist art in all disciplines. This synchronous flowering of feminist culture has been drawn forth by a cultural/political/historical process antithetical to patriarchal culture, which has acted as a catalyst for social change. It is a response to the dead ends into which the current system has led us—a nuclear-powered society, a dying environment, technological control from the birthing room to the workplace.

Canada has been in a particularly advantageous position to engender feminist art due to the co-emergence of Canadian nationalism and feminism in the late sixties. The search for a distinctly Canadian cultural identity calls into question the same colonial and colonizing influences that feminist art challenges. Canadian cultural nationalism was a curiosity to me as an immigrant in 1968. It is of vital interest to me as a lesbian feminist playwright and performer now, since it is my belief that Canadian feminist theatre co-emerged with Canadian nationalism as it was manifested in the alternate theatre movement.

Facts and Fictions

Quebec writer Nicole Brossard has said:

> ...when we are little girls, we perceive reality clearly, as it is, patriarchal. But we are soon told that our perceptions are mistaken. What is first perception becomes impression and then is called imagination... our certainties slowly become fiction... this is the knot that feminist writers have untied in their work.
>
> For women, so-called reality is a fiction because it is not made up of their perceptions... Reality is constructed, reproduced, and transformed by a patriarchal mind... Let's name some fictions: the military complex, the price of gold, the television news, pornography.
>
> On the other hand, women's realities have been perceived as fictions. Let's name some realities: maternity, abortion, rape, prostitution, physical violence. The newspapers will tell you that these are news items and not information. So if you are writing with a feminist conscious-

ness, you suddenly find yourself writing at the edge, at the very limits of fiction and reality. (11)

Under patriarchy our experience has been denied and internalized. The rich inner worlds which result from this denial, threaded as they are with pain and secrecy, may be used as creative resources or may fester into neuroses. In the late sixties the second wave of feminism crashed on our consciousness, shattering our isolation. Women began to make the first tentative moves towards more direct communication with each other, externalizing inner worlds and discovering common experience. The process of factualizing our "fictions" and countering the patriarchal "facts" which are embodied in the structures of an inverted society constitutes the beginning of a feminist cultural (r)evolution, the bottom line of which is aesthetics.

In a 1983 *Room of One's Own* interview, west coast writer Betty Lambert has said of her work:

> I wanted a new form of tragedy. I wanted to battle Aristotle… when Oedipus tears out his eyes, that's it. Even though Sophocles is going to write *Return to Colonus*, you've got this tragic moment. Women know something that maybe men don't know. We know that after the death, somebody cooks bacon and eggs. And that suicide is not an answer, because life bloody goes on. And on some fundamental level, I wanted to break the tragic code. (63–64)

I think Lambert understood the beginnings of a feminist aesthetic in breaking the Greek-based cultural code which pits "man" against fate, and glories in the resulting tragedy. Western drama is based on Aristotelean aesthetic philosophy. The highest ideal of Greek culture was the formation of perfect human character through the fusion of character with fate. Individual destiny was to be transcended in the service of the community. From the first Greek tragedies to the Victorian novel, thousands of fictional characters have suffered tragic ends because the assertion of their individuality (or tragic flaws) conflicted with the moral and philosophical power structures of Church and State.

But why the necessity of suffering? Surely the Greek concept of an immutable fate (which conveniently results in an immutable aesthetic philosophy) is suspect. Nietzsche, writing about Greek tragedy, laments "what suffering must this race have endured to achieve such beauty" (146). In "A Letter on Corsets" (1870) in *The Englishwoman's Domestic Magazine*, the pains of corseting are justified with the quote "*Qu'il faut souffrir pour être belle*" (qtd. in Murray 67). [One must suffer to be beautiful.] For men, clearly, aesthetics meant creating works of art external to themselves. For women, clearly, it meant moulding their bodies into the form of the governing aesthetic. When Dorothea Brooke, heroine of George Eliot's *Middlemarch*, bemoans her inability to become a poet, the hero assures her that she *is* a poem (cited in Gubar 293). Man does, woman is. If you embody poetry then you don't have to write it. But, while we do reject the objectification of women that the structure of this dichotomy implies, simply inverting the equation is not enough. There is a dialectical pattern inherent in the creative process. We can characterize it by the phrase "dobedobedo." Doing is a form of becoming; in the creative act doing and becoming occur simultaneously, the one feeding the other, back and forth.

When a woman sits at a typewriter today it is *her* choice whether to twist herself into the shape of the male aesthetic (i.e., lace up her corsets), or to wrench from within her own buried aesthetic. The twist resonates with centuries of similarly patterned "fictional" pursuits undertaken in the cause of fashionable self-objectification. We have seen the development and perpetuation over centuries of an alien objectifying aesthetic. Their absorption of this ubiquitous and iniquitous aesthetic has slowed women down and controlled them from within. The current redefinition of how a woman should look and what is beautiful goes beyond fashion. It is part of a cultural revolution: the de-objectification of woman and the search for a fluid aesthetic consonant with the growing awareness of our time.

Colonial Culture: The Regionals

Prior to the seventies' renaissance of Canadian culture, the Canadian theatre network consisted of regional theatres run exclusively by men. The big-budget organizational structures of these mainstream theatres were and continue to be funded by the federal and provincial arts councils to produce seasons of plays which will draw as large an audience as possible, and build a subscription series. Until the seventies the general fare was British and American plays which, having proven successful abroad, were acceptable to a middle-class Canadian audience. A typical season might include works by Harold Pinter, Neil Simon, Chekhov, Shakespeare, and a Broadway musical. The emphasis was on comedy and musicals. This conservative, commercially-motivated policy meant that the regionals rarely, if ever, produced a play by a woman, or by a Canadian of either gender.

Because theatre is collaborative and transient, it is particularly dependent on funding and on a support network. In her report, "The Status of Women in Canadian Theatre," Rina Fraticelli explains the continuing female invisibility factor.

> The high cost of producing theatre is a significant factor in the general conservatism of the industry. Theatre is a high-risk, labour-intensive operation in which only the most commercially successful productions can break even or, even more rarely, generate profit... What makes a woman a risk *now* is that there haven't been women before; the historical exclusion from the mainstream of theatre thus becomes an intangible factor affecting a board of directors' or artistic director's decision to risk their money, resources, or artistic reputations... [Ironically,] the worst offenders in terms of the employment of women are to be found among that group of theatres which receives the highest level of Canada Council subsidization. ("Invisibility," 118–19)

Canadian Cultural Nationalism

1974. Canadian nationalism is at its height. I am a student at Concordia University in Montreal, taking my first playwriting course. That winter a theatre conference was held at Concordia. All the pioneers of Canadian alternate theatre were there: Paul Thompson of Theatre Passe Muraille, John Juliani of Savage God, George Luscombe of Toronto Workshop Productions, Ken Gass of Factory Theatre Lab, Martin Kinch of Toronto Free Theatre; playwrights such as Carol Bolt, George Ryga, David Freeman. Sparks of nationalist passion flew in all directions. The boys were frustrated. They wanted recognition for their work. The general consensus was that Canadian theatrical content should be legislated. The male voices were loud. Word went out to the regional theatres that they would no longer receive funding unless a percentage of Canadian plays appeared in programming. The regional theatres complied in order to maintain their funding base.

But let's take a closer look at the nationalist revolution and examine both the contributions it made to the subsequent development of feminist theatre and the continuing structural biases which resulted in the continued exclusion of women from theatre.

In addition to promoting Canadian content, alternate theatre was an innovative stylistic force. Many of the values promoted by alternate theatre are shared by feminist theatre. Theatre Passe Muraille's artistic director Paul Thompson was one of the pioneers of Canadian collective creation. Collective creation was to become a popular format for both alternate and feminist theatre. The collective process engages a group of actors in research into a certain subject through reading, interviews, films, and videos. (In the case of the groundbreaking theatre piece *The Farm Show*, the actors lived in the farming community of Clinton and worked with the people whose lives they subsequently documented in the show.) Then, through group discussion and improvisation, a play is created collectively. Either the script is written collectively with contributions from each actor or an individual writer takes that responsibility, using notes taken during improvisations. The collective creation de-emphasizes specialization, breaking down the hierarchical structure of traditional theatre. In traditional theatre, the director controls and manipulates *his* actors and the writer puts words in their mouths. In collective creation, the power of decision-making is balanced out as far as possible among the group to allow fuller participation. It is a difficult but rewarding process.

With the flowering of alternate theatre, Canadians began to see more political content on stage, a content often framed by a Brechtian episodic structure. Historical events are the basis of such plays as Michael Ondaatje's *Billy the Kid*, Rick Salutin's *1837: The Farmers' Revolt*, Carol Bolt's *Buffalo Jump* and *Red Emma*. Brechtian theatre is named for Bertolt Brecht, the German playwright whose theories revolutionized modern theatre. Brechtian theatre is anti-Aristotelean and is characterized by incitement to action rather than emotional catharsis. This is achieved by the *verfremdungseffekt* (distancing effect) which facilitates objective political analysis. There is a stylistic tendency towards layering, collage and assemblage—all methods of getting away from the traditional Aristotelean structure of explication, complication, and denouement, with its accompanying rising action, climax, and resolution. The epic structure and political content of Brecht's work is intended to provide a historical overview and to open audience awareness to the possibility of social change. This technique is directly opposed to the audience identification with fate-bound characters which traditional Greek drama encourages. The Brechtian narrative moves imagistically, making frequent use of music and song, and smashing the convention of linear time.

Much alternate theatre emphasized, as feminist theatre does, process rather than product. John Juliani's company, Savage God, which originated from the theatre department of Simon Fraser University in 1966, is a prime example. Juliani's work was not unique; he, like other Canadians in alternate theatre, was influenced by eastern European theatre and by New York's Living Theatre company. Juliani represents, however, an extreme in that he viewed process as product. No two performances by Savage God were the same. Their process was dynamic and open to continuous experimentation and evolution. To quote Juliani, "Deliberate public mistake is the essence of experimental theatre. All theatre is experimental. Experimental means 'Process as Product'" (qtd. in Usmiani 77).

A further link between alternate and feminist theatre is the attempt to demystify and popularize what has traditionally been an elitist art form. Tight or non-existent budgets for alternate theatre have forced performers onto the street, into parks, into factories, warehouses, and other no-frills locations. These alternate theatre spaces prove to be less intimidating in both price and appearance to novice theatre-goers than, for example, Toronto's Royal Alex Theatre. Taking theatre *to* the people—touring union halls, community centres, church basements, schools or prisons with material relevant to the specific audience—will often provide the audience with their first experience of live theatre.

After the Renaissance: Where Are the Women?

Despite the innovative influence of the alternate theatre movement in terms of Canadian content and experimental forms, the great male revolution of the sixties and seventies did not improve the status of women in theatre. Alternate theatre, like the mainstream, was male-dominated. Wives, girlfriends, and female friends were included, but the boys were in control, and still are. In a National Survey of 1,156 productions staged at 104 Canadian theatres between 1978 and 1981, women represent only 10 percent of playwrights, 13 percent of directors, and 11 percent of artistic directors (Fraticelli, "Invisibility" 114). The pattern is familiar: the Leftist movements of the sixties—Black Power, Peace, Human Potential—all have failed to make gender equality a priority. But perhaps equality is not precisely the point. Rina Fraticelli puts her finger on the equality issue in her *Room of One's Own* article, "Any Black Crippled Woman Can":

I want to make it clear that I am a committed supporter of affirmative action: I recognize the therapeutic value of treating symptoms to keep the body alive while working at healing the root condition. However, I don't believe that having more women positioned in conventionally structured theatrical institutions is going to radically improve the status of women in a society which accords women such a low status in the first place. (16)

Despite the dismal statistics of Fraticelli's 1982 report (which has provided an invaluable reference point in an unchanged situation), there have been the exceptions: women who developed as playwrights and directors concurrently with the development of alternate theatre, and others who have since benefitted from the context it established. We see ample evidence of women's talent and achievement in the successes of playwrights such as Beverley Simons, Margaret Hollingsworth, Sharon Pollock, Judith Thompson, Linda Griffiths, Carol Bolt, Marie-Lynn Hammond; directors such as Jackie Maxwell and Svetlana Zylin; and artistic directors such as Pamela Hawthorne of the New Play Centre in Vancouver. Much work, however, is considered feminist by association because the characters and the writer are female. Some strong feminist work, on the other hand, is not named as such because successful writers are reluctant to risk the status they have gained in the mainstream by committing themselves to feminist culture. Sharon Pollock, quoted in *Canadian Theatre Review,* says "that she is a feminist 'in the sense of general concern for women,' but she resists ideological labels that infringe on the rights of the independent artist" (qtd. in Bessai 41).

The Feminist Companies

In the seventies, in response to this exclusion, feminists began forming their own companies. Toronto has seen two significant feminist theatres established: Red Light Theatre, which appeared in January 1974 and played three seasons; and Nightwood Theatre, established in 1978 and still going strong. Red Light Theatre, founded by Francine Volker, Marcella Lustig, and Diane Grant, provided a vital precedent back in 1974. Starting with a federally-funded LIP (Local Initiatives Program) grant, Red Light subsequently survived on an average of $10,000 a year to fund three or four annual productions. The male-dominated Toronto alternate theatres such as Factory Theatre Lab, Tarragon, Passe Muraille, Toronto Free, and Toronto Workshop Productions received significantly more funding at that time. (Now having moved into the mainstream with expanded budgets, they receive total government funding of, on average, $375,000 and up.) Red Light provided experience for women in the technical field, producing new scripts and collective creations as well as previously produced plays. They disbanded because financial strictures and lack of community support led to emotional burnout among the members. Francine Volker's experience makes her sympathetic to the struggle of the feminist theatre community. "Nothing has changed in ten years," she says. "Nightwood is having the same struggle, but they have a good support system." [2] Volker is justifiably proud of the fact that Red Light was the first Toronto theatre to name itself as feminist. This kind of creation of precedent and context, even though a company disappears, is critical.

Toronto's longest surviving all-woman theatre, Nightwood, was established in 1978 by Cynthia Grant, Mary Vingoe, Maureen White, and Kim Renders. Although Nightwood has evolved into what is generally seen as feminist theatre, Grant says "in 1978 we were very anxious that people not consider Nightwood a 'women's theatre'" (45). Although Grant was clearly defined and out as a feminist, she understood the derogatory implication of the term, and the consequent risk to Nightwood. Ironically, the existence of women's theatres led to potential ghettoizing because male artistic directors on the fringe, instead of incorporating women's work, tended to refer all feminists to the women's theatres. The fact that Nightwood is today recognized and respected as a feminist theatre shows how far we have come in naming ourselves.

Nightwood was launched with an adaptation of Sharon Riis's book, *The True Story of Ida Johnson*. Riis's book had been published by The Women's Press, with whom Grant had been associated. Over the years Nightwood has produced an impressive variety of original works and adaptations such as *The Yellow Wallpaper*, adapted from Charlotte Perkins Gilman's novel; *Glazed Tempera*, based on the paintings of Alex Colville; *Mass/Age*, a multimedia collage of nuclear age images; *Peace Banquet*, loosely adapted from Aristophanes; *Smoke Damage* (originally *Burning Times*, conceived by Mary-Ann Lambooy and written by Baņuta Rubess with the collective); *Pope Joan* by Baņuta Rubess, which ran during the Pope's 1984 visit to Toronto; *Antigone*, which featured a twin-imaged female Tiresias; *Penelope*, based on Margaret Atwood's *Circe Mud Poems*; and *Love and Work Enough*, winner of the 1985 Dora Mavor Moore Award for children's theatre. Commitment to community/popular theatre drew Nightwood into work within the Latin American and Greek communities in Toronto on shows such as *Memorias del Mañana*, which was produced with the Latin American music group Compañeros. Their first scripted work was the May 1986 English-language premiere of Jovette Marchessault's *The Edge of the Earth is Too Near, Violette Leduc*, directed by Cynthia Grant (who directed the majority of Nightwood's productions).

Nightwood's work has, for the most part, reflected Grant's commitment to the development of new feminist work and aesthetic innovations. "What we want to do," said Grant at the August 1985 Women in Theatre conference at York University, "is revolutionize form as well as content. We do not want to imitate the institutions or catch up with anyone. Women want to alter the current state of values." As artistic director and administrator/fundraiser (until her recent resignation), Grant spent years submitting project grants every few months until the company was eligible for a stable operating budget from the arts councils. After several years of working project by project on a budget of less than $10,000 per play, Nightwood can now afford one $25,000 production per season. In addition, they produce several developmental workshops and a modestly funded festival of new works. Nightwood has provided opportunities for many women in all areas of theatre. In welcoming novices, it has acted as training ground as well as production vehicle for the more experienced.

Although the company is still struggling financially, it has a solid support system and an expanded board of directors. Ironically, this sense of relative security may be backfiring. Nightwood appears to be moving in the direction of scripted, previously-produced work. The group is becoming more mainstream by profiling the work of established writers such as Judith Thompson and Margaret Hollingsworth, who arguably don't need Nightwood when they have already been produced at an established theatre like Tarragon. [...]

The lesbian community has also provided a rich source of theatre. The lesbian theatre group Atthis Theatre was formed in June 1979 by Keltie Creed. The Toronto group produced script-based lesbian work with high aesthetic standards. Atthis was named for the woman to whom Sappho dedicated her poetry, as a symbol of women's culture inspired by women. Although Atthis was short-lived, they did some important productions, notably Jane Chambers's *A Late Snow* in June 1979 and Jovette Marchessault's *Night Cows* in 1981, produced both in Toronto and at the Boston Theatre Festival. Atthis also produced several workshops and readings organized by Creed and Lyne Waddington. Atthis was amateur in the sense that it operated without funding. (Only in its final year did it receive a grant from the Gay Community Appeal.) The amateur/professional distinction breaks down with the advent of feminist theatre, where so many professionally trained theatre artists operate on their own time without public funding. Professional status is tied to financial status and the ability to pay Actors' Equity union rates.

Pelican Players is a Toronto multicultural, neighbourhood-based professional theatre founded by Robin Belitsky Endres. Pelican has done fine work bringing theatre into the lives of many people and encouraging participation from non-professionals. As an educational tool, this kind of popular theatre is an important element in feminist theatre. Pelican's most memorable shows are *Ancestor Stick*, a play about cultural and spiritual roots; *Sardines and Salami*, a piece describing Italian and West Indian immigrant families; and two short plays about Black Caribbean and American immigrants to Canada: *Cherry, Remember the Ginger Wine*, and *Martha and Elvira*. These last two plays toured England in 1985 and played at the Edinburgh Festival and in Amsterdam. Pelican, renamed Imani, is now under the direction of Diana Braithwaite, who is active in Black women's theatre.

Endres herself has made a considerable contribution to feminist culture, both as artistic director of Pelican and as an independent writer and performer. Her play *Ghost Dance* was produced in Fireworks, a 1980 festival of women's plays selected from the *Fireweed Feminist Quarterly* playwriting contest. (Fireworks arose partly as a response to the plaints of male artistic directors that they weren't producing women's plays because there simply *were* none.) In December 1980, Endres and her baby, Ivana, presented *A Pelican in Her Piety*, an extraordinary performance piece. It consisted of monologues, songs, and stand-up comedy about having a baby. Also notable was *Integrated Circuits*, written and performed by Endres. *Integrated Circuits* was first seen as a work-in-progress at the Toronto Women's Perspectives Festival in 1983 and was also performed at the Women and Words conference in Vancouver.

Pelican Players' *Holy Cow Goddess Bazaar,* a twelve-hour spectacle, was presented at the 1984 Toronto Women's Alter Eros Festival. It was worked on for six months and presented twice. It was not documented in any way in the news media, yet made a considerable impact upon the lives of the women involved, and upon the audience. I frequently hear reference made to *Holy Cow* by women working in Toronto theatre, and see its influence from time to time in new feminist theatre pieces. The process of development of *Holy Cow* involved research on six Greek goddesses: Demeter, Persephone, Artemis, Athena, Aphrodite, and Hera. The goddesses were intended to represent six different aspects of women's lives. Research was also done on antecedents and equivalents from other cultures such as the pantheon of Egyptian and Hindu goddesses. The process was collective throughout, with direction by Endres. The performers made masks for each goddess and found characters through the masks. They regularly did feminist spiritual rituals which were largely based on Starhawk's *Dreaming the Dark.* Ultimately they developed individual and collective performance pieces which constituted contemporary manifestations of the Goddess in their own lives. *The Holy Cow Goddess Bazaar,* structured as a celebration, took place in a non-traditional space with virtually no separation between performers and audience. The audience sat on cushions scattered on the floor, eating and drinking, with children running around. *Holy Cow* was intended as a spiritual linking of past and present. Using a collage of material, comic and erotic, the Goddess immanent in women was made intelligible in a contemporary sense. [...]

Toronto's newest feminist theatre is the Company of Sirens, formed in June 1986 with a mandate to produce feminist theatre, lesbian theatre, community/popular theatre, and performance art. The Company of Sirens is a collective of six women: Cynthia Grant, Shawna Dempsey, Peggy Sample, Lina Chartrand, Lib Spry, and myself. The emergence of the Sirens is an example of what can grow out of the feminist theatre context which has been in the making over the past dozen years, and shows the effect of feminist culture on the broadening of the women's cultural environment. Sirens did not assemble as the result of an idea, but rather named what already existed; members had already been working together for several years on various projects, either independent, collective, Nightwood-produced, or as part of a women's festival.

During their first year Sirens have produced a variety of shows including *Sex-Réalité,* an installation with performance on female sexuality, including the lesbian perspective, and with a serious attempt at presenting a multicultural perspective. Held in a Toronto basement theatre every three months, the group's *Siren Soirées* provide women with the opportunity to present new work in an informal atmosphere.

The Working People's Picture Show, a piece which focuses on women in the workforce, was developed collectively in response to requests to perform at union conventions and conferences. The Sirens make this kind of work a priority, as it is seen as key to reaching non-traditional audiences. *The Working People's Picture Show* has played to labour audiences and women's groups throughout Ontario, toured Toronto high schools, and represented Toronto at the May 1987 Canadian Popular Theatre

Festival in Cape Breton. The show is structured in interchangeable units which can be adapted according to audience and venue. It uses a variety of styles, including dramatic monologue, popular street theatre, and satirical vignettes using reworded popular songs. Sirens' aim is to present women with a humorous, insightful dramatization of their experience in the workplace and to be both critical and positive in showing the necessity and possibility of affirmative action.

Creating a Context

From the above discussion it is clear that it is impossible to talk about the development of feminist theatre in Canada without referring constantly to the feminist festivals, conferences, and community groups which nurtured that development. The formation of a Toronto feminist theatre network in particular, shaped by hard economic facts, has been sparked by women's cultural festivals. These were, typically, community events. All were welcome to participate: the priority requirements were personal initiative and having something to say. These festivals have included all branches of the arts—painting, sculpture, theatre, performance art, music, poetry, film, and video. Arranged around feminist themes, they prompted exploration and a breaking of boundaries between artistic disciplines.

In March/April 1983 the Women's Cultural Building, a multi-disciplinary group, organized a festival of the arts. In May 1983 the Women's Perspectives group held a festival at Partisan Gallery, following up a year later with the Alter Eros Festival. In spring of 1985 the artist-run Gallery 940 organized FemFest. The tradition of spring festivals broke down in 1986 due to organizational burnout and the increasing difficulty of obtaining funds, even the minimal kind of funding on which the festivals had operated. However, the collaborations formed during these festivals endure. A women's artistic network exists; women working in different genres are aware of each other's work and provide for each other a kind of human resource account which supplements the meagre bank account.

Feminist theatre events are often held, out of economic necessity, in alternate venues such as art galleries, bars, restaurants, and coffee houses. There are, in addition, frequent conferences across Canada on woman-related topics, which feature performance evenings and invite women to participate. Examples are the National Association of Women and the Law Conference on Reproductive Technology held in Ottawa, February 1985, and the Women's Counselling, Referral & Education Centre Conference held in Toronto, November 1985. These alternate venues have led to a broader cross-genre definition of theatre. Also, the frequently imagistic, expressionist style of feminist theatre has attracted women from other disciplines such as dance, the visual arts, music, poetry, and video; women who, with the advent of feminism, have become politicized and sought personal and political expression in their work. These cross-disciplinary collaborations have helped to break boundaries between disciplines and have contributed to the development of performance art.

Performance Art

Performance art evolved out of "Happenings" which were generated by the European and American art scene of the late fifties and early sixties. "Happenings" had their roots in Dadaism, and took the visual artist out of the studio into the public arena. In this new environment, her/his work expanded to include a collage of environmental elements such as sound, smell, tactile sensation, and time duration. A typical "Happening" was Allan Kaprow's *The Courtyard*, performed outdoors. In it a man rode a bicycle in slow circles. In an early piece, performance artist Laurie Anderson played her violin on a New York City street corner wearing skating boots encased in blocks of ice. Performance art has become a genre in itself, both overlapping with and influencing feminist theatre in terms of the development of a feminist aesthetic. Lucy Lippard, American art critic, says of performance art:

> ...your subject is your form... The subject matter is your raw material, and then you transcend that to get to the content, which is spiritual or universal as well as political... Performance art also affected the outside community in a political way by bringing the feminist emphasis on process and public vulnerability and the importance of private experience and autobiography out of the closet and into an art world arena. (24)

As a vital and innovative form of feminist artistic expression, performance art reflects the narrative of autobiography, the mysticism and ritual of the human potential and women's spirituality movements, and political activism in the form of agit-prop street theatre. It embodies the feminist slogan "the personal is political" and shows the impact society has on our lives. While performance art evolved from visual artists moving towards the theatrical, it has been embraced by feminist theatre workers, resulting in some innovative multi-disciplinary productions. May Chan is a Canadian visual artist who lives in Kingston. Her performances and installations use ritual and diaries to communicate her experience as an immigrant. Much of Chan's work explores her relationship with her mother. The ritualized repetition she uses carries a strong emotional quality which is alleviated by a subtle sense of humour. Chan's installation at the Art and Community show at Toronto's artist-run A Space Gallery in September 1985 consisted of a circle on the floor made up of place settings, each with a cushion and a diary documenting in minute detail a segment of Chan's trip to Hong Kong to visit her ailing mother. Scattered around the place settings were broken crab claws, lemon rinds, and other food fragments which were echoed by delicate, water-colour representations on the wall above.

Elizabeth Chitty comes from a dance background and expanded into video and performance in 1975. Her twelve-scene performance piece, *Moral/Passion*, presented in Toronto in 1985, featured four performers in a rich, sensuous blend of dance, visuals, poetic prose, music and technological tricks. Focussing on the subject of love, *Moral/Passion* shows the transition from states of physical, emotional, and ideological loss to a spiritual mending and holistic transcendence of duality. "*Moral/Passion* is a statement of hope and affirmation for our age," says Chitty. "Our Western legacy has given us a dualistic outlook on the world—good and evil, heaven and hell, right and wrong—a high-contrast viewpoint on life which instructs us towards conflict."[3]

Lillian Allen introduced Dub poetry to Canada. She has been performing regularly in Toronto for years and has also been much in demand at women's festivals across Canada and in the States. Her work, a blend of intensely political content and personal warmth, has made a powerful contribution to feminist culture. Allen's evolution from poet to performance artist has been dramatic, culminating in the July 1986 launching of her record, *Revolutionary Tea Party*. With musical and technological backing, Allen's singing/chanting delivery transcends the poems on the page. Her subject matter ranges from the oppression of the Black immigrant who "Fights Back," to the "Revolutionary Tea Party" where we "criticize, analyze, strategize," to the riveting "Birth Poem" about the birth of her daughter Anta (see Allen). Allen has her entire audience pulsating in a celebration and acknowledgement of the power of childbirth with the repetitious "and me labour, and me labour, and me labour … and Bops, she born."

Toronto's feminist girl trio, The Clichettes, have been delighting audiences for years with their cross-dressing and lip-synching to popular songs. They synchronize their exaggerated male gestures and body language, parodying the macho image and undercutting the misconception of liberation as equality with men. Their rendition of the fifties song, "You Can't Go Home Again," complete with ultra-"feminine" gestures and beehive hairdos, is pure hilarious nostalgia. In The Clichettes' performance we see the redefinition of woman in progress, content, and form uniting in a popularly accessible, politicizing leap.

The Hummer Sisters are three women who have developed an extremely sophisticated style of performance art which blends cabaret, rock, theatre, and video. They challenged incumbent Art Eggleton in the 1983 Toronto mayoral election with the slogan "art versus Art" and came in second. Their campaign created a continuing city-wide performance in which the public participated with enthusiasm.

English-Canadian feminism has not really had a separatist phase in which to express the uninhibited rawness of initial feminist consciousness. Any separatism tended to occur in French Canada, in tandem with national separatism. The general tone in English Canada, particularly in Toronto, was caution, moderation, cover yourself against accusations of being anti-male. However, in terms of the seventies/eighties agitprop and feminist political street theatre, it is no coincidence that the little that Toronto had came from the extremity of the lesbian perspective.

Gay Bell has been a key mover in this type of theatre, which makes political content a priority. Among her many projects put together with performer Marcia Cannon and others are *Sizzle City* and *Pink Triangle Tears*. *Sizzle City*, a forty-five minute guerilla play, to quote Bell, "concerned itself with popularizing anti-nuclear arguments, but at the same time, lots of lesbian propaganda was inserted for comic relief."[4]

Pink Triangle Tears (1981) was a lesbian view of the notorious Toronto bath raids. Bell's political theatre reveals a broad political perspective, not limiting itself to "feminism" or "gay rights" or "the anti-nuke peace movement." Bell understands the links and shows them in her work. She calls her work lesbian theatre, believing that lesbianism as a political choice means much more than sexual orientation: it is indicative of a revolutionary, radically politically aware view of society.

Another example of Bell's integrated vision is *Danger/Anger*, a play she wrote, produced and directed during the summer 1985 International Gay Association Conference. Moving away from her earlier agitprop style, Bell's play was structured by a dual plot line consisting of a lesbian love story and the dilemma of a woman dealing with both an unwanted pregnancy and a right-to-life boyfriend. In it, Bell documented Toronto feminist history with scenes of the burning of the Toronto Women's Bookstore, of pro-choice rallies and demonstrations, and of the raid on the Morgentaler Clinic, all integrated into a dramatically entertaining form.

Artistic Excellence and the Myth of Perfection

Clearly a great deal has happened in the development of feminist theatre in the past ten years or more; it has been an exciting time. But it is not enough. The aesthetic revolution is only beginning, and it is important to evaluate in order to continue. A certain polarization has arisen among feminist theatre workers, both in Canada and abroad, regarding the issue of "artistic excellence." But to frame the discussion in these terms is in some ways beside the point. What we are really talking about is a mismatching of form and content. Feminist theatre and innovative theatre *demand* new forms to contain the new content. And those who continue to insist on traditional artistic excellence deny women the necessary period of grace to discover their own aesthetic—an aesthetic not so bound to the strictures of naturalistic theatre. It is unrealistic to expect revolutionary feminist theatre to spring forth with a feminist aesthetic complete and ready-made. Content always precedes form. Feminist theatre begins with women's experience. If you try to squash women's experience into traditional male structures you silence the voice. You have to *search* for the appropriate form, and in the interim you have to live with the mess and confusion which accompany experimental, innovative work.

In theatre everyone wants every show to be the best. Because we have been conditioned to associate imperfection with failure, it is very difficult to relax into the risks inherent in experimental work. Some of the most interesting feminist performers, writers, and directors are quite volatile in terms of the quality of their work because they take risks. Most have found their style within the mainstream training ground, and now they have to start all over again, finding their inherent feminist style. It is difficult. We have been culturally censored by the prevailing value system for so long that self-censorship is ingrained in us. Because we are afraid, there is a tendency to fall back on the known and accepted male values, aesthetics, and ideas.

Another factor contributing to the breakdown of perfectionism is time. Financial strictures mean less development and rehearsal time, but the current pace of global events creates an even greater time pressure. When the content of the theatre piece concerns issues of immediate social relevance, the slow crafting approach would result in the play being out of date by the time it reached the stage.

Mira Friedlander has said that "performers on the cutting edge are distinguished from those in the mainstream by their political analysis and dedication to effecting change" (57). The key word here is dedication. Indeed, to work and remain working in feminist theatre requires dedication and passion, backed by a thorough understanding of feminist politics and the place of feminism in the world today. Feminist theatre is by definition a political activity and a politicizing force. In understanding and naming our experience, we become aware of negative influences—tic tac—changing our tactics to evade trivialization and the seduction of approval.

(1987)

Notes

[1] I would like to acknowledge Rhea Tregebov, Lina Chartrand, Cynthia Grant, Gay Bell, and Mariana Valverde for their editorial assistance in writing this article.

[2] The source of this quotation is unrecoverable—ed.

[3] The source of this quotation is unrecoverable—ed.

[4] The source of this quotation is unrecoverable—ed.

Works Cited

Allen, Lillian. *Revolutionary Tea Party* (LP). Toronto: Verse to Vinyl, 1986.

Bell, Gay. "From a Resistance to Lesbian Theatre to a Lesbian Theatre of Resistance." *Resources for Feminist Research: The Lesbian Issue* 12.1 (1983): 30–34.

Bessai, Diane. "A Survey Report: Women, Feminism and Prairie Theatre." *Canadian Theatre Review* 43 (1985): 28–43.

Brossard, Nicole. "Fictions & Realities: Jean Wilson Interviews Nicole Brossard." *Broadside* 2.8 (1981): 11, 18.

Fraticelli, Rina. "Any Black Crippled Woman Can! or A Feminist's Notes from Outside the Sheltered Workshop." *Room of One's Own* 8.2 (1983): 7–19.

———. "The Invisibility Factor: Status of Women in Canadian Theatre." *Fuse* (September 1982): 112–25.

Friedlander, Mira. "Feminist Performance: On the Cutting Edge." *Canadian Theatre Review* 43 (1985): 52–58.

Grant, Cynthia. "Nightwood Theatre: Notes From the Front Line." *Canadian Theatre Review* 43 (1985): 44–51.

———. Presentation. Women in Theatre Conference. York University. August 1985.

Gubar, Susan. "The Blank Page and the Issues of Female Creativity." *The New Feminist Criticism: Essays on Women, Literature and Theory.* Ed. Elaine Showalter. New York: Pantheon, 1985. 292–314.

Lambert, Betty. "Battling Aristotle: A Conversation with Betty Lambert." *Room of One's Own* 8.2 (1983): 55–66.

Lippard, Lucy. "Political Performance Art: A Discussion by Suzanne Lacy and Lucy Lippard." *Heresies* 17 (1984): 22–25.

Murray, Janet. *Strong Minded Women & Other Lost Voices From 19th Century England.* New York: Pantheon, 1982.

Nietzche, Friedrich. *The Birth of Tragedy.* New York: Doubleday Anchor, 1956.

Usmiani, Renate. *Second Stage: The Alternate Theatre Movement in Canada.* Vancouver: U of British Columbia P, 1983.

Erasing Historical Difference:
The Alternative Orthodoxy in Canadian Theatre

by Alan Filewod

The construct of an alternative theatre as the radical aesthetic and structural challenge to an established "mainstream" informs the most common perception of modern Canadian theatre history. It is inscribed in critical discourse, in the funding policies and assessment procedures of the federal and provincial arts councils, in the rhetoric of the theatres and, for most of its history, in the editorial analysis of the *Canadian Theatre Review*. By questioning the critical paradigm of alternative theatre I wish to suggest a need to reappraise the ideological forms by which the recent history of Canadian theatre has been constructed, and in the process of that argument, I want to reconsider the general usefulness of "alternative theatre" as a critical term. This inquiry begins with the idea that in the context of Canadian theatre at least, terms like "alternative" and "mainstream" obscure rather than clarify historical forces. These terms enabled critics to define an emerging movement a decade ago but they have outlived their function, and their continued use draws attention to their essentially metaphoric nature. Rather than constantly redefining such terms to align them with changing conditions, perhaps their fundamental validity should be questioned.

My analysis is based on the English-Canadian experience because the rhetorical formation of alternativeness was different in Quebec, where the term *jeune théâtre* played a parallel identifying role. The material and structural principles may have been in most respects similar—bearing in mind that the *jeune théâtre* comprised many more part-time troupes, and had the advantages of a more centralized culture and ideology—but the political determination of the theatre differed greatly between francophone (primarily but not exclusively Québécois) and anglophone Canada. [1]

Critical orthodoxy of the alternative theatre in English Canada locates the period of the late 1960s to the mid 1970s as a point of historical crisis during which the mainstream regional theatre system was challenged and overshadowed by the emerging alternates. The regionals are usually characterized by conservative repertoires, a mistrust of Canadian drama, middle-class audiences, and a marked tendency to prefer foreign, usually British, artistic directors. The alternates are the heroes in this cultural drama: nationalistic, committed to Canadian playwrights, young, radical, and self-consciously experimental. [2] As convention has it, they began as expressions of the familiar American concept of radical theatre, and evolved a nationalist ideology: the weak faded away and the strong survived; they legitimized playwriting as a profession in this country; they spawned a generation of new actors, designers, and directors, and eventually they ate the mainstream. This version of history locates its climax in the merger in 1988 of the "alternate" Toronto Free Theatre with the "regional" CentreStage to form the Canadian Stage Company, now one of the three largest theatres in Canada; the alternates have transformed the conditions of their existence to become the new mainstream.

During the struggle for cultural nationalism in the 1970s that reading of emerging history was necessary, and it may still be useful. Recently I've become dissatisfied with it, because there are too many unresolved questions and contradictions. I am uncomfortable with the implied analysis of what is termed "mainstream," a term that does not imply anything as marginal as the theatre in Canada today and simplifies the complex class allegiances that institutionalize the theatre in North America. This entire mainstream/alternative paradigm progresses with no explicit reference to class or audience. It constructs the audience not as an active presence but as an ahistorical mass that is acted upon, a target for subscription drives and publicity campaigns. The terms are employed with virtually no reference to the cultural formation of the theatre as an expression of community. Their pretension to dialectical coherence, and their bipolar axis mean that these terms do not admit analyses based on criteria other than their own premises. The most obvious exclusion is a consideration of the role of gender: when recent Canadian theatre history is analysed in terms of the politics of gender and sexuality (and it rarely is) the dialectic of mainstream/alternative as it has been constructed is extremely dubious.[3] Even within its own ideological paradigm, it fails to investigate the historical mechanisms by which change is effected. Ultimately it precedes a kind of cultural Darwinism.

I want to begin to unwind the central problem that I perceive by looking at the initial conflict posited between the mainstream and its radical opposition. The mainstream refers to the regional theatres—the system of civic theatres that came into being during the 1950s and 1960s in most major Canadian cities.[4] It is difficult to generalize about these theatres: some embodied bourgeois cultural principles; others declared themselves as politically engaged. What they had in common was the agreement of the Canada Council that they would develop as the flagship theatres of their respective regions. This agreement translated into capital funding to construct or renovate large physical plants. Some of them were constructed by coalitions of various civic groups and community theatres with a strong ingredient of boosterism; others survived because of the dedication of a few founding individuals. What is important here is that it is difficult to impose uniformity: the histories of Regina's Globe Theatre, or Montreal's Centaur Theatre, for example, have more in common with the so-called alternates than with regionals like the Citadel Theatre in Edmonton or Toronto Arts Productions, precursor of CentreStage in the St. Lawrence Centre for the Arts in Toronto.

Despite these disparities, critics perceived the regional theatres as a system, one that consumed the lion's share of government funding. The arts councils for their part inherited in the mid 1970s dozens of small theatres that had begun on easily obtained but short-lived make-work LIP (Local Initiatives Projects) and OFY (Opportunities for Youth) grants from the relatively nationalistic Liberal government of Pierre

Trudeau. The councils, led by the Canada Council, encouraged the establishment of new theatres, but at the same time sought rational models of development. What they evolved through trial and error was a model that placed the alternates as satellites to the regional theatre, locked into place by funding categories. On paper, this model looked right: in the centre the regional theatre would act as a catalyst to validate the alternates. This model was dynamic and it admitted controversy. What could be better? It was the institutional realization of an ideological relationship between mainstream (which means big) and alternative (which means small), and which accorded with a bourgeois model that understands culture in terms of polarities: high/low, establishment/avant-garde, commercial/experimental. In the theatre community, this model came to represent the institutionalization of an ideological debate about culture situated on the issue of the Canadian playwright. The regionals were perceived as anglomaniac and hostile to indigenous playwriting, and the alternatives pro-Canadian. That perception was fuelled by the fact that the larger theatres were generally run by community boards rather than artists, and thus had less interest in the development of new work than in the advancement of subscription sales. The equation of nationalism with alternative perhaps reached its apogee in the middle of the decade when a group of nationalist academics in Ottawa founded the Great Canadian Theatre Company with the mandate of performing only Canadian plays and hiring only Canadian artists. Reflecting on this in 1979, one of the founders wrote that

> I regret that this insistence upon doing Canadian theatre was, and to some extent, is radical. But it is. As we observed time and again; when companies in Ottawa didn't do anything Canadian for three, four, or five years no critic or commentator turned a hair. But when we decided to do only Canadian theatre we were described as that "narrowly nationalistic," that "chauvinistic," that "militantly nationalist" company. (Matthews 134)

From a distance the concentric model of mainstream theatres and satellite alternates seemed to describe the situation adequately. However, it did not describe the situation in Newfoundland, where there was no regional theatre and where Actors' Equity refused the "alternate" Mummers Troupe, a political intervention theatre, the standard studio contract given to small theatres because Newfoundland had no regional theatre to which the Mummers might be considered an alternative. Nor did it describe the situation in New Brunswick where the regional theatre, Theatre New Brunswick, behaved more like an alternate by encouraging local playwrights and decentralizing its operation in several small cities; nor in Toronto where rapid changes invalidated it almost as soon as it was proposed; nor in Manitoba, where the Manitoba Theatre Centre pursued an erratic course, depending on the artistic director; nor in British Columbia where the same could be said of the Vancouver Playhouse. The only place where that model seemed to work was in Edmonton where Joe Shoctor, the powerful lawyer who founded and still governs the Citadel Theatre, straddled the mainstream and defied anyone else to "jump his claim."

This model of alternative and mainstream seemed to make sense when the lines were drawn on the issue of Canadian playwrights, but that was not an institutional condition; it was a matter of how the institutions were used. After all, there were self-defined alternates that expressed less interest in Canadian drama than many of the so-called regionals. The construction of the mainstream was in effect an ideological fiction that rationalized larger grants to certain theatres on the basis of box office sales (or community penetration) and physical assets. Beyond that, the stream became a confusing delta: any category that lumps the left-wing populism of the Globe Theatre with the Stratford Festival is obviously problematic. Yet it is this category that under-lies the whole concept of the alternative theatre, which is commonly represented as the radical challenge to a bourgeois model of theatre.

Part of the problem can be attributed to critical tradition, which has a demon-strated need to reconcile the Canadian experience with a Eurocentric historical discourse.[5] Because the Canadian theatre carries references to the European model of bourgeois and avant-garde art and the postmodern tradition, critics have attempted to transpose their analyses. The Eurocentric discourse is an essentially colonial revival of the idea of a New World that extends the experience of the old. It seeks to explain the development of Canadian theatre in terms of a dialectic that explains particularly European affinities of aesthetics and institutional structures.

Perhaps more importantly, the problem is geographical: if the Canadian theatre cannot be understood by the experience of other societies, neither have all areas of the country followed the same development pattern. Nevertheless, the attempt to define the Canadian experience has tended to impose an ideological uniformity. The recog-nition of this paradox has led to a general acceptance of the theory of regionalism to explain the significant differences encountered across the country (see Bessai, Wallace). Regionalism is an attempt, an imperfect one I believe, to reconcile institu-tional and thematic structures. It only works in reference to an implied centre that is in critical practice, as opposed to theory, usually located in Toronto. That in turn con-structs Toronto as the paradigm of Canadian culture by which regional variations can be measured.

This condition is built into the formulation of the alternative/mainstream prob-lematic, because the labels are themselves taken from the Toronto experience. Because Toronto is the defacto cultural capital of Canada (which may only mean that it has the largest concentration of critics) its development is taken as representative of the coun-try at large. Although the opposite is more likely the case, I want to focus on the Toronto experience, not because I think it is more important or more central than that of any other city, but because it is from Toronto that the mostly Toronto-based critics have drawn their normative principles.

It is generally conceded that the Toronto alternate theatre had its sources in polit-ical radicalism. Certainly something happened in those signal years of 1970 and 1972. In 1970 the three major hits of the Toronto theatre scene were all expressions of the so-called radical spirit at Toronto Workshop Productions. *Chicago '70*, a documentary satire of the Chicago Seven conspiracy trial, ran for three months; at Studio Lab

Theatre *Dionysus in 69* (the first professional production of the play outside of New York) had become *Dionysus in 70*; and at the Royal Alexandra Theatre, Toronto's oldest commercial house, *Hair* still celebrated an ideal that died that same year at Kent State. 1970 was also the year of the Festival of Underground Theatre, during which the new St. Lawrence Centre played inadvertent host to groups as diverse as Bread & Puppet Theatre and le Theatre de la Panique. In 1970, alternate theatre was underground (at times literally: Theatre Passe Muraille originally performed in an underground garage), "off-Yonge," and consciously radical, its politics and much of its repertoire informed by the American experience. It described itself as "experimental," appropriating that term to mean iconoclastic. Ironically, the nationalist axis that characterized the later alternate theatre movement was inverted in 1970, when Toronto Arts Productions, the St. Lawrence Centre's main tenant which grew to be the bogey of the alternate theatres, initiated itself with an all-Canadian premiere season.

By 1972, Toronto Arts Productions was leaning heavily towards the classics and the alternate theatre appeared very different: it was nationalistic—detractors called it xenophobic—and it expressed its nationalism in a rediscovery of self. This was a theatre of collective creations and documentaries that articulated the Canadian voice, and of kitchen-sink naturalism that returned a distinctly Canadian gaze. It was the theatre of Passe Muraille's groundbreaking rural documentary *The Farm Show* and David French's naturalistic melodrama *Leaving Home*. This was a theatre of cultural reclamation and postcolonial consolidation which sought to express its difference from the American experience that had originally informed it. [6]

This change in the project of the alternate theatre was the result of an overdetermination in the theatre at a time of cultural contradiction between colonialism and nationalism in the arts. The alternative theatre appropriated the aesthetics of the "international" avant-garde as a means of expressing its difference and autonomy. The convergence of several social crises—of nationalism, of the counter-culture movement, and of a generational surge resulted in a theatre that perceived itself in terms of its difference from a social mainstream that it rejected as colonised, middle-class, and middle-aged. This overdetermination, which identified alternative aesthetics with alternative politics (and which ironically accorded with the federal government's expressed interest in cultural nationalism in the early 1970s), established a myth of the alternate theatre at odds with the facts. This myth accepts the evolutionary fallacy that describes cultural development in generational and anthropomorphic terms, constructed Canadian culture as something that grows from colonial infantilism to an undefined "world-class" maturity. This same principle is at work in the hypothetical convergence of alternate and mainstream that is said to typify the theatre of the present day.

It is commonly stated then that the experience of the alternate theatre in Toronto saw a shift in ideological emphasis from generational ("radical") to nationalist politics (see e.g., Johnston). The problem is that this model cannot account for its contradictions, particularly those which attempt to equate the institutional placement of various theatres with their ideological alignment. To mention only one example, if the so-called radical theatre of 1970 is the source of the alternate theatre in Toronto, then Ed Mirvish's overtly commercial Royal Alexandra Theatre must be considered a forerunner of the alternate theatre because *Hair* was no less (in retrospect, perhaps no more) radical that *Tom Paine* and *Futz*, the two performances that established a radical reputation for the early Theatre Passe Muraille. What differed was that *Hair* was a business venture and *Tom Paine* was not. To reject the Royal Alex as a forerunner of the alternate theatre, then, is to put the defining criteria not on repertoire but on the context of production. By the mid 1970s, however, the definition of alternate theatre in Toronto was normally based on repertoire, or more precisely, the nationality of the repertoire.

If the original criteria for alternate status were contextual, then it is clear that the alternate theatre in Toronto preceded the so-called mainstream not just by a few years but by several decades. Its origins lie in the Workers' Experimental Theatre and its successor, the Theatre of Action in the 1930s.[7] The workers' theatres sought new ideological and structural contexts for the making of theatre. Their emphases on collectivity and cultural politics established a tradition that George Luscombe carried on when he founded Toronto Workshop Productions in 1959. Luscombe, who had travelled to England to spend five years with Joan Littlewood's Theatre Workshop in the 1950s and who founded his theatre on her model, trained a generation of artists and infused the theatre around him with a radical spirit, both in terms of external politics and the politics of the theatre. In 1970, the alternate theatres were clearly the successors of the political theatre that had if not thrived at least struggled in Toronto for forty years.

The theatre of the mid-1970s represented more than a maturation of that political alternative theatre, and to argue that the one grew into the other confuses the issue and invalidates the work of subsequent political theatres as undeveloped and immature. The sources of the nationalist theatre can also be traced back to the 1930s, to a time when the vision of a network of civic regional theatres across the country was challenged by a populist alternative. The regional theatre system had been anticipated as early as 1897, when Hector Charlesworth, critic for the *Toronto Evening News*, called for government subsidies as a corrective to the inanity of the commercial stage. The civic theatre ideal was commonly expressed in the subsequent decades by critics and cultural politicians—foremost among them B.K. Sandwell and Vincent Massey, who adapted the nascent British model of subsidized civic theatre as an alternative to American monopoly control of the theatre in Canada.[8] This proposal evolved into the system of regional civic theatre recommended in 1952 in the report of the Massey Commission, which in turn was the model encouraged by the Canada Council in its first decades. The nationalist alternative theatre of the 1970s was not an overnight conversion of politically radical theatres. It was the modern articulation of a challenge first envisioned in 1933, when Archibald Key, writing in *Canadian Forum*, envisioned that Canada's national theatre would be a little red schoolhouse and a Ford van somewhere in the Prairies (Key 462). This was a vision of a postcolonial theatre that rejected imported models of development and sought its structures in the audiences it was designed to serve. Although many of the alternate theatres of the 1970s never visited that little schoolhouse, the majority of them shared that commitment to an autonomous postcolonial theatre. For most of them that meant a commitment to the Canadian playwright.

I am left at this point then with two models of the alternate theatre that overlap but do not accord. On the one hand, there is the theatre that defines itself as alternative by virtue of its expressed values. This is the political theatre that speaks for a defined constituency, and which may include a variety of institutional structures and aesthetic approaches. On the other hand, there is the theatre that defines alternative in terms of its relations to the institutional structures of Canadian culture: this is the theatre of postcolonial nationalism. When these two tendencies overlap, as they did in Toronto in the early 1970s, that overdetermination can engender a critical confusion that tries to comprehend both under the one label of alternative. If the idea of an alternative theatre is a determining factor in contemporary Canadian theatre history, then the idea of a mainstream is a necessary corollary that is equally confusing, because of the false unity it imposes on a complex reality.

Even as the dialectic of alternate/mainstream is enshrined in the discourse of theatre criticism in this country, it is challenged in the theatre itself by terms that undermine that dialectic. The first of these terms is "the fringe." It too accepts marginalization as a condition of its formation, but its metaphor is posited in terms of spatial centrality rather than bipolarity. The fringe perceives theatrical difference in structural and institutional terms, a perception that has definite aesthetic implications but no necessary aesthetic coherence or unity. The second term also expands a tendency obscured by the alternative label: that is the popular theatre. As it has come to be known, popular theatre refers not to a genre or form in itself, but the application of theatre as a tool of political or social development. Much of the energy behind the popular theatre movement comes from the development education sector; at present there are countless community groups—a large proportion of them initiated by women and Native peoples—across Canada that use theatre as a means of empowerment in political struggle. Some of them are professional theatres, like Edmonton's Catalyst Theatre, which initiates projects with marginalized and disenfranchised communities; most however are one-time grassroots projects working on grants from social agencies and government action programs.[9]

Both the fringe and popular theatre have developed rapidly in the last decade and both are celebrated by regular national festivals, chief among them the annual Fringe festivals in Victoria, Vancouver, Edmonton, and Winnipeg, and the biannual festivals of the Canadian Popular Theatre Alliance. Implicit in the acceptance of these terms (which themselves need to be challenged as reductive) is the recognition that the label of alternative theatre no longer suffices to express the particular characteristics of these tendencies. In fact, it never did suffice. The idea of the alternative theatre is a rhetorical strategy which erases the fact that what is constituted as fringe and popular today were integral, overlapping, but essentially contradictory elements in the very formation of the independent theatre of the 1970s.

(1989)

Notes

1 By the mid-seventies there were approximately one hundred "alternate" theatre companies in English-speaking Canada, and roughly the same number of francophone troupes in Quebec. For two different perspectives on the parallels of the alternate theatre and the Quebec *jeune théâtre*, see Filewod, "Ideological Formation," and Usmiani.

2 Although the terms "alternate theatre" and "alternative theatre" have been used indiscriminately in Canada, the generation of theatres that emerged in the early 1970s have been known as "the alternates," following the usage most common in Toronto at that time.

3 That there has been very little work on Canadian theatre history from a feminist analysis is problematic considering the important role feminist theatres have played in the last two decades, and considering that one of the earliest political performances in Canada was Nellie McClung's *Parliament of Women* in Winnipeg in 1903. For an analysis of women in contemporary Canadian theatre, see Fraticelli. The report is discussed in Lushington.

4 The "regionals" were generally understood to include: in Nova Scotia, Neptune Theatre (Halifax); in Prince Edward Island, the Charlottetown Festival; in New Brunswick, Theatre New Brunswick (Fredericton); in anglophone Quebec, Centaur Theatre (Montreal); in Ontario, Toronto Arts Productions (later CentreStage), National Arts Centre (Ottawa), Sudbury Theatre Centre; Grand Theatre (London); the Stratford Shakespearean Festival, Shaw Festival (Niagara-on-the-Lake), Magnus Theatre (Thunder Bay); in Manitoba, Manitoba Theatre Centre (Winnipeg); in Saskatchewan, the Globe Theatre (Regina); in Alberta, Theatre Calgary, Citadel Theatre (Edmonton); in British Columbia, Vancouver Playhouse and Bastion Theatre (Victoria). There were no theatres in this category in Newfoundland, the Yukon, or the Northwest Territories.

5 This is the thesis of Usmiani's *Second Stage*. She precedes her analysis by placing it in the European context of alternative theatre with its major references to the Artaudian and Brechtian traditions.

6 The evolution of Canadian theatre, and particularly of collective creation, is discussed as a strategy of postcolonial definition in Filewod, *Collective Encounters*.

7 Critics have accepted as a truism the hypothesis that the Workers Theatre Movement of the 1930s offers no direct links with the postwar alternative theatre. See "Introduction" by Endres. That proposition needs to be challenged because of the number of activists who overlapped both periods, because the concept of "direct links" is the product of an empiricist historiographic method that is unable to account for ideological developments in society, and because it marginalizes the ongoing project of political intervention theatre.

8 The nationalist argument against American financial control of the theatres is stated in Sandwell (1911). Sandwell, editor of *Saturday Night*, and Massey, a leading diplomat and later Governor General of Canada, were both influenced by William Archer and Granville-Barker's scheme for a national theatre in Britain. From this they extracted the principle of publicly subsidized theatres. They recognized, however, that because of geographical conditions, Canada's national theatre must be a decentralized geographical network of theatres across the land. Massey built upon this idea in the Report of The Royal Commission on National Development in the Arts, Letters, and Sciences (see Canada). The Massey Report became the guiding document of the Canada Council, which was established to implement the recommendations of his commission. It can be argued that these critics responded to the perceived colonization of Canadian culture by American monopoly capital by reverting to an older colonial allegiance to a cultural model derived from Britain.

9 For a survey of popular theatre in Canada, see *Canadian Theatre Review* 53 (1987). The issue includes articles on popular theatre projects with Inuit and Dene women in the arctic; with striking workers in Alberta; with homeless shelter projects in Toronto; and with women in the workplace. See also *Participatory Research Group Newsletter* (Spring 1987) special issue on Popular Theatre.

Works Cited

Bessai, Diane. "The Regionalism of Canadian Drama." *Canadian Literature* 85 (1980): 7–20.

Canada. Report of the Royal Commission on National Development in the Arts, Letters and Sciences, 1949–1951 (Massey Commission Report). Ottawa: King's Printer, 1951.

Charlesworth, Hector. "Touchstone." *Toronto Evening News* 5 June 1897.

Endres, Robin. "Introduction." *Eight Men Speak and Other Plays from the Canadian Workers' Theatre.* Ed. Richard Wright. Toronto: New Hogtown, 1976. xi–xxxvi.

Filewod, Alan. *Collective Encounters: Documentary Theatre in English Canada.* Toronto: U of Toronto P, 1987.

———. "The Ideological Formation of Political Theatre In Canada." *Theatre History in Canada* 8.2 (1987): 254–63.

Fraticelli, Rina. "The Status of Women in the Canadian Theatre." Report prepared for The Status of Women Canada, June 1982, unpublished.

Johnston, Denis. "Diverting the Mainstream: Bill Glassco and the Early Years of Tarragon Theatre." *Canadian Drama* 13.2 (1987): 121–74.

Key, Archibald. "The Theatre on Wheels." *Canadian Forum* 13 (1933): 462–63.

Lushington, Kate. "Fear of Feminism." *Canadian Theatre Review* 43 (1988): 5–11.

Mathews, Robin. "Letter to the Editor." *Canadian Theatre Review* 24 (1979): 134.

Participatory Research Group. Special Issue on Popular Theatre. *Participatory Research Group Newsletter* 4.2 (1987).

Sandwell, B.K. "The Annexation of our Stage." *Canadian Magazine* 38.1 (1911): 22–26.

Usmiani, Renate. *Second Stage: The Alternative Theatre Movement in Canada.* Vancouver: U of British Columbia P, 1983.

Wallace, Robert. "Writing the Land Alive: The Playwright's Vision in English Canada." *Contemporary Canadian Theatre: New World Visions.* Ed. Anton Wagner. Toronto: Simon and Pierre, 1985. 69–81.

Six Million Dollars and Still Counting

by M. NourbeSe Philip

Six million dollars! As of the week before the October 17, 1993, opening of *Show Boat*, this amount was reportedly sold in advance ticket sales. *The Globe and Mail* described these figures as "encouraging" given that *Show Boat* was a revival and not a "much-bally-hooed new work" (Enchin). ("Much-ballyhooed" is, in fact, exactly how I would have described the media coverage of *Show Boat*.) On Friday, October 16, 1993, Livent share prices closed at $16.00 on the Toronto Stock Exchange, reflecting a $1.50 increase (Enchin).

Alongside television images of opening night festivities reflecting the theme of travelling up the Mississippi, this sort of hard factual information (or is it disinformation?) representing tangible evidence of Garth Drabinsky and Livent's "success," could very easily have the impact of making those who opposed this production of *Show Boat* feel that they had lost the fight. Not to mention the chortling on the part of the media, including dismissive references, at the small number of demonstrators at the previews and the opening night. In these apparent zero sum games there appear to be only winners and losers, and the Coalition to Stop *Show Boat* (The Coalition), along with those opposing this production of *Show Boat* certainly appear to have lost.

Imagine for the moment, however, the following scene and its development: it has come to the attention of the Black and African Canadian communities that the well-known impresario Garth Drabinsky and his company Livent are producing the musical *Show Boat* in which they have already invested a considerable sum of money. Various members of the Black communities meet with him and, through a series of meetings, he is convinced that the production of *Show Boat* will create great pain and hurt to African Canadian communities. He is concerned that he and his company might be associated with a show that is racist, and whose production will affect African Canadians negatively. He meets with his shareholders and with the Mayor of North York. With the exception of a few shareholders, there is general agreement that this show cannot go on. Drabinsky realizes that the opening of the North York Performing Arts Centre (NYPAC) will have to be postponed for another six months, while he arranges for another musical to open the centre. North York has agreed to bear 50% of the financial cost of this postponement.

> Fairy tale? Yes.
> Romantic hogwash? Yes.
> True or false? False.

Would that such a scenario could play itself out in the Toronto of the 1990s. It would be illustrative of a very different society from the one in which we presently live; it would be representative of a society which valued all its peoples equally. A society which didn't need the lubrication of power or money to work. As this one does. A society which understood the collective pain of African peoples. But if we lived in such a society, then Black children would not be being streamed into vocational programs; we would need no affirmative action programs to ensure that African Canadians were hired; we would not have Black people being shot by the police in circumstances which did not warrant it; nor would we have strip searches of Black women in public.

What has played itself out over the last several months in North York and Toronto around the production of *Show Boat* is all of a piece with how African Canadians are positioned in a society which consistently dismisses them and their concerns. For instance, in the October 16, 1993, issue of *The Globe and Mail*, William Thorsell, Editor-in-Chief, writes that the only game in town is one of power—"The apparent issue is race—the allegation by some black people in Toronto that *Show Boat* demeans them. But the real issue is power. *Show Boat* is really just a vehicle to advance the campaign of some blacks in Toronto for more power in the life of the city, in particular the City of North York."

Mr. Thorsell not only dismisses the most consistently and publicly expressed concern of all those opposed to *Show Boat*—its demeaning treatment of Blacks—he also suggests that in expressing this concern, Blacks are being less than honest and, as all good white fathers are wont to do, he tells his audience what the *real* issue is. Power.

Accepting for the moment Thorsell's argument that power is the issue, there is a further implication by him that there is something amiss in Blacks seeking to gain power. In as rapacious a society as ours, where power—and primarily financial power—*is* the only language understood, surely its pursuit would be seen as a respectable and acceptable act. Not, however, when it comes to Blacks. The acquisition, maintenance, and abuse of power by individuals like Garth Drabinsky and his corporation are commendable and remain unquestioned; the acquisition of power by Blacks—whether or not we agree with Thorsell's analysis of the issues behind the opposition to *Show Boat*—always remains questionable. Once again we see the double bind of being Black: not only are we dishonest in identifying what we find demeaning in a show, but we also have no business trying to achieve power.

All the World's a Play

There have always been two "plays" in rehearsal around the present production of *Show Boat*. One is the Garth Drabinsky/Livent-produced show; the other, the "play" of events around the production.[1] At issue in the latter "play" have been the following: the inappropriateness of using a racist production to open a multimillion dollar, municipal flagship facility which was also publicly funded; the public and private challenges and objections to the production made by Blacks and African Canadians;

and the wholeheartedly negative responses to those challenges by the producers and the media—in short, by the powerful.

The nub of the issue in this latter production is the refusal on the part of Canadian society to take seriously the issues Blacks and African Canadians define as important to themselves including their histories, their cultures, and their representation in society. This refusal is integrally linked to their social position in Canadian society. With the opening of *Show Boat*, Garth Drabinsky and Livent have attempted to shift the ground of the debate from this central issue to whether or not the production is racist. This being a democratic society, the argument goes, we must see for ourselves and make up our own minds. The unstated corollary to this argument is that if you decide the play is, as we have been told repeatedly, a paean to racial tolerance and anti-racism, then the issues which have been the focus of the "play" around the play immediately become non-issues. They fade to black with the last curtain call.

It is, therefore, crucial that we look backwards and forwards simultaneously in order to remain centred on the issue—that even if the present production of *Show Boat* were *the* most anti-racist piece of work since *The Autobiography of Malcolm X*, it in no way alleviates the up-front-out-there racism on the part of the producers, the media, and other institutions like the United Way during its production. It in no way cures the disrespect meted out to Blacks and African Canadians, neither does it repair the grave damage done to race relations in this city. The black of six million dollars does not appear on the only relevant balance sheet—the one that tallies relations between whites and African Canadians. By my reckoning, this balance sheet remains deeply in the red to Black and African Canadians.

If we see this struggle as merely one between winners and losers and believe that winning equates with the opening of *Show Boat*, then we have, indeed, lost. Those losses, however, translate into gains when we acknowledge the strenuous work on the part of The Coalition in a variety of areas, including making representations to various school boards. Further gains are to be found in the individual and collective acts of resistance and courage, in the face of powerful institutions, resulting in mass resignations by Blacks and African Canadians from the United Way committees and board.

There are also some lessons to be learnt. While physical demonstration of Black protest is important, to rely primarily on public demonstrations to convey our concerns is, to some degree, to speak a language that can be easily dismissed as outmoded particularly if numbers remain small. The weekly pickets demonstrated an overwhelming commitment and helped to keep attention focussed on the issues. However, strategies like boycotts, lobbying, and legal actions need to become a greater part of how Black communities function in their struggles. The Coalition's attempt to have criminal charges laid under hate-crime legislation, and to involve the Human Rights Commission represents the beginning of just such a development. A mass return of American Express credit cards and a one-day-a-week boycott of the *Toronto Star* were among some of the possibilities raised in discussions I have had with others. Such actions, however, require a great deal of coordination and work to convince Black and non-Black people of their appropriateness. At the higher levels of the economy, Blacks as a group may not exert much economic leverage; our purchasing power is, however, by no means insignificant. It is a weapon we should focus on increasingly; it speaks the only language this society understands.

As we tally the balance sheet, we notice that overt government support for the position of those opposing the production of *Show Boat* has been virtually non-existent, although the absence of the Ontario premier Bob Rae, from the opening-night celebrations represents a small public relations victory. The Anti-Racism Secretariat has made no public statement on the issue. While giving money to The Coalition, it has remained assiduously low-keyed, not wishing to be seen to be taking sides. This *is* the Anti-Racism Secretariat after all.

At a recent lecture in Toronto, sponsored by the B'nai B'rith Garth Drabinsky Lecture Series, Harvard professor Henry Louis Gates Jr. described this production of *Show Boat* as "a victory of tolerance and sensitivity to the feelings of an important segment of the community" (qtd. in Hudson). [2] In his May 12, 1993, written presentation to the North York Board of Education trustees, however, we can see what Garth Drabinsky and Livent thought of the concerns of this "important segment of the community." In his submission Drabinsky describes those opposing the production as "using *Show Boat* as a platform to promote their own agenda and causes which have nothing whatsoever to do with this show" (Drabinsky, "Statement" 63). He dismissed legitimate concerns as "shouted slogans, mob rule and wild accusations which have no substance behind them." In an accompanying document in which he responds to community concerns, he writes: "We believe that the protests that have been raised about the script's purported racial stereotyping and its alleged contribution to the perpetuation of negative images of people of African-American ancestry, are *vague, misconceived, and inaccurate*" (Livent, "Community"; emphasis added). Drabinsky criticizes those opposing the show *prior* to its staging: "we have the right to be judged on our works," he argues, "only after they have been presented for public scrutiny... and not a minute before." Simultaneously, however, Drabinsky uncritically accepts the support of "the media, the general public and... even educators, (who) have expressed their full support of this production." *This without their having seen the Livent production.*

According to Drabinsky, those objecting to a show which had already been performed countless times, filmed three times, and based on a book which is undeniably racist, indulge in "mob rule" and "wild accusations," while those supporting a yet unproduced show are a "largely silent majority" supporting the "right of the free exchange of ideas, opinions and information."

Despite his condemnation of those criticizing *Show Boat*, within the same document Drabinsky writes that "all of the concerns which have been raised about *Show Boat* have been and will be considered as our production is developed," a production which, he assures us, will carry a "message of racial harmony and understanding."

If there were no validity to the arguments of those challenging *Show Boat*, if those concerns were "vague, misconceived and inaccurate," if those challenging this production were interested in "mob rule," why did Livent think it necessary to state that it would consider all the concerns raised and to emphasize the show's "racial harmony and understanding"? Why has Livent produced a television program on the making of *Show Boat*, narrated by Black actor James Earl Jones, which tries to show how racially sensitive and respectful it has been to issues around race (*Show Boat: Journey*)? Why was it necessary to bring in personalities of the stature of Oscar Peterson to validate the show and the production? If accusations were "wild" and lacked substance, why go to the trouble and expense? If nothing else, Livent and Garth Drabinsky owe an apology to those who have opposed this show for the kind of contemptuous statements they have written about them, since from all reports the production now seems all set to win a Tony for the most "socially acceptable," if not politically correct version, of *Show Boat* ever produced.

Further to the issue of the dismissal of Black concerns and requests, Drabinsky, in his response to community concerns mentioned above, gave reasons for refusing to release the script for public scrutiny. To do so, he argued, would be an "abrogation of the right of free speech… [w]hat the show will be, cannot be fully ascertained from the script alone," since levels of meaning could be added through "directorial embellishments, underscoring, stage action and other theatrical techniques." How then do we explain the fact that *without having seen the show* and *only having read the script*, Henry Louis Gates Jr. was able to declare the show non-racist?

Despite protestations to the contrary, Livent's attempts to discredit the protesters and their opinions, and to take the high moral road have been driven by the morality of the bottom line. With eight million dollars at risk, not to mention the possibility of a Broadway run, the juggernaut that is Live Entertainment Corporation of Canada could not risk the possibility that "shouted slogans," "mob rule," and "wild accusations" might hinder its progress. And so, despite the genuine and very real concerns of African Canadians, advance ticket sales have reached six million dollars and Livent share prices have increased.

The Culture of Contempt

In a racist society such as Canada, it is a common practice to isolate issues of racism so that they appear to have relevance only for Africans, Asians, or First Nations people. Links between these groups and the larger society only surface when the need arises to manipulate the latent and, more recently, not-so-latent racism around issues of immigration, crime, and welfare fraud. While the issues around *Show Boat* may appear to have relevance primarily for African Canadians, its opening during the height of the 1993 election campaign has highlighted the connections between apparently "Blacks only" issues and the seemingly larger issues like the deficit.

These links and connections have to do with how ideas are legitimized or delegitimized, and while I have more questions than I do answers, it is all the more important to ask these questions. For instance, how does one explain the apparently meteoric rise of the Reform party? Is it simply populist fervour, or are there other fac-

tors at work? How have the ideas of a party that, not too long ago, the media presented as fringe, racist, sexist, and fundamentalist, become mainstream? How has a party
that many in the media appeared to have had to hold their collective noses in order to
write about become the main player in the 1993 elections? Did the media malign them
in their earlier coverage? Or, is it that the media have realized the error of their ways
and now understand the validity of what the Reform Party truly stands for? Whatever
the reasons, what is almost miraculous is how a party like the Reform Party has been
able to come in from the cold to a position of respectability, where reporters have by
and large failed to challenge its spokespeople on issues that as little as two years ago
were grounds to dismiss it. Where have all the investigative journalists gone to? Why
hasn't there been a major article about the racist roots of Reform? Or, was discussion
of the deficit—that supposedly colourless, classless, genderless issue sufficient to legit-
imize its more unsavoury antecedents?

Since beginning this epilogue, the Liberal Party has become the government of
Canada with an overwhelming majority. The Conservatives—may they rest in
peace—have been vanquished, and Reform, some two seats short of the official opposition party, the Bloc Québécois, will remain a significant force in Parliament.

What does all this have to do with *Show Boat* and opposition to its production?
A great deal, indeed. Alongside the redemption, sanitizing, and recuperation of
socially repugnant ideas such as those espoused by the Reform Party, have been the
demonizing and discrediting of ideas such as anti-racism, feminism, and respect for
one's history and culture—despite the fact that all levels of government pay lip service to these ideals, not to mention those of multiculturalism. The success of these
processes runs the gamut from the national to the local level, so that the Reform Party
has now become a major player on the national scene, while one of the most blatant
exercises of how the powerful trample on the concerns of the powerless—the production of *Show Boat*—is heralded as the second coming.

With the catch-all epithet and slur "politically correct," the media—no doubt
speaking for their audience—is able to effectively discredit and dismiss every progressive idea and ideal. And they do. Could it be because those so-called politically correct
ideals can only be realized with real and fundamental change—the yielding of power
to the powerless; the democratic control of the powerful, and a more equitable distribution of power? Is it that these ideas truly challenge the powerful (as mentioned
above, Mr. Thorsell clearly had some difficulty with Blacks seeking power), while the
ideas of the Reform Party, all talk of populism and the deficit to the contrary, appeal
to those who see the powerful as victims of the "politically correct," and the powerless
as deserving of, and at fault for, their position in life.

All this constitutes the backdrop, setting, and context of the 1993 production of
Show Boat and its sycophantic support by the media. "When the NYPAC opens on
October 17, the self-proclaimed City with Heart will become the City with Culture."
So wrote Christopher Hume in an advertising section of the October 2, 1993, *Toronto
Star*, masquerading as news. With the building of the new Princess of Wales theatre
for the Canadian launch of *Miss Saigon*, and now NYPAC, culture has become syn-

onymous with big buildings, just as it did during the heyday of imperialism. It is an impoverished definition of culture that fails to encompass those artists who, year after year and with very little funding, make their art, put on their plays, perform their dance and keep the cultural heart of this city beating. Caribana, for instance, remains *the* most outstanding example of culture without walls or buildings. With very little support from either government or the private sector, in excess of a million people are entertained and some 200 million dollars pumped into the economy within seven to ten days.

The equation of culture with big buildings is an integral part of a long and impe-rial tradition that equated civilization with big stone buildings. By this definition, India and China were "civilized," while Africa was not. At least south of the Sahara. When great stone buildings stopped (beyond Egypt), so did civilization. The only explanation, therefore, according to European scholars, of archaeological ruins of great stone buildings such as Great Zimbabwe found in sub-Saharan Africa, must be that non-Africans had built them. Despite evidence to the contrary—that Africans had, in fact, built these buildings, this remained the entrenched and irrational belief of many European scholars. The script has remained the same: Europeans are civilized and Africans not at all. Consider, for instance, the language used by Drabinsky and Livent to describe Blacks objecting to the production: "mob rule," "wild accusations," "vague, misconceived and inaccurate." All connote qualities of the primitive, the une-ducated, and the unsophisticated—in general, an absence of civility.

Culture is, however, far broader than the arts—big buildings included; it includes the mores, customs, and behaviour of individuals in society—how we settle disputes; how close we stand to people when we talk to them; how we marry and so on. We in Canada, for instance, believe our culture to be a kinder, gentler one than America's, where violence appears to be more endemic. The hotly defended right to bear arms and the frequency of assassinations are but two examples of this culture of violence. However, within the context of a shift to the right throughout Canada, as reflected in the success of the Reform Party in the 1993 federal elections, the "play" of events around the opening of NYPAC and the production of *Show Boat* symbolize, if not rep-resent and illustrate, the development of a different kind of culture in Canada—the culture of contempt.

This culture of contempt is a burgeoning one: it sees the weak, the helpless, the unemployed, the aged, the sick, and the potentially sick as being at fault for their plight; immigrants, women, lesbians, gays, Africans, Asians, and First Nations are parasitic groups feeding off the country. It is a culture of the powerful dismissing the powerless, a culture that says the less powerful can be ignored and dismissed with impunity. The very ideals that Canadians cherished, which they saw as setting them apart culturally from Americans, for instance—the culture of caring, of compassion if you will, the culture of the peacekeeper (now also damaged, perhaps fatally, by the killings of Somalis by Canadian peacekeepers)—are now all under threat if not per-manently destroyed. Many, if not all, of these beliefs, were myths in the first place, but myths are the lifeblood of cultures and no less powerful for it. Their value lies in their ability to generate a certain belief system that shapes a culture indelibly. These myths—the myth of multiculturalism included—have now all been exposed for what they are, at least in relation to Black and African Canadians; they have been effectively laid to rest with the production of *Show Boat*. May they rest in peace. Long live the culture of contempt—Canadian style!

Nobody Knows the Trouble I Know

When his father wrote "Ol' Man River" a sombre-faced William Hammerstein (Oscar Hammerstein's son) tells the audience during the October 26, 1993, CBC special (*Show Boat: Journey*), he "expressed things that nobody had expressed before." Hammerstein was gracious enough to qualify this statement by adding, "certainly no white man." Naturally, creativity only begins when the white man or woman creates or composes. Not a minute before. But who composed the spirituals and gospels? Nobody, of course. Who sang them? Nobody. From whom did Magnolia learn her "coon" songs? From Nobody, naturally. And Kern himself, when he used black syncopation and gapped sevenths to convey black melodies and rhythms in *Show Boat* and in particular "Ol' Man River," from whom did he learn them? Why, Nobody! Since Blacks were all Nobody. And Nobody knows the trouble I know. The words of the spiritual by the same name take on a new and deeper meaning if we understand Nobody to mean not "no one" but Blacks themselves, since in the hearts and minds of most whites they were all, individually and collectively, Nobody. And isn't this still the case today when we remain Nobody in trying to get our voices and concerns heard? And Nobody knows the trouble I know—words bearing the possibility for generating solidarity work in two senses: (a) only other Nobodys will understand the trouble Blacks experience—through similar suffering, and (b) to understand the trouble Blacks experience, one had to be prepared to risk becoming a Nobody.

It is probably unlikely that Hammerstein junior consciously *intended* any deliberate disrespect for Blacks. It is also irrelevant. What *is* relevant is how statements like these reveal the commonsensical and organic nature of racism, resulting in racist statements even when individuals are trying to show how kind and good they are or were towards Blacks.

False News Syndrome[3]

Newspaper reports to the contrary, the production of *Show Boat* is not a victory for free speech and freedom from censorship. Rather, it is an expression of how money talks, of how when one is able to control the media, one's position can be articulated apparently endlessly—in advertisements masquerading as news specials. The press, both print and electronic, have slavered over this production of *Show Boat*. Even *Share* newspaper: "…if there are the equivalents of Oscars for theatre set designers… then Eugene Lee, who conceptualized, designed and developed these *Show Boat* sets, should get two" (Greene 1). For eight million dollars what did we expect? And can form be so neatly separated from content? While the verdict of this newspaper was that *Show Boat* was "implicitly" racist, it failed to explain how, suggesting instead that we not take the writer's word for it but look to *The Globe and Mail*'s review for verification.

The overall effect of media response to the production, including articles such as this, was to make one wonder what all the fuss had been about. Garth Drabinsky and Livent had urged us to have faith in them; assured us that they knew what was best for us, and promised us that they would clean up the production so that Blacks would find it acceptable. And so they have, from all reports to date.

As argued earlier, the issues have shifted ground: instead of the focus being on the racism inherent in using this type of production to open a publicly funded arts centre, *over the legitimate objections of African Canadians*, or the racism manifest in the dismissive attitudes shown towards Black concerns on the part of institutions like the United Way, the issue has been transformed into a debate: is or isn't the Hal Prince-Garth Drabinsky production of *Show Boat* racist? (I too have gone through the should-or-shouldn't-I-go arguments with myself—how else could I critique it if I didn't see it?) Further, the implication is that if you can only get enough people to come forward and say that the production isn't racist, then that will lay the issue to rest. Particularly if you can get enough "respected" and respectable Black-skinned people to argue how ill-informed and misguided those who object to the production are, and a few powerful whites to urge Blacks to spend their time doing something else.

The spectacle and farce of newspapers quoting other newspapers to prove the racist or non-racist nature of the show would be risible if it didn't underscore the essentially colonial status of Canada. How many drama critics does it take to convince us that this performance is truly non-racist? Sid Adilman of the *Toronto Star* quotes five—the *New York Post*, the *New York Times*, the *New York Daily News*, the *New Yorker*, and *Variety*. Does the recommendation carry more weight if its source is American? Possibly, since received opinion holds that their experience with racism is far more extensive than ours. And can you score extra points if the recommender/critic is Black? Like James Earl Jones, Henry Louis Gates Jr., Sandi Ross, or Lonette McKee? Does an American Black carry more weight than a Canadian Black? There could be a whole new genre of light bulb jokes: how many critics does Garth Drabinsky need to convince us that *Show Boat* is not racist? The process is as whimsical as the s/he-loves-me-s/he-loves-me-not daisy test. Depending on which petal remains, you have your opinion.

Racism, however, is not merely a matter of whimsy and unsubstantiated opinion. It is a highly developed, finely tuned system; it is a matter of historical fact as well as present-day reality. If we understand how it has worked, and continues to work right up to the very present reality of Black concerns around *Show Boat* being dismissed, then we understand how this production is all of a piece with the tradition and practice of racism. In its very underpinning the work remains what it has always been—a work *by* white people who have used Black creativity to enrich themselves; a work *about* white people whose very lives as characters depend on their Black characters whose function is to sing and dance and disappear so that whites can prosper.

"Censorship is to art as lynching is to justice." Henry Louis Gates Jr. is reported as saying (qtd. in Hudson). "We ought to fight the former as ardently as the latter." Many see this production of *Show Boat* as a successful fight against censorship. For others it is a victory of right thinking (no pun intended) over the forces of political correctness and "mob rule." The media's insistence on the unblemished quality of this production, their role in attempting to convince the public that Blacks and Africans are ill-informed about protesting this production, and their insistence that *Show Boat* is a miracle of tolerance, underscore the adage that he who pays the piper calls the tune.

Promotion of *Show Boat* has relied heavily on the use of "specials" which cloak advertisements in a news format. As mentioned above, the *Toronto Star* special section in its October 2, 1993, issue was entirely devoted to NYPAC, *Show Boat,* and Garth Drabinsky. What was essentially advertisement for Garth Drabinsky and Livent was presented by the *Star* to the public as news, with articles by art critics like Christopher Hume. Given that the *Toronto Star* is one of the investors in this production, it calls into question the objectivity of the "reporting."

On October 18, 1993, during its *Prime Time News,* CBC aired clips of the opening night festivities along with interviews of some of the main "players" in the "play" around the play. With the exception of Jeff Henry, Chair of The Coalition, all the "players" Black and white expressed support for the production and contempt for the position of those opposing it.

On October 26, 1993, CBC television featured a special, produced by Garth Drabinsky and narrated by James Earl Jones: *Show Boat: Journey of an Epic Musical.* The unrelenting message presented to the audience by individuals of the stature of Oscar Peterson was that *Show Boat* was non-racist, and that this production had gone to great lengths to redeem the negative stereotypes. In an attempt, no doubt intended to show how generous the production team was in giving credit where credit was due, choreographer Susan Stroman tells us that African Americans created the Charleston dance, along with many other American dance styles. "Whites," she adds straight-faced, "stiffened it up and *took it to another dimension*" (*Show Boat: Journey*). Is this theft masquerading as appropriation masquerading as imitation being the highest form of praise? Or, just theft? Or is it, as Ntozake Shange writes in *For Colored Girls who have Considered Suicide when the Rainbow is Enuf* that "…somebody almost walked off wid alla my stuff… you cant have them or do nothin with them / stealin my shit from me / dont make it yrs / makes it stolen / somebody almost run off wit all my stuff/…" (50).

On October 29, 1993, once again in its *Prime Time News* slot, CBC Television aired yet another program on *Show Boat,* billed as a feature on Hal Prince. The latter suggested that there were better things that African and Black Canadians could be doing than protesting *Show Boat.* Lonette McKee, the mixed-race African American actress who plays Julie, assured listeners that because she was Black *and* performing in *Show Boat* this meant that there was nothing wrong with it! Ms. McKee may be Black and American but her comments reveal an astonishing lack of knowledge about a significant development in Black politics—Black conservatism as epitomised by

Clarence Thomas. Black skin is no longer a marker of anything except Black skin. No longer can we assume that because someone is Black their actions will be helpful to Black people. As in the case of Clarence Thomas, the work of such people will often be actively harmful to Blacks. At best, Ms. McKee's position is problematic; her Blackness neither explains nor justifies anything.

The mutual back scratching between the *Toronto Star* and Livent, while not acceptable, is understandable. The one-sided and, therefore, biased coverage by our national broadcasting agency, CBC, is entirely unacceptable and must be in breach of both CBC guidelines for fair coverage and CRTC licensing requirements. These advertisements, masquerading as news, all feature spokespeople for Livent with Nobody representing the position of those opposed to the production. The one exception to this was Jeff Henry's appearance on the October 18, 1993, feature, but he was entirely outnumbered. The format requires that questions be put to Livent supporters on behalf of Nobody, and the answers come back rejecting Nobody's position. Nobody, of course, never appears to speak for him or herself.

Surprisingly, there has been some criticism of the present production of *Show Boat* in the mainstream press, surfacing in the most unexpected of places—*The Globe and Mail*. Critics of the present production of *Show Boat* do not necessarily agree on the reasons for objecting to it, however Bronwyn Drainie's objections to the overwhelming American nature of the production (*The Globe and Mail*, October 30, 1993) bears noting. So too do Michael Valpy's (*The Globe and Mail*, October 19, 1993) strongly worded criticism of the production for its insensitivity, and Liam Lacey's (*The Globe and Mail*, November 2, 1993) targeting of the blurring of the lines between news and advertisement that the CBC has indulged in.

The Globe and Mail has, in fact, gone on record as identifying the show as racist: "Is the Hal Prince-directed *Show Boat* racist?" theatre critic Jack Kirchhoff asks. "Sure, and probably sexist and ageist, too," he answers. Could this statement be used, I wondered, to launch a complaint with the Ontario Human Rights Commission? My mind buzzed with possibilities. I read on in surprise, recognizing many of the arguments, albeit unacknowledged, made in this work, *Showing Grit*.[4] But. And there is always a "but." "Is *Show Boat* appropriate for the 1990s?" Jack Kirchhoff asks again: "I think so," he answers, "at least as much as any other 65-year-old piece of theatre." I was to hear others—on CBC Radio, for instance—repeat this argument. Age, it appears, has now become the rationale for racism and sexism. The argument, astonishing in its banality, goes something like this: what do you expect from something that is 65 years old? Would such an argument be acceptable enough to justify the promotion of works such as *Mein Kampf* today? Or, is it because *Show Boat* is a "work of art" that such arguments apply? There are some who might object to the comparison between a work of reprehensible hate literature and a piece of theatre, but the argument holds.

If age becomes the primary criterion by which we assess the acceptability of material, then even the very society around us should escape our judgments. In seven years, the year 2000, racism, classism, and sexism and their manifold practices will be at least two millennia old. Ought we, therefore, to use the age of these belief systems to excuse them today? Surely, the relevance of the age of these systems lies in helping us to understand how embedded they are in the cultures of the world and, therefore, how difficult it is to eradicate them. To use age to excuse the inexcusable—the present production of *Show Boat*, for instance—is, at best, lazy thinking; at worst, it is to be an apologist for Livent and Garth Drabinsky.

Before leaving the subject of the media it is worth noting the double standards that are blatantly applied when issues of concern to Blacks arise. The *New York Times* dismissed the protesters against *Show Boat* as "ill-informed," individuals who "accused the show of racism without bothering to see it" (Rich C17). This same newspaper carried but one small informational column on the closing of the multi-media show *Jesus Was His Name* (The Associated Press C17) […] scheduled to open in New York at Radio City Music Hall last June. The *New York Times*, at that time, expressed no opinion on the events surrounding the closing of that show; it described none of the objectors to the show—Jews and Christians alike as "ill-informed"; it blamed no one for accusing the show of racism "without bothering to see it." Unlike *Jesus Was His Name*, however, *Show Boat* has had a 65-year track record of indisputably racist productions, of which at least three versions are preserved on film. Despite this we remain, according to the *New York Times*, "polite, ill-informed local protesters" (Rich C17).

Be it American or Canadian, white society, by and large, ignores the concerns and issues of its African citizens. This remains *the* central issue around this production of *Show Boat*—that the concerns raised by many African Canadians were dismissed as "mob rule" and "wild accusations." The concerns of other groups, however, are always seen as more important, more valid, more worthy than those of Blacks and African Canadians and Americans. The approach of the *New York Times* underscores this fact.

To Redeem or Not to Redeem

There has been much talk about the possibility of redeeming stereotypes in this production of *Show Boat*. Did I think negative stereotypes could be redeemed, a reporter asked me recently. In other words, did I think that Garth Drabinsky could sufficiently "clean up" the negative stereotypes in *Show Boat* to make it acceptable to those who were objecting to the production? If we accept that the central issue in this particular set of events is to be found in the "play" around the play—namely the dismissal of Black concerns, then this question becomes irrelevant. Within the context of the larger issue of "race and representation" however, the issue does bear some looking at.

The first issue that comes to mind is whether a white person can ever redeem a stereotype about Black people, or whether a white person should even be trying to do so. Some years ago, the African American artist Betye Saar "liberated" the image of Aunt Jemima in a work in which the latter carries a broom *and* a machine gun. [5] The image, at once powerful and immediate, completely subverts and, therefore, redeems the stereotype of the mammy, the fat Black woman, whose role is one of universal nurturer. In its subversion, the image becomes overwhelmingly empowering.

Any redemption of stereotypes that may have taken place in *Show Boat* has only occurred *because* of the outcry around this production. Livent's aim has always been to make money for Livent and Garth Drabinsky, *not* to redeem negative stereotypes of Black people, as in the case of the Betye Saar's work. And most certainly not to empower Black people. Being concerned only about box office profits, Garth Drabinsky and Livent had no recourse but to minimize the financial effect of those criticisms. Hence the company's attempts to discredit critics of the show and "prove" how non-racist *Show Boat* is.

What has *always* been at stake here is the bottom line: the Livent corporation has never been concerned about the feelings, opinions, concerns, or pain of Black people, except as these might prove to be inconvenient for them and lose them money. Black pain, provided it does not become Black anger, is tolerable, particularly if it reinforces the liberalism of whites. This explains the existence and persistence of the language of hand-outs and charity, rather than reparations in matters relating to Africa and Blacks. Black pain is acceptable if it can be turned to a profit for whites, as all productions of *Show Boat* have done. Black pain is unacceptable if it turns to anger and demands not pity but respect as The Coalition and other African Canadians have done. The only opinions of Blacks that Livent and those supporting this production, such as Mayor Mel Lastman, have been willing to listen to were of those who supported their position.

There is, however, another sort of bottom line—another type of tallying that needs to happen. On the one side of the balance sheet are the powerful with their advance ticket sales of six million dollars, the increase in Livent share issue prices and news that *Show Boat* will open in New York in the spring or fall of 1994. On the other side is the heightened tension and anger on the part of many Blacks in this city, at the flagrant disrespect and disregard for their concerns. No *one* should equate the paucity of numbers at the demonstrations and pickets—more a reflection of over-extended activists—with a lack of support for the issue by many, many people in Black communities in Toronto. For instance, the annual cricket match, a major fundraiser by the United Way, and organized by Black member organizations of that organization, did not take place this year. Contrary to what many want to believe, there *has* been a cost—a cost in social tensions that Toronto will have to bear long after *Show Boat* has gone to the Big (rotten) Apple. Which was always the goal of this enterprise. The deficit that presently exists in the provincial and federal economies is paralleled by an even larger social deficit that has been created in relations between Blacks and whites in Toronto.

Not With My Child

While tallying balance sheets we must keep in mind the attempts being made by Livent to expose students to this production. If the issue around this production of *Show Boat* continues to focus on whether or not the production is racist, or whether Livent has adequately cleaned up the stereotypes, the larger *and more important issue* of how Blacks and Black concerns are treated will be lost. Once that happens, and it is in danger of happening, then it all becomes a matter of whose opinion carries more weight. Further, an entire struggle will be obliterated and the impulse to social amnesia so pervasive in modern society will carry the day. In the vacuum so created, it will be extraordinarily easy to justify taking students to this show.

Garth Drabinsky and Livent's response to community concerns presented to the North York Board of Education, and mentioned above, states that it "offers comprehensive educational programs to students from across Canada and the US border states" (Livent, "Community"). According to Livent, "[m]ore than 400,000 students" have participated in these programs. "Livent considers it important that young audiences be given an opportunity to experience the world of live theatre." Given the exorbitant price of tickets to these shows—an average of $50.00; given that it is only the well-to-do who can afford them, is this an accurate experience of "the world of live theatre"? Isn't this a brazen attempt to influence the thinking of students so that they come to equate live theatre with these "blockbuster" types of shows—often American and trans-Atlantic imports? This type of experience fails to provide students with an understanding and knowledge that much good, and often great, theatre takes place around them month after month, year after year, put on by small and often struggling theatres like Tarragon, Theatre Passe Muraille, or the now defunct Black Theatre Canada and Theatre Fountainhead.

For teachers, many of whom are already juggling several tasks, the ready-made packages provided by Livent are undoubtedly attractive. The preparatory work is already done for them, and school boards will already have approved the shows, so the possibility of offending parents is lessened.

In the case of *Show Boat*, the "world of live theatre" to which Garth Drabinsky and Livent wish to expose Canadian students comprises an imported show, thoroughly American in its racist script, its cast, and its production team, not to mention the racism in the "play" around this production. And to explain it all to Canadian students, no less a figure than the eminent Harvard professor Henry Louis Gates Jr. with his educational "anti-racist" material paid for by Livent and Garth Drabinsky. Corporate involvement in schools has gained increasing acceptance over the last few years, particularly in the US. This involvement includes food concessions and direct linking of curricula to business needs. The most reprehensible of these incursions take the form of companies contracting with schools for which schools are paid—to have students watch televised material, complete with advertisements prepared by them.

The process is not so far along in Canada, but with school boards facing shrinking budgets, there is increasing pressure for them to seek this solution. There is, in fact, at least one recorded attempt to introduce advertisements into the school system in Alberta. At present, the linking of business and education in Canada manifests itself primarily as the tailoring of curricula, at the secondary and university levels, to fit the needs of business.

Livent represents the cultural manifestation of this now burgeoning movement of corporate involvement in schools. In their own words: "As government arts programs have been drastically cut back due to budgetary constraints, Livent considers it important that young audiences be given an opportunity to experience the world of live theatre" ("Community"). "Budgetary constraints" and cuts are the very arguments used by businesses and schools as rationales for forging closer links. While the dangers of this new alliance appear sharper with respect to business, it *appears* to be less so in areas of culture—it is, after all, only entertainment. But as argued earlier in this work, culture "works" best when it does not appear to be "working" at all. In racially toxic societies such as Canada and the US, shows like *Miss Saigon* and *Show Boat*, both implicitly and explicitly racist, become even more pernicious. To allow corporations like Livent, which have demonstrated contempt for concerns of Blacks and African Canadians, to control anti-racist education of students is a frightening and unacceptable development.

The Emperor Has No Clothes

A great deal more than negative factors exist on the Black side of the balance sheet, however. Despite all that has been written about the evils of political correctness, including the media's attempts to dismiss the protests and protesters, the latter have had an impact: the sheer amount of media time spent justifying the production is proof of this. The Coalition, which kept up pressure through weekly demonstrations, must be given credit for this. If opposition to the show had had no effect on public opinion, Garth Drabinsky and Livent would not have spent money producing a show to prove how entirely non-racist this production of *Show Boat* is. Neither would he have brought Henry Louis Gates Jr. to Toronto to tell us country Canuck Caribbean Blacks just how ill-informed we really are. Nor would that backsliding anti-Semite, William F. Buckley have come, courtesy of B'nai B'rith, to tell us why Jews deserve special treatment and Blacks don't. Neither of these individuals comes exactly cheaply.

Those of us—African, Asian, First Nations, and white—who have opposed the productions of *Show Boat* and *Miss Saigon* have succeeded in pushing the boundaries of the debate concerning issues such as racism and culture and that post-modernist mantra, "race and representation." In short, we have, collectively, put the issue of culture, one of the linchpins of racist structures, on the table. The mandarins of high culture and the media can try, and how they have, to dismiss us as typifying "mob rule" and rabid purveyors of political correctness. They can no longer ignore the arguments, rooted as they are in fact. The best *The Globe and Mail* could do, after admitting that the show was racist, was to drag out the age of the work to justify it.

One argument, however, made earlier in *Showing Grit* bears repeating. It is the argument, made equally often by Blacks and whites, that *Show Boat* is acceptable because it is historically accurate. The history that *Show Boat* reflects is a one-sided history, written, as often history is, by the victors. It is a history that omits—deliberately—the anguish, the pain, and the trauma of a people. It is a history that, in an attempt to cover its bloody tracks, portrays Blacks as happy singing "darkies." It is a twisting and warping of history that in 1993 results in the son of Oscar Hammerstein, William Hammerstein, describing his father as having a strong sense of "unpleasant experiences such as being Black in the South 100 years ago" (*Show Boat: Journey*). Somehow the words "unpleasant experience" do not begin to capture the experience of the holocaust that was slavery in the South and its aftermath. It is but a short step from "unpleasant experiences" to portraying Blacks as essentially happy-go-lucky workers content with their lot.

While we continue to engage in the debate about whether or not *Show Boat* is racist, we continue to play by the rules of the game laid down by Garth Drabinsky and Livent. It is crucial that we not lose sight of the larger issue located in that "play" around the play—the adamant refusal of white Canadian society to take seriously, or treat with respect, the needs of its Black citizens and residents. This is manifest in *all* aspects of Canadian life beginning with the education of Black children, through issues of policing and the justice system, to larger issues like immigration. This ought not to surprise us, however, when we reflect on how Canada, a white supremacist society, has treated, and continues to treat, its First Nations people. The benchmark for the treatment of all other peoples of colour coming to this land is the attempted genocide of Native peoples by Europeans. *That* is what links this struggle by Blacks and African Canadians against the production of *Show Boat*, to the opposition to *Miss Saigon* and to the many struggles of Asians, First Nations, and other peoples of colour—the struggles of all Nobodys—against a system and systems that appear poised to claw back the tiny and very recent gains made by them.

These systems *are* powerful, they appear to have unlimited financial resources and, allied as they are to the mainstream media, they seem invincible. They are, however, morally repugnant, politically bankrupt, and spiritually dead. Despite the many many tailors—the emperor has no clothes.

No walls will come toppling down with the death of capitalism; there will be no media gathered to witness its demise. But we *are* living it, if not witnessing it, as economies shrink, unemployment rolls grow, violence multiplies, and we continue to poison our environment. Hence the need for anodynes like *Show Boat* and *Miss Saigon*.

The fairy tale described earlier of Garth Drabinsky cancelling the production of *Show Boat* would have had astoundingly long-term benefits for race relations in this city; it would have gone a long way towards convincing Blacks that lacking financial clout does not mean that they are at the mercy of the powerful. What we have had instead is an exercise of raw, naked power—*Show Boat* must open and hang the costs of increased resentment and anger on the part of African Canadians—masquerading as a "victory of tolerance and sensitivity." In their gospels of power, the powerful always win; the powerless remain losers. However, the powerful are not the only ones who tally balance sheets: resentment, anger, perceived contempt and limited educational, social, and employment horizons, eventually and inevitably lead to explosions. Unfortunately, rioting is still one of the most frequent ways in which Blacks attempt to exercise power and exorcise the disrespect and abuse meted out to them in white societies. Yonge Street was just such an attempt to balance the inequities.[6] And while that "ol' man river" of racism continues to run, other Yonge Streets are inevitable.

To ensure a balance sheet that results in the Black, however, it is essential that those opposed to *Show Boat* continue their opposition during the run of this show. Since there has been so much talk of redeeming the stereotypes of *Show Boat*, I determined to explore the possibilities of truly subverting these stereotypes. The play *The Redemption of Al Bumen*[7] is the result of that attempt. I hope it succeeds, as "The Liberation of Aunt Jemima" has, in empowering readers and revealing the emancipatory possibilities when we take control of our own images. The following are other suggestion for continued resistance:

1. Parents should refuse to allow their children to attend *Miss Saigon* and *Show Boat* if their school organizes such a trip. They should also make their protests known at the school and board level.
2. Individuals or groups should write to the Anti-racism Secretariat *and* the Minister of Citizenship to express their concerns and opinions over *Miss Saigon* and *Show Boat*, including the treatment of Blacks and Africans in the events leading up to the production of the latter.
3. Individuals or groups should complain to the CBC's ombudsman and the CRTC regarding the lack of representation of the views and opinions of The Coalition and those opposed to the production.
4. Contact The Coalition or the Black Secretariat to see how you could be of assistance.
5. Continue to educate yourself and others about the issues.

(1993)

Notes

[1] This idea of the "play" within a play came after a discussion with Enid Lee. Credit for the idea rests with her.

[2] The B'nai B'rith Garth H. Drabinsky Lecture Series invited Dr. Henry Louis Gates Jr. to speak in Toronto on 28 October 1993.

[3] This expression was coined by the artist Robin Pacific and plays off the expression, "false memory syndrome."

[4] *Showing Grit: Showboating North of the 44th Parallel* is the title of the book by Marlene NourbeSe Philip in which this essay first appeared—ed.

[5] "The Liberation of Aunt Jemima," 1972, mixed media. Joe Overstreet and Murray DePillars have also produced work on Aunt Jemima in 1964 and 1968 respectively. See also Cathy Campbell, "A Battered Woman Rises," for a discussion of the changing image of Aunt Jemima.

[6] The so-called "Yonge Street Riots" took place on 4 May 1992 after an anti-racist rally organized in response to the acquittal of the LAPD officers who were caught on videotape beating Rodney King as well as several incidents of police brutality in Toronto (in particular a police shooting of a young black man—Raymond Constantine Lawrence—a few days earlier). Riots broke out along Yonge Street and at city hall after a peaceful protest at the US consulate, a march up Yonge Street, and sit-in at Yonge and Bloor—ed.

[7] By Marlene NourbeSe Philip, published in the second edition of Philip, *Showing Grit.*

Works Cited

Adilman, Sid. "New York critics proclaim Show Boat as see worthy." *Toronto Star* 25 October 1993: E1.

The Associated Press, "Anti-Semitism Charge Delays a Show on Jesus." *New York Times* 28 May 1993: C17.

Campbell, Cathy. "A Battered Woman Rises." *The Village Voice* 7 November 1989: 45–46.

Drabinsky, Garth H. Statement to a Meeting of the North York Board of Education Trustees. 12 May 1993. Written Submission.

Drainie, Bronwyn. "Show Boat's Billing as Canadian Holds No Water." *The Globe and Mail* 30 October 1993: C7.

Enchin, Harvey. "Livent Plays Lead in Stage Revival." *The Globe and Mail* 16 October 1993: B1.

Greene, Fitzroy. "Show Boating in North York." *Share* 16.27 (October 21, 1993): 1, 4.

Hudson, Kellie. "Show Boat row 'misguided,' historian says." *Toronto Star* 29 October 1993: A11.

Hume, Christopher. "North York: The City with Art." *Toronto Star* 2 October 1993: S1.

Kirchhoff, H.J. "Theatre Review: Showboat." *The Globe and Mail* 18 October 1993: C1.

Lacey, Liam. "CBC's documentary doublespeak COMMENT: When it comes to information programming, there cannot be different levels of legitimacy for news and culture." *The Globe and Mail* 2 November 1993.

Livent. "Community Concerns and Live Entertainment Corporation of Canada's Responses." 12 May 1993. Written Submission.

Philip, Marlene NourbeSe. *Showing Grit: Showboating North of the 44th Parallel.* 2nd edition. Toronto: Poui, 1993.

Rich, Frank. "The Seminal American Musical is Rebuilt From the Ground Up." *New York Times* 20 October 1993: C15, C17.

Shange, Ntozake. *For Colored Girls Who Have Considered Suicide When The Rainbow Is Enuf.* New York: Macmillian Publishing, 1977.

Show Boat: Journey of an Epic Musical. CBC Television, 26 October 1993.

Thorsell, William. "In America's bazaar of competing interests, power is the only currency." *The Globe and Mail* 16 October 1993: D1.

Valpy, Michael. "STREETS Surely there's something better than Show Boat." *The Globe and Mail* 19 October 1993: A2.

Space Administration:
Rereading the Material History of
Theatre Passe Muraille in Toronto [1]

by Michael McKinnie

A dominant feature of contemporary theatre work in Toronto is that a significant portion of it has been undertaken in performance spaces that are former industrial buildings. The company that most explicitly draws attention to this industrial-spatial history is Factory Theatre, which first produced plays in a former candle factory above a car repair garage on Dupont Street, northwest of downtown. Tarragon Theatre, two blocks from Factory's original home, resides in a former cribbage board factory, and the Canadian Stage Company's Berkeley Street theatres became performance spaces when Toronto Free Theatre took over a former gasworks at the southeast edge of downtown. Young People's Theatre is nearby, operating out of an old Toronto Transit Commission building.

The fifth company that works in a former industrial space is Theatre Passe Muraille, which, some critics argue, led Toronto's so-called alternative theatre movement in the 1970s (Johnston; Rubin, "Toronto Movement"; Usmiani). The alternatives (or "alternates," as they are sometimes called) were Passe Muraille (founded in 1968), Factory Theatre Lab (1970), Tarragon Theatre (1971), and Toronto Free Theatre (1972), a group of companies founded in response to the large regional theatre network established according to the recommendations of the Massey Commission report of 1951. As Richard Paul Knowles and Jennifer Fletcher comment, the regionals, initiated with the creation of the Manitoba Theatre Centre in 1958, were often criticized for functioning on an industrial and bureaucratic model of culture, "as 'branch-plant' operations, taking Art and Culture from the Centre to the supposedly culturally impoverished regions" (209). Knowles and Fletcher also note that the label "alternative theatre movement" implies a common purpose that simply did not exist. The "mandates and practices of the so-called 'alternates'... in fact varied considerably" (210), and the rather crude schema of "alternative" versus "mainstream" has, as I will discuss later, led a significant body of theatre historiography about these companies to adopt a simplistic teleological model of their historical development.

The regional theatre network can be seen as a Fordist model of theatrical production. By Fordist, I mean the system of economic production organized on the basis of routine industrial labour in service of the mass creation of commodities for circulation within nation-states. The regional theatre network provided a structure through which the production and distribution of relatively homogeneous high-cultural commodities could be coordinated. The built forms of these theatres, often styled in the massive, poured-concrete vernacular of state-sponsored testaments to the public good, confirmed their dominance and their interchangeability. John Juliani, who formed the experimental performance company Savage God in Vancouver, witheringly—and correctly—described the Canadian high-cultural industry as suffering from an "edifice complex" (qtd. in Usmiani 24).

Many of the theatres that grew up in response to this system, however, are better considered not as "alternative" but as post-Fordist. By post-Fordist, I mean a system of economic production that occurs when capital floats freely across national borders, structuring production and labour according to the needs of transnational financial speculation.[2] The theatres that flourished in Toronto in the 1960s and 1970s (we may include Toronto Workshop Productions here, though its relationship to the "alternative" movement is in dispute) can be seen as the kind of intensely local, small-scale enterprises linked through informal alliances established in the interstices of national and transnational cultural mass production. Whatever their artistic virtues, these theatres have often been forced to use the tools of late capitalism to ensure their survival. "Alternative" and "mainstream" are simply inadequate representations of either a trajectory of artistic development or as a way to classify economic modes of theatrical production; the categories cannot account for the ways in which late capitalism reconfigures Manichean binaries of margin and centre.

My case study here is Theatre Passe Muraille, perhaps the paradigmatic post-Fordist theatre in Toronto. In its shift from a conception of performance space as a creative and political issue to a conception of performance space as an administrative issue, Passe Muraille best articulates the difficulties of trying to reconcile contradictions within performance ideology and private property in contemporary Toronto. This shift, however, cannot elide the significant transformation in the performance work that Passe Muraille produces. My analysis hinges on 16 Ryerson Avenue, the former industrial building that the company purchased in 1975 and has occupied since 1976. Passe Muraille was not the first theatre company to occupy a former factory (that was Factory Theatre), it is not the longest-resident company in a former factory (that is Tarragon Theatre), and it is not the building that has been "gentrified" most extensively (that would be the Canadian Stage Company at Berkeley Street). But Passe Muraille was the first of these companies to own its performance space, and, for more than any other mid-sized company in Toronto, its building can be read as an index of the ways in which theatres have been forced to incorporate the urban political economy of a late capitalist city into the heart of their work.

A Brief History of Theatre Passe Muraille

Theatre Passe Muraille was founded in 1968 by Jim Garrard at Rochdale College, the now-defunct housing and educational laboratory affiliated with the University of Toronto. Garrard was heavily influenced by the theatre experiments of La Mama in New York, and he saw Passe Muraille as a similar response to conventional naturalist

ind the Canadian theatre mainstream, with its focus on building
iments to bureaucratic culture. Garrard's first show, Paul Foster's
......, received only one "private" performance in the underground parking
garage of Rochdale. He followed that performance in March 1969 with *Futz*, a love
story between a farmer and a pig. Passe Muraille's notoriety in Toronto was cemented
when the actors in *Futz* were charged and convicted of staging an indecent performance (they were acquitted on appeal), and the show inaugurated a provocative
stylistic and political pose that became popularly associated, for better and worse,
with the "alternative" theatres.

When Paul Thompson took over the artistic directorship in 1970, he moved the
Theatre Passe Muraille acting ensemble into the collective creation of plays, a mode of
dramaturgy and performance style in which Thompson and the actors created productions through research and improvisation in rehearsal. This approach often
involved a complete rethinking of the way in which performance space contributes to
the creation and reception of theatre. *The Farm Show* (1972), for example, was developed as a play about farm life by Passe Muraille actors living and working on farms
near Clinton, Ontario. The show played in Toronto and toured widely, with the actors
at one point taking to a barn near Clinton and performing to the people on whom
their characters were based. *1837* (1973), created by the Passe Muraille company and
writer Rick Salutin, reread the Upper Canada Rebellion as an allegory for Canadian
cultural and economic independence in the 1970s. The play was rewritten for rural
audiences as *1837: The Farmers' Revolt*, however, with the "left-of-liberal politics" of
the Toronto production toned down and the emphasis on the farmers' role in the
revolt strengthened.

Although Theatre Passe Muraille produced the work of individual playwrights,
the company became best known for combining its method of developing plays
collectively (though Thompson was firmly in the driver's seat) with a concern for
"ordinary (even banal) Canadians as their central figures" (Johnston 107). The work
of Passe Muraille in the early 1970s used collective creation to yoke together an
intensely local dramaturgy with national(ist) commentary: theatrical location,
method, subject matter, and political imperative seemed to converge more immediately than in the established theatres. In Toronto, Passe Muraille best exemplified the
cultural nationalist ideal of "*Canadian theatre* as something distinct from the more
traditional notion of *theatre in Canada*" (Rubin, "Toronto Movement" 396).

For the first nine years of its existence, Theatre Passe Muraille operated out of a
variety of performance spaces in downtown Toronto, all of which it rented. The production of *I Love You, Baby Blue*, however, provided Passe Muraille with the capital
necessary to purchase its present home at 16 Ryerson Avenue. *I Love You, Baby Blue*
was a 1975 collective creation that examined sexual attitudes in Toronto, taking
CityTV's popular late-night soft-porn movies as its point of departure. The show contained nudity and sexually explicit material and was shut down twice by the morality
squad of the Toronto police. In a rerun of the *Futz* case, Thompson and cast members
were eventually acquitted of obscenity charges, but the play's notoriety ensured a

lengthy and enormously profitable run. Passe Muraille located a vacant warehouse in a residential neighbourhood at the west end of downtown near the intersection of Queen Street and Bathurst Street and purchased the building for $100,000. Passe Muraille became the first "alternative" theatre in Toronto to own its own home, and this ownership testified to the company's apparent fitness and stability.

It is illuminating to consider Theatre Passe Muraille not as an enterprise in tele-ological development but as a post-Fordist theatrical formation that necessarily changes as it attempts to reconcile internal and external contradictions. The nature of these contradictions, and the theatre's methods of attempted resolution, define a dialectical process of historical transformation. A dialectical analysis of Passe Muraille reveals a company that, from its inception, has grappled with a spatial contradiction within contemporary performance ideology. On the one hand, performance space was coded in late 1960s Canada as the "edifice complex," as the architectural expres-sion of theatrical ossification and social privilege. Brutalist theatre buildings seemed to enforce boundaries and hierarchies between stage, audience, and world, making them appear immutable and impermeable. On the other hand, experimental theatre of the late 1960s saw performance space (broadly defined) as the site of theatrical and social contest, and, if the space itself was subject to a consistent retheorization, then the theatrical event could be artistically and socially liberatory. In Jim Garrard's con-ception at the founding of Passe Muraille, this ideal was posited as "a theatre free of distinctions between actor and spectator, between 'inside' and 'outside' the theatre, between drama as one art form, music as another and dancing as yet another" (qtd. in Johnston 34). One could argue that Paul Thompson's period as artistic director at Passe Muraille, usually considered as a break from Garrard's experimentation, was in fact the logical deepening of those ideals, at least in spatial terms. Passe Muraille's col-lective creations during Thompson's tenure were a more rigorous examination of what it meant to perform in certain spaces, particularly those not conventionally deemed "theatrical" (the best-known example is depicted in a photograph of *The Farm Show* in a barn near Clinton, where the audience sat on hay bales and in the rafters).

Theatre Passe Muraille used the motto "theatre through walls" and "theatre with-out walls" on much of its correspondence in the 1970s, and it used "theatre beyond walls" in its public transit advertising campaign in the mid-1990s. Promotional brochures for the 1998–1999 and 1999–2000 seasons contrast the title "Theatre Beyond Walls" with a photograph of a corner of 16 Ryerson Avenue. The photograph depicts a "THEATRE PASSE MURAILLE" sign bolted to the building, illustrating the way in which the company has stamped itself on the walls of its workplace. That the building has become a promotional tool implies that the phrase "theatre beyond walls" reveals a different understanding of the company's relationship to physical space than it once did.

Garrard's notion of a "plastic theatre" and the company's emphasis in the early 1970s on touring and seeding shows across the country demanded a constant re-evaluation of the location of performance. Such a continuous retheorization of performance space, however, is difficult to reconcile with the administrative demands of an expanding theatre company. Although Theatre Passe Muraille's use of multiple and flexible performance spaces was a productive response to the way in which the Canadian theatrical establishment used performance space, the contentious nature of those flexible spaces was not only a virtue but also a problem. At a certain point, resituating a company in unstable spaces understandably becomes tiring, expensive, and, most importantly, difficult to manage. By the mid 1970s, the company focused on creating a comprehensive theatre complex that could function as a "home for its administration" (Theatre Passe Muraille, "Request" 6). Passe Muraille's purchase of 16 Ryerson Avenue should be seen as an attempt to divide spatial considerations from artistic considerations or, better, to make performance space assume a predictable consistency through monopoly control. Instead of becoming a creative issue, performance space became an administrative issue, solving the spatial problem in one location by moving it to another. This relocation, however, created a new set of pitfalls to manage. Passe Muraille has become the paradigmatic post-Fordist theatre because its ownership of 16 Ryerson Avenue has entrenched the company in Toronto's volatile contemporary urban political economy and because of the particular ways in which this involvement has forced the building itself to become a spatial-administrative instrument of the theatrical labour process and the site of an increasingly insistent commemoration of the company's history in performance.

Built in 1902 as a commercial bakery, complete with stables for delivery horses, 16 Ryerson Avenue is a competently designed but now slightly shabby example of Toronto's small industrial architecture styled in beaux-arts neoclassicism. The Toronto Historical Board described the building as "a notable example of a small industrial building of the period. The skillful use of brick and classical architectural design elements in the facade gives it a prominence in the neighbourhood that is usually found only in public buildings" (Council 1235). The building was listed in the City of Toronto's Inventory of Heritage Properties in 1974, and it was subsequently designated as a historical property "of architectural value" by Toronto City Council in 1977 (under the Ontario Heritage Act, the city can refuse to issue permits for demolition or for alterations that modify the architectural or historical character of a designated building). The value of the building was not only aesthetic. The building site was relatively large for the neighbourhood: at sixty feet wide by one hundred feet long, the lot was three times the width of the neighbourhood average. In 1902, the City of Toronto assessed the building's value at $9,000; most of the houses in this working-class neighbourhood were valued at between $250 and $600 (City of Toronto 233–34).

The building housed bakeries and confectioneries until 1926, and in 1927 Wilkinson and Kompass of Hamilton took over the space, manufacturing and wholesaling hardware until 1957. Sol Friendly Sheet Metal Works, which manufactured heating supplies, occupied the vacant building in 1959 and remained there until 1967, after which the building sat empty until Theatre Passe Muraille purchased it in 1975. Following repairs to bring the space into compliance with building codes for theatres, Passe Muraille opened its doors on Ryerson Avenue in 1976. The workplace of bakers and machinists was now a theatre workplace.

Canadian Theatre History, Urban Geography, and the Labour Process

My challenge is to arrive at a narrative that can adequately account for the way in which Theatre Passe Muraille and Toronto's urban political economy intersect through 16 Ryerson Avenue as both administrative and performance concerns. David Harvey writes that a central challenge of dialectical analysis is to represent the relationship between "things" and "the structured system" of which they are a part (*Justice* 50). Dialectics, he writes, sees this process as one of mutual constitution. There are three bodies of work that logically inform an analysis of Passe Muraille and contemporary Toronto: Canadian theatre historiography, specifically case studies about theatre in Toronto; Marx's examination of the labour process under capitalism in the first volume of *Capital: A Critique of Political Economy*; and urban geography, which may include urban theory, sociology, and political economy. By drawing on and writing against work done in these fields, I can extend what might be called a materialist cultural economy of Theatre Passe Muraille.

There is not much theorized theatre historiography about Toronto and the 1970s. A large body of criticism about the plays of the period exists, but there is a relatively small amount of analysis that claims to examine the conditions of theatre practice in Toronto in the late 1960s and 1970s. As a result, Toronto theatre historiography about this period often appears critically monolithic and dominated by idealist representational strategies. Theatre practice is frequently represented in humanist, masculinist, and teleological terms. These narratives may emphasize various moments, may not be exclusively nationalist, and may evaluate theatrical impact differently, but common to all is a representational methodology premised on contemporary Toronto theatre being produced by individual practitioners (largely male artistic directors) leading a handful of key companies through a process of artistic influence, experimentation, and consolidation.

An illustrative sample of idealist historiography about Toronto theatre in the 1970s includes work by Don Rubin, Renate Usmiani, and Denis Johnston. Their historiographies appear in three forms: as nationalist-ontological teleologies (Rubin), as aesthetic-epidemiological teleologies (Usmiani), and as anthropomorphic teleologies (Johnston). Although I disagree with their methods and conclusions, each of these critics provides a wealth of historical data and attempts to set the terms of analysis for Toronto theatre in the 1970s in provocative and productive ways.

Don Rubin was a key agitator for a nationalist Canadian theatre from his post as founding editor of the quarterly periodical *Canadian Theatre Review*. His work advocates a theatre that is the unmediated expression of national identity, the performative answer to the question "Who are we as Canadians?" In the first issue of *Canadian Theatre Review* in 1974, Rubin published an essay entitled "Creeping toward a Culture: The Theatre in English Canada since 1945," in which he attempts to locate the "impressive development" of Canadian theatre in an emerging "national awareness and identity" (319, 323). He accepts unquestioningly the idea advanced by the Massey Commission that, at the end of the Second World War,

> Canada was fast becoming an empty shell. While it had managed to
> retain its own government, its own leaders and its own buildings
> through the years, there was precious little that could be called Canadian
> in many of those people, and precious little that could be called
> Canadian inhabiting those buildings. (319)

The expanding postwar theatre, most visibly illustrated by the regionals and the
Stratford Festival, helped to establish a professional industry in Canada but only mar-
ginally contributed to a distinct Canadian "culture." Prior to 1967, Canada was a
"young giant" trapped in a "colonial identity" (323). After the centennial and
Montreal's Expo, however "the current concern with a viable Canadian national identity was born. For it was during this period that Canada began to realize... that the
country not only had stature and size but that it could have the respect and envy of
the world as well" (323). The best theatrical expression of this self-awareness was
Theatre Passe Muraille, "an experimental house" that later became "a Canadian experimental house" when Paul Thompson assumed the artistic directorship (326). By
1983, Rubin looked back on the "Toronto Movement" with some lament as a move
from "innocence" to "matur[ity]" ("Toronto Movement" 402). He represented
Canadian theatre in general, and Toronto theatre in particular, as a trajectory toward
national culture and identity, moving progressively through a national metaphysics:
from backward colonialism through nationalist restlessness to a self-aware maturity.[3]

Renate Usmiani, on the other hand, locates the "alternative theatre movement"
within the avant-garde. Where Rubin is nationalist, Usmiani is internationalist, but
her narrative has structural similarities in its representation of theatrical development; it also progresses from influence through experimentation to consolidation. For
Usmiani, the mechanical influence of the European and American avant-garde is key
to understanding the creation of smaller theatres across Canada in the late 1960s and
early 1970s. Her discussion of Paul Thompson emphasizes the time that he spent
working under Roger Planchon in Paris in 1964 and 1965, and it gives Thompson singular credit for Theatre Passe Muraille's development: Usmiani claims that with *The
Farm Show* Passe Muraille "achieved its artistic identity," which, though created
collectively, was "largely due to the vision and labour of its director" (45). In her narrative, a Canadian director trained abroad brings techniques back with him to Canada
and then spreads them among theatre practitioners. She likens this process to an
experiment through which techniques are perfected in the performance laboratory
and a complete theatrical style and identity come into being.

Denis Johnston's *Up the Mainstream: The Rise of Toronto's Alternative Theatres* is
the most comprehensive account of Toronto theatre production from 1968 to 1975.
Johnston places Theatre Passe Muraille in the vanguard of the "alternative theatre
movement," and his historiography focuses on companies rather than on texts,
accomplishing what he terms a "historical" as opposed to a "literary" survey. Johnston
is the critic who makes his liberal ideals most explicit; his goal, he writes, is to create
a "consensual history" (x), a "foundation of agreed-upon knowledge on which other

scholars and researchers may build" (ix). In his narrative, influence is figured as a broadly defined zeitgeist channelled through prominent artists:

> The leaders of Toronto's alternative theatres, like educated people every-where, were heavily influenced by the American "counter-culture" of the 1960s, an alternative expression to mainstream mores that found public focus in the civil rights movement and the anti-Vietnam War protests. Canada's aspiring theatre artists were steeped in this liberal/radical sen-sibility of the 1960s and its anti-establishment catchphrases: Marshall McLuhan's "global village," Fritz Perls's "do your own thing," Timothy Leary's "turn on, tune in, drop out." (5)

The metaphor for Johnston's narrative is of a youth growing up in "stages" (6). The first stage is his (and, given Johnston's strong focus on male artistic directors, it is always his) "radical" phase, then his "nationalist" stage, then his "mainstream" stage. By 1975, Toronto theatre had grown up, and Passe Muraille "was the fountainhead of a new style of Canadian performance" (138).

However lively and informative these historiographies are, their liberalism tends to privilege individual progress, reify male artistic directors, and mystify the complex conditions of theatrical production. These theatre historiographies hinge on a series of notions—national identity, aesthetic lineage, the zeitgeist—presumed to be trans-parent but ultimately difficult, if not impossible, to define. Each notion becomes a fetish—a catchphrase whose explanatory capacity is supposedly self-evident but whose meaning cannot be theorized. A welcome corrective, however, is Alan Filewod's *Collective Encounters: Documentary Theatre in English Canada*. His discussion of Theatre Passe Muraille focuses on the collective method of play creation. His histori-ography is productive because it moves beyond a catalogue of identity, influence, and personality into the relationship between the performance event and the organization of theatrical labour. This focus on the theatrical labour process is worth retaining and pushing to different ends.

Performance, the Labour Process, and Materialist Geography

Theatre historiography without a theory of the labour process can too easily become a list of names and functions, a description of who did what where and when told in the mystifying and cosseting voice of "consensus," liberal history. In the first volume of *Capital*, Marx makes a tripartite division in his discussion of labour: there is the labourer, the social subject; there is labour power, the ability to work; and there is the labour process, the structured system by which the worker puts his or her labour to use in service of the production of an object. The labourer and labour power are potential resources but are not actually labour practice until structured through some sort of process. The labour process, in turn, is comprised of three parts: "(1) pur-poseful activity, that is work itself, (2) the object on which that work is performed, and (3) the instruments of that work" (284). For my analysis of Theatre Passe Muraille, the relationship between performance space and the instruments of labour is important. Marx defines an instrument of labour in the following way:

> a thing, or a complex of things, which the worker interposes between himself and the object of his labour and which serves as a conductor, directing his activity onto that object. He makes use of the mechanical, physical and chemical properties of some substances in order to set them to work on other substances as instruments of his power, and in accordance with his purposes… In a wider sense we may include among the instruments of labour, in addition to things through which the impact of labour on its object is mediated, and which therefore in one way or another, serve as conductors of activity, all the objective conditions necessary for carrying on the labour process. (285–86)

By becoming an owner of private property in 1975, Passe Muraille redefined performance space from a creative instrument of its labour to an administrative instrument of its labour. Passe Muraille's work, then, has been spatialized along different lines since 1975, and this transition marked the company's full subsumption under a post-Fordist urban political economy.

Space in this sense, then, is something that is made and remade. Space should not be reduced simply to the physical setting of performance or, worse, the physical means by which performance naturalizes existing social relations. Edward Soja argues that an "essentially physical view of space… has tended to imbue all things spatial with a lingering sense of primordiality and physical composition, an aura of objectivity, inevitability, and reification" (79). This view, which recurs periodically in the Chicago School of urban sociology, for example, fails to acknowledge spatial relations as being in dialectical relationship with social relations, with each being mutually constituent, but neither being synonymous with each other. [4] Soja calls this "the distinction between space per se, space as a contextual given, and socially-based spatiality, the created space of social organization and production" (79).

Toronto theatre historiography can learn a great deal from materialist geography, since its narratives have tended to represent the production of performance space either not at all or in crudely physical ways. Materialist geographers such as Edward Soja, Doreen Massey, and David Harvey have attempted to overturn the presumption in positivist geography that to consider the spatial is, at base, to measure types and effects of existing physical boundaries and properties. They have also attempted to use geography to spatialize Marxist analysis, trying to correct a tendency within Marxism (and within Marx's writings themselves) to privilege historical time over historical space or to treat space as the unmediated physical reflection of a capitalist mode of production. The conceptual language that Massey uses attempts to resolve this problem by taking space into the labour process: she proposes "spatial divisions of labour" in which space functions as a necessary and frequently disciplinary part of the organization of the labour process.

Materialist geography grappled uneasily with the "physical problem" through the 1960s and 1970s, since the role of space in Western Marxist theory was somewhat ambiguous and ambivalent. Harvey notes the difficulty of teasing out theorized spatial concerns in Marx's writings and points to the way in which Marx, like most modern social theorists, tends to privilege change through time (whether as "progress" or "revolution") rather than change through space (*Condition* 205). [5] Geography, like liberal theatre history, also tended toward a positivist empiricism. Massey comments that, until the 1960s, geography focused on "the region," a "distinct area of the earth's surface" that was the geological circumscription of political change. Geography rested on a disciplinary understanding of the "natural" and the "social" as complementary but discrete essentialisms (50). Bringing the spatial into dialectical relationship with the social required a move beyond the physical that materialist geography began to make through its leading practitioners in the 1970s and 1980s. This conceptual shift is best described by Soja:

> Space as a physical context has generated broad philosophical interest and lengthy discussions of its absolute and relative properties (a debate which goes back to Leibniz and beyond), its characteristics as environmental "container" of human life, its objectifiable geometry, and its phenomenological essences. But this physical space has been a misleading epistemological foundation upon which to analyze the concrete and subjective meaning of human spatiality. Space in itself may be primordially given, but the organization, and meaning of space is a product of social translation, transformation, and experience... Lefebvre distinguishes between Nature as naively given context and what can be termed "second nature", the transformed and social concretized spatiality arising from the application of purposeful human labour. It is this second nature that becomes the geographical subject and object of historical materialist analysis, of a materialist interpretation of spatiality. (79–80)

The physical may be material put to work within a sociospatial dialectic, but it is no longer the "natural" basis, boundary, and measure of human activity. Space has meaning above and beyond its physical contours, and the implications of performance space have to be evaluated by what appears both on and off the stage.

Property Ownership and Post-Fordist Toronto

Under capitalism, the privileged relationship of the subject to urban space is through private property ownership. Harvey notes that private property ownership is the means by which monopoly control is exerted over space. He writes that the "property relationship" (*Social Justice* 14) produces "absolute space" where "'owners' possess monopoly privileges over 'pieces' of space" (168). It is clear from archival records that by 1975 Theatre Passe Muraille was looking for some sort of predictability in its performance space. The company wanted to exert greater control over space, and private property ownership offered the greatest opportunity to do so. But the implications of asserting monopoly control over space under late capitalism posed a new challenge to Passe Muraille's administration of its labour process.

It is no accident that 16 Ryerson Avenue is a former industrial building and that Tarragon, Toronto Free, and Factory Theatres also began producing plays in former industrial spaces. The possibility of occupying—or buying—those spaces was contingent on changes in Toronto's urban political economy, but the role of this historical transition has never been taken into account. In fact, Theatre Passe Muraille could only purchase 16 Ryerson Avenue because industrial production had largely abandoned the downtown core. Fordist suburbanization of manufacturing was well under way by 1975, and 16 Ryerson Avenue was simply impractical economically for industry by the late 1960s. The building had been vacant for almost eight years when Passe Muraille purchased it in 1975. When Wilkinson-Kompass (as Wilkinson and Kompass of Hamilton became) and Sol Friendly Sheet Metal Works left 16 Ryerson Avenue, both moved to larger sites in the rapidly expanding suburb of North York.[6] The industries that formerly would have occupied buildings such as 16 Ryerson Avenue had largely left the downtown core or closed shop permanently; the portion of Canada's economy devoted to industrial production (already small by international standards) had been declining since the end of the Second World War, and Toronto's industrial decline was even greater than the national average. As remaining manufacturing companies such as Wilkinson-Kompass and Sol Friendly moved to greenfield sites and industrial parks near 400-series highways, the majority of the economic activity in the city core became tied to financial services and commercial property development (see Filion; Gad; and Matthew). This transformation depressed the market value of former downtown industrial sites enough that even cash-strapped theatre companies could move into the property market, and it freed up space that, while sometimes uncomfortable, could accommodate the demands of theatre labour and audiences. Indeed, when I look at 16 Ryerson Avenue today, I find it difficult to imagine it as a working factory. This conceptual shift speaks to the way that the postwar economic boom changed our understanding of the amount and type of space needed to do industrial work, and it made such spaces seem entirely appropriate for theatre work. The idea of 16 Ryerson Avenue as a downtown Toronto manufacturing building seems almost quaint now, but as a theatre space it seems entirely natural.

By entering into private property ownership, Theatre Passe Muraille tried to take spatial concerns off the table as a creative issue by transferring them into the administration of its labour process. Performance space remained a key part of theatre work, but in a different way, and the consequences of this transfer have become increasingly manifest in performance. Monopoly control meant that Passe Muraille was forced to find ways to turn 16 Ryerson Avenue into a spatial and administrative instrument of its own labour, but doing so also tied the theatre company more tightly to economic cycles of crisis and consolidation. In order to posit some sort of stability during a time of political, economic, and cultural volatility, 16 Ryerson Avenue has increasingly become a site of commemoration, the spatial means by which the company's own history is nostalgically recuperated to sanction the present-day theatre event.

Spatial Instruments of Performance Labour

16 Ryerson Avenue is a spatial-administrative instrument of performance labour in three ways. First, the building is a *managerial* instrument within a theatrical labour process, invoked as a means of coordinating that labour process spatially. Second, the building is an *institutional* instrument that brings performance labour into complementary political and economic relationships with state capital and trade labour. Third, the building is a *financial* instrument that invokes space as a means of capitalizing the theatrical labour process.

16 Ryerson Avenue as a Managerial Instrument of Labour
As with any mode of production, theatrical production requires that its labour process be organized and administered. It is clear that, for Theatre Passe Muraille, 16 Ryerson Avenue was the spatial means by which to centralize and coordinate its work. A fundraising prospectus circulated in 1978 explicitly linked building renovations to Passe Muraille's labour process: "the growth of this creative and resourceful enterprise, and the flourishing of many affilliated [sic] projects, has necessitated the establishment of a CENTRE, a home for its administration, for the building and storage of sets, and most importantly, for a flexible performance space" (Theatre Passe Muraille, "Request" 6). The practical difficulty of working in rented space at Rochdale College and Trinity Square (let alone the various sites that Passe Muraille had used around the province) made ownership a desirable goal pragmatically; one could, for example, drill holes in the floor and schedule work without worry. But property ownership also brought with it an air of permanence, productively deploying the link that Soja identifies between physicality and perpetuity. By gaining ownership of fixed capital, Passe Muraille was able to lay claim to an ideology of permanence—using space, in effect, to become timeless—that could be mobilized as an administrative tool and virtue. This ideology of permanence would also become important as the spatial basis by which a Passe Muraille "tradition" could be produced in performance, a phenomenon to which I will return later.

16 Ryerson Avenue as an Institutional Instrument of Labour
Theatre Passe Muraille's building played an important role in helping to organize and sustain complementary work investments with the state and with trade labour. The extensive renovations made to 16 Ryerson Avenue in 1983 are illustrative in this regard. Significant funding for the renovations came from the federal and provincial governments through the Canada/Ontario Employment Development Program. It provided wage subsidies for registered businesses, non-profit organizations, partnerships, and corporations to hire the long-term unemployed for specific projects (Reilly). Passe Muraille's successful appeal for funding was made not in artistic language but in administrative language: company correspondence to the federal government stated explicitly that construction "requires at least 22 skilled and semi-skilled tradesmen totalling 221 work-weeks of labour—a significant figure at a time of widespread unemployment" (Theatre Passe Muraille, "Funding"). Passe Muraille used its physical plant in two ways: first, to attract needed investment from the state in the building itself, transforming an industrial space into a space better suited to the-

atre work over the long term; second, to link funding for Passe Muraille's physical plant requirements to state desires to alleviate long-term unemployment during a major economic recession.

We may also say that this state contact used the building to support both an internal labour economy (the company's work in its own space) and an external labour economy (the non-performance labour that the building brought into the theatrical workplace). Archival photographs document how trade workers dismantled and remade the interior of Theatre Passe Muraille during the 1983 renovation (Theatre Passe Muraille and Leonard Kalishenko and Associates Ltd.). This moment embodies a shared work history, in which two types of workers often considered to have little in common create labour bonds through working in and on performance space. This affiliation may be important in "building" labour-based political alliances at a time when historic ties based on large-scale industrial work are weakening.

16 Ryerson Avenue as a Financial Instrument of Labour
Theatre companies need not only to coordinate their labour processes but also to capitalize them. Theatre Passe Muraille used the industrial history of 16 Ryerson Avenue to attract capital investment to finance its work. As I noted above, the building was deemed in 1977 to have "architectural value." When the company first acquired the property, renovations were geared primarily to making the space usable for public performance: fitting fire doors, enclosing stairwells, and installing public washrooms. But the building required substantial reconstruction. Its industrial heritage ensured an appropriate scale and price, but the space was still not ideally suited for a theatrical workplace. For example, the major renovation in the early 1980s removed most of the second floor and many of the building's internal supporting, and therefore obstructing, pillars. It also restored historically "correct" sash windows to the building's second-storey exterior. In fact, the transformation of the interior for theatrical purposes depended on the invocation of the exterior for "heritage" purposes. [7] Persuading the city of the building's heritage value prevented its previous owner from demolishing the empty factory and encouraged him to sell the plant to Passe Muraille (Johnston 136). The official heritage designation, granted later, increased the urban status of the space, allowing Passe Muraille to invoke 16 Ryerson Avenue's protected industrial facade as a means of leveraging capital investment into the theatre company. The 1978 fundraising prospectus offered contributors the opportunity of "INVESTING IN A HANDSOME BUILDING, THE CONTINUED EXISTENCE OF WHICH IS ASSURED BY ITS DESIGNATION UNDER THE ONTARIO HERITAGE ACT," and gave them the chance of "ENHANCING AND PRESERVING A PART OF TORONTO HISTORY" while "PROVIDING AUDIENCES WITH A COMFORTABLE AND ACCESSIBLE THEATRE" (3). The industrial history of the building continued to assert itself after Passe Muraille's ownership, but now as "heritage." The facade helped to smooth a difficult transition from an industrial to a theatrical workplace by turning the building's architectural, aesthetic, and local history into tools of capital investment that allowed Passe Muraille to fund and situate its work.

Theatre Passe Muraille nearly ceased operations when it ran into serious financial difficulty late in 1990. The company had accumulated a deficit of $450,000, and its bank refused to extend its line of credit beyond $200,000. Once again its building allowed access to capital that it would otherwise have been denied; the property value of the building allowed work to continue. The company itself made the link between funding the space and funding operations: "what we're fighting for," its general manager told *Theatrum* magazine in 1991, "is the survival of the facility as a viable theatre space" ("Banking" 6).

Residential property values across the city rose significantly during the 1980s, driving up the potential resale value of 16 Ryerson Avenue to the point where the company could borrow heavily against its equity in the building.[8] Residential prices in both the Toronto Census Metropolitan Area and in the downtown-west district increased almost in lock step through the early 1980s recession and skyrocketed after the recession ended. By the time of an appraisal in early 1983, the market value of 16 Ryerson Avenue had increased to $275,000 (Allen Trent Realty 2). Even though property prices depressed during the early 1990s recession, the building was still highly valuable; *Theatrum* cites the appraisal at the time of bank negotiations in 1991 as $890,000 ("Banking" 6). Johnston comments that, "Because of the equity in the building, Theatre Passe Muraille has been able to carry a deficit which would be alarming for other small theatres" (136), and there is little doubt that the property value of 16 Ryerson Avenue leveraged increasing amounts of capital into the theatre's operating budget, allowing its work to continue when its financial position was poor. But the building also tied Passe Muraille's financial administration to a highly speculative and volatile downtown housing market. Passe Muraille's crisis in 1990 and 1991 coincided with a dramatic drop in the value of residential properties in the Toronto Census Metropolitan Area and an even steeper decline in its immediate area.[9] Property value inflation and deflation, on a scale previously unknown, became a dominant feature of Toronto's post-Fordist urban economy in the 1980s and 1990s. Passe Muraille entered this economy through its building, and the measure of the company's economic integration is the way in which its physical space offered, on the one hand, a means of capitalization and, on the other, an ever greater exposure to the economic shocks of property value speculation. In effect, Passe Muraille internalized post-Fordist property relations through its performance space.

Heritage, Economic Crisis, and the Spatialization of Collective Memory

Although Theatre Passe Muraille focused on theatre space as an administrative issue, theatre space did not disappear as an artistic issue. While "heritage" referred to a particular representation—historical, aesthetic, and symbolic—of the architectural features of 16 Ryerson Avenue in the late 1970s and 1980s, the term took on a different meaning after Passe Muraille's financial crisis in 1990-91. Alongside its functional and administrative significance, the building explicitly became a poetic space or, more precisely, a commemorative site. Curiously, in asserting the importance of space, I have tended to measure that space physically. Doing so seems to go against a central preoccupation of materialist geographers such as Harvey, Massey, Soja, or Henri Lefebvre (and is, to some degree, a response to a modernist aesthetic problem that Passe Muraille has periodically invoked since moving to 16 Ryerson Avenue: physical abnegation as a spatial ideal). I agree wholeheartedly with their case, which argues that it is an epistemological error to assume that the measurement of spatial relationships is necessarily physical and a fetish to make the physical the referent and analytical touchstone of the spatial. Harvey emphasizes as a corrective Bachelard's notion of "poetic space" and Lefebvre's concept of "imagined space," in which space functions as a representational discourse in which "codes, signs, ...utopian plans, imaginary landscapes, and even material constructs such as symbolic spaces, particular built environments, paintings, museums, and the like" produce social meanings above and beyond the physical (*Condition* 218–19). One of the most important functions of poetic space for Passe Muraille is the production of imagined collective memory. "Heritage," after Passe Muraille's financial crisis, increasingly connoted the way in which 16 Ryerson Avenue was becoming a site of spatial commemoration of the theatre's own history. Commemoration, as Susan Bennett points out, is nostalgic; it activates an "imaginary past" as a "stable referent" in order to compensate for a "defective and diminished present" (5). She describes commemoration as functioning on a binary of good past/bad present; I would reframe the binary somewhat in the context of Passe Muraille so that the issue is not only good past/bad present but also stable past/unstable present. As Passe Muraille has weathered the upheavals of a post-Fordist political economy in Toronto in the 1990s, the company's history has become a marker of stability. The theatrical event at 16 Ryerson Avenue increasingly commemorates this stable past, transposing it to the present as a form of theatrical compensation for political and cultural volatility.

The 1990s have been unkind to midsize, not-for-profit theatres across Canada. The recession of the early 1990s was extraordinarily deep and long in Ontario, to a degree unseen since the Depression. Moreover, the political consensus around the desirability of public arts funding in Ontario, on which not-for-profit companies rely heavily, began to break down in that recession and was dismantled completely after the election of Mike Harris's Conservative government in 1995. Without the degree of access to private sponsorship that the regional theatres enjoy, midsize theatres in Toronto, of which Theatre Passe Muraille is only one, have generally been under financial siege for the entire decade.

What makes Theatre Passe Muraille different from these other companies, however, is its ability to recuperate a historical period in the 1970s when it was seen— rightly or wrongly—as "probably the most influential company in Canada" (Johnston 109). To this end, Passe Muraille increasingly refers to its early and most famous collective creations in its recent work. We may include here *The Urban Donnellys* (1993), which resituates some of the themes of the 1973–74 collective creation *Them Donnellys* in inner-city Toronto; a new production of *1837: The Farmers' Revolt* (1998); Michael Healey's *The Drawer Boy* (first produced in the spring of the 1998–1999 season and then remounted in the fall of the 1999–2000 season), based on the making of *The Farm Show*; and *The Rediscovery of Sex* (2000), a collective creation that will revisit the ideas explored in *I Love You, Baby Blue* (at the time of writing, this show has been scheduled but not performed). In addition, many of the practitioners from Passe Muraille's first decade work at the company with greater frequency. They include Paul Thompson, actor David Fox, Jim Garrard, actor-writer Linda Griffiths, and Miles Potter (who acted in *The Farm Show* and *1837* and directed *The Drawer Boy*). Throughout the 1990s, the company's repertoire and personnel have increasingly drawn on what are perceived, and now incontrovertibly inscribed, as Passe Muraille's "golden years."

A performance of *The Drawer Boy* is a particularly powerful commemorative event, in which the company's representation of its past shores up an unsteady present by positing the existence of, and its allegiance to, a Theatre Passe Muraille "tradition" (however ill-defined that tradition may be). The basic plot of the play—an actor named Miles lives and works with a pair of farmers as research for an unnamed play that he is helping to create and in which he will perform—was inspired by the creation of *The Farm Show*. The role of Angus, one of the two farmers in *The Drawer Boy*, was played by David Fox, who also performed in the original production of *The Farm Show*. The director of *The Drawer Boy*, Miles Potter, performed in *The Farm Show*, and the character of Miles in *The Drawer Boy* is a clear reference to Potter and some of his experiences living and working on a farm. The origin of the "haying" scene of *The Farm Show*, which was based on Potter's frustrations with farm labour, is depicted in *The Drawer Boy*. At the performance that I attended, photographs on the wall of the upstairs bar at 16 Ryerson Avenue were largely of 1970s collective creations, privileging this period in Passe Muraille's history as constitutive of the work done that day; photographs from the 1980s and 1990s were largely omitted or included primarily to sustain the particular continuity between past and present that the company desired (as with the photographs of *O.D. on Paradise*, a successful 1982 production that involved Linda Griffiths, Jim Garrard, and present artistic director Layne Coleman).

For those in the audience who saw the original production of *The Farm Show*, *The Drawer Boy* acknowledges their spectatorial history with the company and affirms that this history is constitutive of their present spectatorship. In the same way that a production of the play helps to unify Theatre Passe Muraille's history into "heritage," the production's inclusivity reassures this spectator that the history of Passe Muraille is also his or her own history and, like the company's, is uncontested and stable. For those in the audience who did not see the original production of *The Farm Show*, *The Drawer Boy*'s appeal to the socially affirmative power of theatre is equally inviting; the implication is that, by attending a production of *The Drawer Boy*, one memorializes the theatrical past and through that commemoration assumes a place within the Passe Muraille tradition.

Consequently, this conflation of histories and subjectivities completely refigures the conception of Theatre Passe Muraille's work during the 1970s as "alternative." By deploying Passe Muraille's history as a stable and unifying referent, the theatrical event can no longer conceive of this history as being in formation, dissonant, and anti-institutional. Passe Muraille's production of *The Drawer Boy* strips the company's "alternative" past of its radical content because that past is now bourgeois, hermetic, and accessible through unmediated representation in the present day. And an important part of that radical past—the way in which it was spatially interrogative—is unrepresentable once 16 Ryerson Avenue is imagined as a commemorative site. The nostalgic invocation of a stable past, so reassuring in a particularly uncertain moment of cultural production, is contingent on performance space being conceived of as transhistorically uncontested and infinitely transposable. But this is misleading: 16 Ryerson Avenue is a necessary part of this commemoration because, in the post-Fordist economy, the building itself is reassuring. Its "heritage," in both an architectural and an imaginary sense, commemorates a Fordist age that was ostensibly ordered and coherent and in which the preeminence of the bourgeoisie was secure.

Conclusion

Materialist theatre history has to look for the ways in which performance space is inscribed in theatrical production as more than stage space and beyond the immediate moment of performance. The retheorization of performance space did not cease to be an issue for Theatre Passe Muraille after it purchased 16 Ryerson Avenue; rather, the company first used the building to relocate spatial concerns from an artistic ideal into the structured administration of its labour process. This relocation was possible because of a post-Fordist suburbanization of manufacturing in Toronto's urban political economy, a move that opened former industrial spaces for use by theatre companies. When Passe Muraille purchased 16 Ryerson Avenue, however, it became tightly tied to Toronto's volatile property market. The theatre company has consistently attempted to reconcile administratively the spatial contradictions of the building: while owning it offers inventive modes of capitalization and physically embodies a sense of stability that funding sources and audiences usually welcome, the building also tethers Passe Muraille's financing to wild swings in local property values. In this sense, Passe Muraille has entrenched Toronto's urban political economy in its conception and management of performance space; the theatre workplace is also a marketplace. But while materialist theatre history can use the tools of Marxist geography and political economy to reveal the suppressed history of a theatre industry, it must also work toward an understanding of the ways in which the transformation of performance practice is also part of that history. For Passe Muraille, this transformation increasingly means that 16 Ryerson Avenue is a commemorative site, the spatial means by which histories are collapsed in the theatrical event and cultural tradition is invented and reproduced. A Theatre Passe Muraille that is, in Jim Garrard's words of 1968, "free of distinctions between actor and spectator, between 'inside' and 'outside' the theatre," now implies a very different understanding of the "theatre beyond walls."

(1999)

Notes

1 A revised version of this article appears in: McKinnie, Michael. *City Stages: Theatre and Urban Space in a Global City*. Toronto: U of Toronto P, 2007. I would like to acknowledge research assistance provided by the City of Toronto Archives, the theatre archives in the Special Collections department at the University of Guelph Library, and Theatre Passe Muraille. Early fragments of this paper were presented at the 1999 Association for Canadian Theatre Research national conference and in *Canadian Theatre Review*; I would like to thank the members of ACTR and Alan Filewod for allowing me the opportunity to present this research in progress. I would also like to thank an anonymous reader for *Essays on Canadian Writing* for a thorough and productive analysis of this essay's original draft. The writing of this paper has been supported by a Social Sciences and Humanities Research Council of Canada doctoral fellowship.

2 By using the language of Fordism and post-Fordism, I am employing the conceptual framework of Marxist theorists of economic, urban, labour, and artistic transformation: the Regulation School of French economists (see Boyer), the urban geography of David Harvey, the labour sociology of Harry Braverman, and the cultural criticism of Fredric Jameson. These and other critics do not always employ the same terminology, even when discussing the same phenomena. Terms such as "post-Fordism," "late capitalism," "monopoly capitalism," "postindustrial," and "flexible accumulation" may be considered roughly synonymous if not, in my view, equally accurate. "Fordism" and "Taylorism" roughly correspond as well. The chronological marker for a break from Fordism to post-Fordism is usually held to be the abandonment of the Bretton Woods system of international financial governance and the oil crisis of 1973.

3 It is appropriate that Rubin, in his 1998 collection *Canadian Theatre History: Selected Readings*, groups essays about contemporary Canadian theatre under the chapter title "The Development of Self-Image, 1968–1995." His collection is an excellent source of primary documents about theatre in Canada (and not necessarily Canadian theatre, as he frames it) from 1950 to 1995. Criticism of the contemporary period, however, leans heavily on essays from *Canadian Theatre Review*, which is not a scholarly publication. With one or two exceptions, Rubin's "sourcebook in Canadian theatre history" (xi) constructs the critical field as entirely uninformed by theoretical and/or historiographic debates.

4 In the influential work of Chicago School critics such as Ernest Burgess and Robert Park (see Burgess et al.), space is often the mechanism by which a particularly American mode of capitalist production is naturalized as social relations in general. In Burgess's concentric-ring model of urban development, space is the physical terrain—a kind of geological blank canvas or "environmental 'container' of human life," as Soja would call it (79)—by which the "organic" quality of social relations is realized and through which capitalist development is quantified. In Burgess's nar-

rative of urban civilization, space comes into being as the place where distinctions between capitalist relations and social practice are foreclosed. Burgess represents this development in pseudo-Darwinian language, referring to an "urban metabolism" and calling his analysis an "urban ecology." His model is naturalist, nationalist, and radically ahistorical; in short, it is a liberal model of American capitalist growth that transposes Chicago in the early twentieth century to cities in general and brings space into being only as the physicalization of inevitable and immutable capitalist relations.

5   Soja locates the neglect of space in Western Marxism in three places (see 84–88). First, there is the late appearance of Marx's *Grundrisse*, "which probably contains more explicitly geographical analysis than any of his writings" (85); its two volumes were published first in Russian in 1939 and 1941, the first German edition was published in 1953, and the first English edition was not published until 1973. As a result, materialist analysis tended to draw heavily on the completed volumes of *Capital*, which are theorized largely on the basis of a closed national economy. Marx proposed an analysis of world trade that would take up the problem of commodity circulation in transnational space, but he died before undertaking this project. Second, there is the problem of an antispatialism that results from Marx's attempt to overturn Hegel's reified ontological and phenomenological spatiality by privileging "revolutionary temporality" (Soya 86). Third, there was an assumption that, under developing capitalism, space simply was not as important as we might consider it to be now, since space only became important to capitalist development as a way to circumvent strictures later placed on its operation in a fixed place (such as limits on the working day, minimum wages, unionization, and so on).

6   Wilkinson-Kompass relocated to 167 Bentworth Avenue, and Sol Friendly Sheet Metal Works relocated to 797 Sheppard Avenue West.

7   Under the *Ontario Heritage Act*, changes to the interior of a designated building are allowed, but changes to the exterior must largely reproduce the aesthetic character of the building at the time of its construction.

8   Even though 16 Ryerson Avenue is not a residential building, its appropriate property value comparison is with residential property values. The building has little value as a commercial space for a private developer and would likely never be renovated for commercial use. It is as residential space, likely in the form of condominium development, that the building has the greatest potential value. Demand for housing in central Toronto has outstripped supply for many years, and the neighbourhood is already zoned residential, so conversion to housing would be much more straightforward than it would be, say, along Bathurst Street (though some of this difficulty has been mitigated by recent changes to Toronto's zoning regulations). Contrary to the *Theatrum* article, it is not at all clear that the heritage designation depresses the building's value by placing development restrictions on its exterior. Other industrial-residential conversions in downtown Toronto have marketed the heritage status of their buildings as value-added features.

⁹ The Toronto Census Metropolitan Area (CMA), as of its 1999 boundaries, stretches to the western edge of Burlington, the eastern edge of Durham County, and from Lake Ontario north to Lake Simcoe.

Works Cited

Allen Trent Realty. "Appraisal Report: Theatre Passe Muraille; A Two-Storey Semi-Detached Warehouse Used as a Theatre; 16 Ryerson Avenue in the City of Toronto in the Municipality of Metropolitan Toronto Ontario." 18 January 1983. Theatre Passe Muraille Archives, U of Guelph Library.

Bachelard, Gaston. *The Poetics of Space.* Boston: Beacon, 1994.

"Banking on Theatre." *Theatrum* (February–March 1991): 6.

Bennett, Susan. *Performing Nostalgia: Shifting Shakespeare and the Contemporary Past.* London: Routledge, 1996.

Boyer, Robert. *The Regulation School: A Critical Introduction.* Trans. Craig Charney. New York: Columbia UP, 1990.

Braverman, Harry. *Labor and Monopoly Capital: The Degradation of Work in the Twentieth Century.* New York: Monthly Review, 1974.

Burgess, Ernest W., Roderick D. McKenzie, and Robert E. Park. *The City.* Chicago: U of Chicago P, 1967.

City of Toronto. Assessment Roll, Ward No. 1, Div. No. 1, 1903. Toronto: City of Toronto, 1903.

Council of the Corporation of the City of Toronto. Minutes of Proceedings for the Year 1977; Consisting of By-Laws Passed during the Year; Appendix "B." Toronto: Carswell, 1978.

Filewod, Alan. *Collective Encounters: Documentary Theatre in English Canada.* Toronto: U of Toronto P, 1987.

Filion, P. "Metropolitan Planning Objectives and Implementation Constraints: Planning in a Post-Fordist and Postmodern Age." *Environment and Planning A* 28 (1996): 1637–60.

Gad, Gunter. "Toronto's Financial District." *Canadian Geographer* 35.2 (1991): 203–07.

Harvey, David. *The Condition of Postmodernity: An Enquiry into the Origins of Social Change.* Oxford: Blackwell, 1989.

———. *Justice, Nature, and the Geography of Difference.* Oxford: Blackwell, 1996.

———. *Social Justice and the City*. London: Arnold, 1973.

Jameson, Fredric. *Postmodernism: Or, The Cultural Logic of Late Capitalism*. Durham: Duke UP, 1991.

Johnston, Denis W. *Up the Mainstream: The Rise of Toronto's Alternative Theatres*. Toronto: U of Toronto P, 1991.

Knowles, Richard Paul, with Jennifer Fletcher. "Towards a Materialist Performance Analysis: The Case of Tarragon Theatre." *The Performance Text*. Ed. Domenico Pietropaolo. Toronto: Legas, 1999. 205–26.

Lefebvre, Henri. *The Production of Space*. Oxford: Blackwell, 1991.

Marx, Karl. *Capital: A Critique of Political Economy. Vol. 1*. London: Penguin, 1976.

Massey, Doreen. *Spatial Divisions of Labour: Social Structures and the Geography of Production*. New York: Routledge, 1995.

Matthew, Malcolm R. "The Suburbanization of Toronto Offices." *Canadian Geographer* 37.4 (1993): 293–306.

Reilly, John. Letter to Theatre Passe Muraille outlining the Canada/Ontario Employment Development Program. N.d. Theatre Passe Muraille Archives, U of Guelph Library.

Rubin, Don, ed. *Canadian Theatre History*. Toronto: Copp, 1996.

———. "Creeping Toward a Culture: The Theatre in English Canada since 1945." Rubin, ed. 318–31.

———. "The Toronto Movement." Rubin, ed. 394–403.

Soja, Edward W. *Postmodern Geographies: The Reassertion of Space in Critical Social Theory*. London: Verso, 1989.

Theatre Passe Muraille. "Funding Profile for the Theatre Passe Muraille Renovation Project." 10 September 1983. Theatre Passe Muraille Archives, U of Guelph Library.

———. Promotional brochure, 1998–99 season.

———. Promotional brochure, 1999–2000 season.

———. "A Request for a Contribution towards the Renovation of the New Theatre Passe Muraille 16 Ryerson Avenue, Toronto." N.d. Theatre Passe Muraille Archives, U of Guelph Library.

Theatre Passe Muraille and Leonard Kalishenko and Associates Ltd. "Renovations to Theatre Building, 1983." 1983. Theatre Passe Muraille Archives, U of Guelph Library.

Usmiani, Renate. *Second Stage: The Alternative Theatre Movement in Canada*. Vancouver: UBC P, 1983.

Toronto's Spectacular Stage

by Susan Bennett

> A culture now wholly commodity was bound to become the star com-
> modity of the society of the spectacle. (Debord 137)

If, at the end of the twentieth century, cities recognized the "spectacular value" of their cultural products, this phenomenon might best be explained in how these products contribute to the success of a city in the global market, where tourism has become a significant part of local, regional, and national economies. The promotion and commercialization of cultural attractions therefore plays a vital role in the overall strategy of a city trying to adopt a brand identity that will make it competitive in the tourism business. As Nigel Morgan and Annette Pritchard describe it, a brand identity "is perhaps the most powerful marketing weapon available to contemporary destination marketers confronted by tourists who are increasingly seeking lifestyle fulfilment and experience rather than recognizing differentiation in the more tangible elements of the destination product" (11). A city has to create and market a distinctive identity through a series of cultural criteria that every major tourist city must now fulfill, and here theatre plays a fundamental role as an element of the brand for any tourist destination. Although one could argue that in contemporary culture, while the traditional theatre scene (that is, the production of both classic and new plays) has to fight to bring in its audiences, the large-scale spectacles which characterize commercial theatre (generally, but not exclusively, the "megamusical") prosper precisely because of their ability to attract tourists as well as local theatre audiences. This essay will examine the crucial interrelationship between the commercial, spectacular stage and the city through the role played by theatre in the creation of the brand identity of Toronto as a tourist destination.

In the second edition of his seminal work *The Tourist*, Dean McCannell notes a particularly significant change in the tourism environment between the first publication of his book in 1975 and his revised version which appeared in 1999, namely "an aggressive invasion of the touristic field by corporate entertainment interests" (194). It is in this context of production and reception that commercial theatre has prospered. In other words, these stage successes are not the kinds of performances considered to be "serious theatre," but the decidedly more spectacular shows with high production costs and popular appeal. Requiring a high front-end investment in production, these shows rely on strong box office sales and long runs in large capacity theatres to create profit. Spectacular entertainment can, in this way, serve as an anchor for the brand identity of a city. McCannell has ably illustrated how the success of a tourist destination, the efficacy of the brand identity of a city, depends on the full development of its hospitality and travel sectors. But these sectors, although necessary (and certainly economically significant), do not generate tourism in and of themselves. Thus, as Can-Seng Ooi points out, "cultural products are framed as 'baits' to lure tourists [and] these products contribute indirectly to the economic growth of the tourism industry" (101). More precisely, a report produced by the Culture Division of Toronto City Council notes that "cultural institutions draw millions of tourists, bringing in from $450 to $600 million a year in economic benefits just to the hotel and food sectors" (3).

The city of Toronto has long understood that cultural tourism can serve as a powerful marketing tool (for its cultural products in particular but also for the city in general), to convince the consumer that the experience they will have is the same as— if not better than—the experience they could have in another prime destination. In this sense, then, the city must be spectacular—offering its visitors what Susan Fainstein and Dennis Judd describe as "a complex ecological system" (5). In this context, Fainstein and Judd show how tourists, the tourism industry, and cities are intertwined:

> To appeal to tourists, cities must be consciously molded to create a phys-
> ical landscape that tourists wish to inhabit. No city can afford to stand
> still for a moment, no matter how much it has recently done or how
> much money it has spent doing it. The constant transformation of the
> urban landscape to accommodate tourists has become a permanent fea-
> ture of the political economy of cities. (5–6)

This collusion of culture and capital requires a wide array of attractions in order to stay vital and appealing, and for Toronto, as for other big cities, the theatre scene is crucial to this equation. As it is described in the city council report: "For tourists, Toronto has traditionally had three main attractions: live theatre, distinct neighbourhoods, and festivals" (Culture Division 16). This is particularly important because it gives Toronto a brand identity which might not be so apparent at first glance but as Dennis Judd asserts, "cities that lack powerful symbols or historical and architectural signifiers must devise them" (38). In addition to the brand recognition that a symbol as distinctive as the CN Tower provides for Toronto, the city's identity is produced through the interplay of cultural products (theatre, festivals) and geographical districts (neighbourhoods). Cultural tourism allows for "the instrumental use of places, people and activities" (Meethan 130) and, as Bernard J. Frieden and Lynne B. Sagalyn note, the revitalization of a city requires "at least one restored Victorian neighbourhood" (287).

Theatre and district come together in downtown Toronto, in a Victorian neighbourhood, designated as the city's "entertainment district." Street signs there bear subtitles identifying them as part of the entertainment district so that tourists are literally pointed to experience the city's cultural scene. Likewise, maps and tourist literature direct visitors towards this area. (Other promoted areas are also structured around cultural practices, such as the art gallery district located immediately west of the entertainment district, and still others are promoted for ethnic concentration such as Little Italy or Chinatown.) For both Torontonians and visitors alike, the promotion of the distinct identity of an "entertainment district" depends upon what Alan Blum calls "the scenic promise of its space" (175), an urban landscape which is more than a striking façade. Local architecture, with its own charm, contributes, by way of historical, artistic, and commercial interests, to the creation of the spirit of a district. Even so, a theatre building is not simply its exterior architecture, a presence on the streetscape; it promotes the overarching tourism brand. And this is important, because local audiences alone do not ensure the economic viability of the entertainment district. In order to be profitable, Toronto theatres require tourists with their desire for the typical activities of cultural tourism, so as to ensure sufficient revenue to maintain their big-budget shows. These spectacular performances also contribute symbolically to the city's brand identity, since a flourishing entertainment district is a sign of urbanity—the significant cultural capital of a city, where art and pleasure meet, an economy that extends far beyond the box office and which encompasses and supports other urban spending (outings to bars and restaurants after shows, bookstores and other retail stores, taxis and more). Research in Singapore has shown that for "every tourist dollar spent on a theatre ticket, another $2.80 is spent on ancillary services" (Ooi 97). A study done by the Conference Board of Canada (2000) on the Stratford Festival in Ontario indicated that its annual budget of $35 million generates $346 million in economic activity in the region (qtd. in Taylor). The style of neighbourhoods that appeals to tourists is often necessarily static (the district showcases its own history, evoking a certain nostalgia for the city's past), but, even so, new theatrical productions bring with them a "constant transformation of the urban landscape" (Fainstein and Judd 6) which, as Fainstein and Judd rightly point out, constitutes a fundamental rule of the successful tourist economy.

In order to understand the contribution of commercial theatre to Toronto's tourism sector, there is perhaps no better example than Disney's *The Lion King*. A remarkable theatrical event, *The Lion King* was first staged in May 2000 at the Princess of Wales Theatre located in the heart of Toronto's theatre district. The scale and the extraordinary charm of this show have made it into *the* global success story of recent commercial theatre. Its opening in New York in November 1997 was followed by productions in seven other cities, including Toronto, and by an American tour initiated in 2003, which, in 2005, visited nine cities.[1] As Alan Filewod comments, "megamusicals like *The Lion King* have restructured theatre culture in national metropolises for the past two decades" (221), which, among other things, has produced an inextricable link between the entertainment industry and retailers who profit from this far-reaching tourism impact.

The revitalization of the area at the intersection of 42nd Avenue and Times Square in New York into an entertainment complex was initiated by the Disney Corporation through its renovation of the New Amsterdam Theatre for the first production of *The Lion King*.[2] The success of this enterprise, for New York and for Disney, prompted other major cities, especially places where *The Lion King* was a focus attraction, to do the same. The host city promoted a local signature brand, but the presence of *The Lion King* guaranteed a certain global status—that this city was deemed "good enough" for one of Disney's sought-after shows to play there. The opening scene of *The Lion King* is an exemplary spectacular in that it features extraordinary animal puppets summoned on stage by a magnificent musical call in world music style, sung by the wise spiritual leader of the show, Rafiki (a mandrill). Reviewers, with good reason, commented generously on the workmanship of the splendid masks and puppets that set designer Julie Taymor used to give three-dimensional life to what, originally, were only cartoon characters.[3] Seeing thirty-foot tall giraffes (actors on stilts) or flocks of birds (puppets controlled by long cables) swooping towards the stage at the beginning of the show effectively engages and delights audiences through the scope of Taymor's creativity. The puppets and puppeteers, the music, and the set design establish a level of spectatorial pleasure for audiences of any age and origin, and create a stage world that encompasses a variety of cultural practices. This is a formula that has produced enormous financial success. In this context, Filewod points out that large-scale spectacles like *The Lion King* occupy

> an ambivalent space as products of sophisticated local theatrical industries and as imported valorizing texts; these shows were perceived as neither foreign nor local, they seemed dislocated and deracinated enterprises, "belonging" to no place, but never of this place. (224–25)

As an anchor for the brand identity of the city, Toronto's commercial theatre must constantly remind the local and tourist public of its lineage. The contributions of this theatre to the promotion of Toronto are certainly produced directly (the audience's experience of a live show) as well as through explicit reference to where these theatrical productions have played in the past and their future destinations. *The Lion King* started at the Princess of Wales Theatre almost three years after its New York debut, but only six months after it had gone up in London, and, as one pre-premiere *Toronto Sun* article proclaimed: "It could well be that a lion is destined to reign as king of the box-office jungle worldwide—in New York, in London, in Japan and now here in Toronto" (Coulbourn). Spectacular theatre functions as a kind of cultural support for the overall reputation of a city, as a sign of its calibre and global position. For these reasons, Toronto has, in the past few years, imported productions of many recently successful shows—a long-term run of *The Lion King*, of course, and other box-office giants like *Mamma Mia!*, *The Producers*, and *Hairspray*—as well as more short-term and fixed-term runs of other imports such as *The Graduate*, *Contact*, and *The Rat Pack*. As Filewod indicates, these shows call for "a market that covers the entire Great Lakes heartland of North America" (220).

Mamma Mia!, the hit show based on the music of ABBA, was first mounted in London in 1999. This extremely successful production was followed by a Toronto production, which opened in May 2000. This was several months after the American premiere production in San Francisco that exploited ABBA's popularity with gay audiences and in a city where gay tourism was already well established. Since then, eight other permanent productions have been mounted, including a production in New

York in 2001 and another in Las Vegas in 2002.⁴ The impact of *Mamma Mia!'s* success on the theatre economy in Toronto can be measured by the eight million dollars that the show earned in ticket presales, making it the bestselling show in the 93-year history of the Royal Alexandra Theatre even before opening night (see Clark). Like *The Lion King, Mamma Mia!* constitutes popular entertainment that attracts a broad audience, as this London critic attests:

> *Mamma Mia!* [...] is a surefire hit. Stringing together a large number of Abba songs might alone have guaranteed a success, but Catherine Johnson, who has written the book, has done better than that. She hasn't attempted anything deep, dark, svelte or artistic: there is no contravention of the Abba ethos. She has produced a buoyant, celebratory piece which contains both irony and soppiness, the tacky and the wholesome, and which bounces 22 Abba numbers [...] into the audience. (Clapp)

This show surely has all these elements, but it is perhaps an oversimplification to attribute its success only to these production qualities. To attract such big audiences for such a long run, as *Mamma Mia!* did, demands a complex commercial strategy that goes further than insisting on the spectator's enjoyment by constructing a widely recognized international brand image.

An article in *Performance* magazine (the programme distributed to audiences for the "Mirvish season" in 2002–2003) shows the extent to which spectators were incited, in a light and humorous way, to anticipate the arrival of *Mamma Mia!* at the Royal Alex. Written by the late and respected Canadian theatre critic Mira Friedlander, this piece opens with a personal perspective:

> Let's face it. I was grumpy. There I was, taking my seat in the packed Prince Edward Theatre in London's West End, and resenting being there. I was giving up a *real* night of *real* theatre for a musical of ABBA songs?
>
> Not that I don't like ABBA; I like them well enough, in the proper context. But this was London, the theatre capital of the English-speaking world! Out there was the Royal National theatre's exquisite *The Merchant of Venice*. For a self-respecting theatre critic, *Mamma Mia!*—a musical based on the songs of a spandex-clad 1970s Swedish pop group—seemed likely to be a bit of a comedown. (25)

The last sentence of this otherwise largely descriptive article reads as follows: "By the way, I ended up loving *Mamma Mia!* and saw it twice" (Friedlander 30). What is particularly interesting in the passage between Friedlander's initial remarks and final concession is the presumed uniformity of the Canon Theatre audience members, even though it can include subscribers, occasional spectators from the greater Toronto area, or tourists coming from the central Great Lakes region. Like Friedlander, the intended reader of this article is a regular theatre-goer who would choose Shakespeare (or who knows they *should* choose Shakespeare), but who can appreciate the spectacular entertainment of *Mamma Mia!* Not only does Friedlander's account implicitly affirm

London and Toronto as theatrical cities, but she recognizes (twice) that the show is worth seeing even for a cultivated consumer (who appreciates Shakespeare). In one sense, this article illustrates the macro-tactics used by Toronto to create identity through *one* element of its brandscape: the spectacular stage. Even though you are in Toronto, Friedlander suggests, you can see the same theatre as in London—a fact that both illustrates cultural access and confirms spectatorial taste (along a Shakespeare-*Mamma Mia!* continuum). *Mamma Mia!* also adds its recognizable commodity value to the "entertainment district," as the production is housed in a historical building located directly across from the very modern Roy Thomson Hall, an emblem of high culture and home to the Toronto Symphony Orchestra.

Another recent Toronto show, *The Graduate*, received a much less enthusiastic reception from critics than *The Lion King* or *Mamma Mia!*. Despite this, it generated urban tourism, and achieved, on the sales front, a level of success that was remarkably similar to that of *The Lion King* or *Mamma Mia!*. *The Graduate* played for almost two years in London with stars such as Kathleen Turner or Jerry Hall playing the role of Mrs. Robinson. It played there to a packed audience every night, despite the unanimously bad reviews. As John Peter announced in his review for the London *Sunday Times*: "This is a grim business. The show is like the worst of Broadway, shallow and celebrity-driven, and complete with ghastly merchandise being sold in the foyer. Is this what we are heading for? God, I hope not" (Peter). But *The Graduate* was not only successful in London, it also filled a Toronto theatre for the entire month it was at the Canon Theatre (with Kathleen Turner reprising her West End performance) before leaving for Broadway. It is tempting to conclude that star power in contemporary culture holds more influence than theatre critics in the public's process of selection of theatrical events, but I would also suggest here that the triangulated London, Toronto, New York circuit travelled by the show is just as important for Toronto's audiences. *The Graduate* may lack in its theatrical quality but its attraction, insofar as the Toronto production was concerned, stems from an over-determination of the brand identity of prestigious theatre centres like London and New York, the West End and Broadway, with which Toronto seeks identification.

A recipient of four Tony Awards (including one for best musical), *Contact* by Susan Stroman and John Weidman demonstrated the same formula, but in reverse order. Originally produced at the Lincoln Centre in New York (1999), this show played in the Canon Theatre in Toronto in November and December 2002, before being produced in London's West End. In the ad campaign for the Toronto show, Mirvish Productions made sure to remind the public that Stroman was the director and choreographer for *The Producers*, the Broadway megahit that was scheduled to be produced by the same Toronto theatre in an upcoming season. The use of this network of references made people and places practically interchangeable in the hopes of making the Canon Theatre and Toronto—and their audiences, of course—into symbols of transnational prestige and taste.

Over the course of each of these international theatrical events, Toronto has exploited its apparent equivalence to the two cities that are reference points for theatre in a global marketplace. In two of the cases seen here (*Mamma Mia!* and *The Graduate*), audiences were sold the luxury and distinction of seeing these famous shows before they played on Broadway, and for *Contact*, before the London premiere. This elaborates what Fainstein and Judd consider essential to the tourist experience, in that "the tourist is a consumer away from home" (14). Fainstein and Judd also suggest that "the viewing of a harbor or a walk through downtown is insufficient as a tourist experience. Rather, satisfaction for the visitor and profit for the investor require that place become transformed into an object" (14). Thus, not only has Toronto, or at least the Toronto experience, been transformed into spectacular entertainment by way of *Mamma Mia!* (as Friedlander's article explicitly demonstrates, this spectacular entertainment is always already London, or at least the London experience), but it has also been displayed as commodity goods: the souvenir T-shirts and other spin-off products that are designed to remind audiences of the show they attend. In a sense, the spin-off products that tourists bring home indicate not only that they visited Toronto and saw *Mamma Mia!*, but also that they experienced something that New Yorkers and visitors to New York were still waiting for. The effect of this is to spectacularize Toronto's tourist economy; through spin-off products, the city accrues distinctive brand identity. As *The Lion King* T-shirts bear the name of the city where they were bought, imagine the cultural capital earned by wearing a t-shirt that says "*The Lion King* New York City" to the Toronto premiere. In a similar way, *The Graduate* offered its audiences pleasure by proxy by way of owning Mrs. Robinson's handkerchief, and the program for *Contact* invited audiences to "dance to the music of *Contact* on CD or RCA Victor CDs and Cassettes" (2). And this doesn't even take into account the other spin-off products sold in the lobby, that threshold space in which the spectator moves between the stage and the city. But the transformation of city-to-spectacle-to-souvenir is not limited to these specific movements. In a more significant way, this transformation enables duration, when the spectacular experience of tourism and of the theatrical entertainment is, at its core, ephemeral.

Theatre has, it seems, come to occupy a privileged position in what cities have developed as a standard commercial strategy aimed at potential tourist markets. Frieden and Sagalyn suggest that a city's obligatory tourist infrastructure, a mayor's "trophy collection," typically comprises an atrium hotel, festival mall, convention centre, gentrified historic neighborhood, domed sports stadium, aquarium, new office towers, and waterfront development (qtd. in Judd 39). Toronto has just such a set of trophies; only an aquarium is missing. And its entertainment district development is a deliberate part of this plan. The result is, as Saskia Sassen and Frank Roost point out, that "urban culture becomes an exotic object of tourism increasingly mediated through the entertainment industry. This outcome undercuts old distinctions between sites of production and sites of consumption, a point that may apply to urban tourism everywhere" (154). And, of course, the interdependence of commercial theatre and urban tourism manifested itself in a spectacular way in 2003 in Toronto.

The Severe Acute Respiratory Syndrome (SARS) epidemic that hit Toronto at the beginning of 2003 had a fast and devastating impact on the city's tourism industry, especially when the World Health Organization issued a notice suggesting that people should avoid staying in the Toronto area. With low occupancy rates in hotels, empty restaurants (especially in Chinatown), and few reservations planned for leisure visits or conventions, both immediate and long-term economic consequences of SARS quickly became evident. The government and business world realized that tourists would need a significant amount of encouragement to once again start thinking of Toronto as an attractive and safe urban tourism destination. And it was definitely no surprise that Mirvish Productions[5] launched the campaign "It's Time for a Little T.O." the day after the World Health Organization's warning. In that first day, Mirvish Productions fielded more than 4,000 calls a minute and sold 12,000 package deals "which include tickets to dinner at a top restaurant, a voucher for a Toronto Blue Jays [baseball] game and a choice of seeing [...] *The Lion King* or *Mamma Mia!* for $85–$125 if you stay overnight in a hotel" (McGran and Perry). The $500,000 that the promotional campaign for the "It's Time for a Little T.O." event cost was covered by the Ontario Commercial Tourism Partnership (See Knelman, "SARS Tourism"). In this attempt to reinvent Toronto's brand identity, tourists were offered three kinds of activity—fine dining, professional sports, large-scale spectacular performance—at the lowest possible prices. And, at first, when the campaign was targeted to attract tourists from other parts of Ontario, the strategy seemed to have been a success, with more than 100,000 package deals sold.

A second promotional campaign, targeting potential tourists from the proximate states of Michigan, Ohio, and New York, was developed when the second SARS epidemic was reported. But it was not pursued given the costs of buying advertising time from American television channels, when their news was showing in detail the high number of new cases (or suspected new cases) of SARS in Toronto. As Martin Knelman reported in the *Toronto Star*,

> David Mirvish had enjoyed huge success selling theatre tickets for May and June through his "Time for a Little T.O." promotional bargain package, including hotel rooms and restaurant meals. He was going to do something similar for July and August targeted at Americans—until research indicated resistance to Toronto is so high that bargain prices wouldn't help. Instead, he announced *The Lion King* will close on Sept. 28. ("RATS")

This article appeared June 4th. On June 6th, David Mirvish announced a "voluntary quarantine for three months" (Knelman, "SARS puts") for *Mamma Mia!*, putting an end, after the show presented on the Canada Day holiday, to a production which had until then been sold out, only to open again 13 weeks later, on September 30, two days after the finale of *The Lion King*. All things considered, *Mamma Mia!* was not as dependant on tourist ticket sales as the Disney production, with the exception of the summer months when 65% of sales were generated by tourists, generally Americans.[6] If the promotion of the "It's Time for a Little T.O." event provides a dramatic illustration of the crucial contribution of theatre to the commercialization of Toronto, then the second SARS epidemic demonstrates even more dramatically the contribution of the tourism sector to the success of these same shows. In the end,

SARS gave Toronto the worst kind of brand identity, and no commercial strategy could have counteracted this deterrent to travel.

Moreover, the collapse of the brand identity of both the theatres and the city was devastating and its impact on other business sectors quickly became apparent. For example, in July and August, the rate of occupancy in hotels was around 40% (when the normal rate was 90%) and the Conference Board of Canada estimated that the Toronto economy suffered more than $570 million worth of losses because of SARS, and Toronto's GDP was reduced by a million dollars for the year 2003.[7] When SARS finally disappeared from the news, representatives of both government and business demonstrated a bold optimism, stating that there would be no SARS epidemic in the upcoming months (thankfully, this prediction has proved accurate to this day) and that the city would recover completely by 2004, thanks especially to productions of *The Producers* (at the Canon Theatre) and *Hairspray* (at the Princess of Wales Theatre). Tourism in Toronto picked up again, but not to the level it was at before SARS. *The Lion King* closed at the beginning of 2004, and *Mamma Mia!* closed in May 2005. The highly anticipated productions of *Hairspray* and *The Producers* did not bring in the hoped-for audiences and thus profits. Although *Hairspray* stayed open for an eleven-month run, and *The Producers* for a little less than seven months, the two productions still lost money for their New York investors, and as Martin Knelman put it, this "gives Toronto a bit of a black eye" ("Since when"). What Knelman suggests here is that the city's brand identity was damaged—not only in the wake of SARS, but also by the city's inability to ensure a level of return for the investors who underwrote its theatrical recovery. With production costs running between $8 and $10 million per show, *Hairspray* and *The Producers* were seen as failures.

All in all, the consequences of the SARS epidemic serve as a warning to tourist destinations about their commercial practices. As Bud Purves, the president and general manager of Toronto's main monument, the CN Tower, puts it, "Tourism is about sustaining the brand of a city. Flash-in-the-pan products [referring to the "SARS-Stock" concert in 2003 starring the Rolling Stones] are interesting, but they don't recapture that sustaining image" (qtd. in Lu A01). Toronto did nevertheless start to recover its brand identity by marketing the city's attractions to appeal to their traditional tourist clientele, namely American visitors, but also, I believe, to reinforce and to encourage more local tourism, including the population of the greater Toronto area and southern Ontario. For all intents and purposes, this means an increase of cultural "baits" in order to revitalize Toronto's image. This was brought about initially by the development of a new architecture to reinforce the pillars of the city brand through ambitious plans for new urban infrastructure that announced a level of commitment never before seen so as to re-establish the city's local, national, and international prestige. These projects included the expansion of the Royal Ontario Museum (fuelled by a $200 million donation from the Watson family) and the Four Seasons Centre for the Performing Arts, a home for the Canadian Opera Company, which is scheduled to open in 2006. Other development projects plan $195 million worth of renovations for the Art Gallery of Ontario, the Celia Franca Centre (for the National Ballet School), and the Royal Conservatory of Music's learning centre (see Knelman, "Buildings").

A new neighbourhood—The Historic Distillery District—has also been actively promoted as "Canada's premier arts, culture and entertainment destination" (Distillery).
The attractions of this district include art galleries, craft workshops, shops and restaurants, as well as performance space. This new destination district has also become a
prime setting for another staple of Toronto's established brand identity: the festival.
The highly respected annual jazz festival (in its third year in 2005) has relocated to the
Historic Distillery District, attracting audiences not just to listen to jazz and blues
music, but to dance, to eat, and to drink. The reconfiguration of a Victorian neighbourhood into a quintessential entertainment site shows the energy that Toronto has
devoted to diversification of its tourist attractions. As shown in its festival calendar,
the Historic Distillery District presented, for two months in 2005, *Cavalia*, a show
played in the largest big-top tent touring in North America. This show combines
artists and horses (twenty riders and acrobats, thirty-three horses) in a spectacular
performance created by Normand Latourelle, one of the founding members of Cirque
du Soleil. Ambitious renovation and construction projects, like the Historic Distillery
District, display Toronto's commitment to what Derek Wynne and Justin O'Connor
call "a culturally based urban regeneration strategy" (845).

If these new developments add capital to Toronto's brand identity, other indica-
tors suggest that tourism there is still fragile. *We Will Rock You*, the Queen/Ben Elton
musical that has been playing in London's Dominion Theatre for four years and for a
year at the Paris Las Vegas Hotel & Casino, was scheduled to be staged in the summer
of 2005 at the Canon Theatre in Toronto, but the production was cancelled. Following
the recent closure of *Mamma Mia!* (the last musical to have a long run in Toronto),
the confidence to produce expensive commercial theatre seems to have been replaced
by the development of its two other distinctive traits—districts and festivals. But
Toronto's importance in the transnational entertainment circuit was renewed in a
spectacular way by the announcement of the world premiere of the stage adaptation
of *The Lord of the Rings*, with a scheduled opening at the Princess of Wales Theatre
(which presented *The Lion King* and which seats almost 2,000) early in 2006. With a
$30 million budget, it is an extraordinary coup for Toronto to have beaten out London
in staging the first production of this show (and with a contract clause that states there
will be no other North American productions for at least eighteen months after the
Toronto premiere). It came as no surprise that, at the press conference announcing the
event in March 2005, the mayor of Toronto, David Miller, and official government and
tourism industry representatives were present, since the Ontario government contributed a remarkable $3 million to help secure the production, and Tourism Toronto
"committed to provide $3 million in marketing support" (Dixon R2). The president
of the Greater Toronto Hotel Association, Rod Seiling "predicted a major '*Rings*'-
driven boom in visitors to Toronto thanks to proven drawing power of the fantasy
franchise [...] adding that the show would attract not only Canadian and American
audiences but theatregoers from around the world." Seiling continues: "They have to
eat here, they have to shop here, they have to sleep here. [...] The spinoff goes right
across the whole tourism industry" (qtd. in Gray). The day after the press conference,

the newspaper described the show as "being billed as the city's biggest hope to restore its theatre and tourism industries to their pre-SARS financial health" (Dixon R1).

The large-scale spectaculars of commercial theatre are without a doubt at the heart of tourist activity in the city, and tourist audiences ensure that these theatres are profitable. It is culture and performance, not geography and infrastructure, that sells the city to itself and to the rest of the world. But with SARS, the tourism economy discovered the dangers of this logic: the city is extremely vulnerable to the failure of its star merchandise. This essay might also serve as a reminder that SARS cost Toronto dearly: the many horrible deaths and the stress and the pain endured by families and communities were very real. Beyond the tragic consequences that SARS held for Toronto, it substantially changed the circumstances that dictate how a city perceives itself and how it is perceived by the rest of the world. At the same time, it is important to understand the crucial connection between local economies and cultural practices, which produce not only the identity of the city necessary for a viable, indeed robust tourist industry, but which also allow its more spectacular symbolic representation in the context of the twenty-first century global marketplace.

(2005)

Notes

I would like to thank Meg Moran for assistance in preparing the English version of this article.

[1] See Disney for details on the American, international, and touring productions as of December 2010. Besides New York and Toronto, productions were mounted in Hamburg (Germany), Scheveningen (Netherlands), Tokyo, Nagoya, Sydney/ Melbourne (played in both cities for a limited time), and London.

[2] For a complete examination of the Broadway production of *The Lion King*, see the excellent article by Maurya Wickstrom, "Commodities, Mimesis, and *The Lion King*: Retail Theatre for the 1990s."

[3] See my account of the Toronto production (Bennett). In this article, I adopt a different mode of analysis, since my concern is how this production contributes to Canadian theatre. In it I propose that the hiring of Canadian actors (some of whom are well known to Canadian audiences) and references to well-known Canadians (including Ed Mirvish, whose production company directed the play) give the production local meaning. Although I believe that these elements of Canadian content are significant, it is nonetheless essential, in terms of financial success, that *The Lion King* operates as the kind of transnational show that Filewod discusses.

⁴ In 2010 there are eight permanent and five touring productions of the show; see Littlestar Services.

⁵ Mirvish Productions is the most influential theatre production company in Toronto. Founded by Ed Mirvish, a local entrepreneur who made his fortune with Honest Ed's, a store that sells low-priced products, and run by his son David Mirvish, the company has, among other things, brought *Mamma Mia!* and *The Lion King* to Toronto.

⁶ See the previously cited Knelman article. The author suggests that the war in Iraq and an "endless winter" had already reduced sales, even before the devastating effects of the two SARS epidemics were felt.

⁷ See Lu. Lu remarks that the Conference Board of Canada's statistics were generated before the second SARS epidemic outbreak, and that the final impact on the Toronto economy could be much worse.

Works Cited

Bennett, Susan. "Disney North: The Lion King." *Canadian Theatre Review* 105 (2001): 67–68.

Blum, Alan. *The Imaginative Structure of the City.* Montreal and Kingston: McGill-Queen's UP, 2003.

Clapp, Susannah. "Great Dane, super Swedes: London goes Scandinavian with a new Hamlet and a celebration of Abba." *The Observer* 11 April 1999: 10.

Clark, Andrew. "ABBA-solutely fabulous: Mamma Mia! features a light plot, an old-fashioned ending and 22 songs from the group that defined a decade for many." *Maclean's* 112.21 (22 May 2000): 48.

Contact Program (magazine insert). *Performance* (September/November 2002): 2.

Coulbourn, John. "Royal Triumph: Taymor's Vision Unleashes a Spectacular *Lion King*." *Toronto Sun* 26 April 2000: 74.

Culture Division of Toronto, City Council. "The Creative City: A Workprint." April 2001.

Debord, Guy. *The Society of the Spectacle.* Trans. Donald Nicholson-Smith. New York: Zone Books, 1995.

Disney. *The Lion King: The Official Site of the Musical.* 14 December 2010. http://disney.go.com/theatre/thelionking.

Distillery Historic District, The. 14 December 2010. http://www.thedistillery district.com/about.php.

Dixon, Guy. "Can a Hobbit Save Hogtown?" *The Globe and Mail* 17 March 2005: R1–R2.

Fainstein, Susan and Dennis R. Judd. "Global Forces, Local Strategies, and Urban Tourism." *The Tourist City.* Ed. Dennis R. Judd and Susan S. Fainstein. New Haven and London: Yale UP, 1999.

Filewod, Alan. "Theatre Capitalism, Imagined Theatres and the Reclaimed Authenticities of the Spectacular." *Crucible of Cultures: Anglophone Drama at the Dawn of a New Millennium.* Ed. Marc Maufort and Franca Bellarsi. Bruxelles: Peter Lang, 2002.

Frieden, Bernard J. and Lynne B. Sagalyn. *Downtown Inc.: How America Rebuilds Cities.* Cambridge and London: The MIT P, 1989.

Friedlander, Mira. "Mamma Mia! What a Surprise." *Performance* (September/November 2002): 25, 26, 29, 30.

Gray, J. "Lord of the Rings Musical to Premiere in Toronto." *The Globe and Mail* 16 March 2005: A6.

Judd, Dennis. "Constructing the Tourist Bubble". *The Tourist City.* Ed. Dennis R. Judd and Susan S. Fainstein. New Haven and London: Yale UP, 1999.

Knelman, Martin. "Buildings Going up as Hollywood North Sinks." *Toronto Star* 26 December 2004: C02.

———. "RATS (Reluctant American Tourist Syndrome)." *Toronto Star* 4 June 2003: F02.

———."SARS puts Mamma Mia! into Quarantine." *Toronto Star* 6 June 2003: C12.

———."SARS Tourism Recovery Plans Not Going Anywhere." *Toronto Star* 24 May 2003.

———."Since When is $30M in Revenues a Flop?" *Toronto Star* 9 October 2004: A26.

Littlestar Services Ltd. *Mamma Mia!* 14 December 2010. http://www.mamma-mia.com.

Lu, Vanessa. "Tourism Slump 'Urgent'." *Toronto Star* 12 July 2003: A01.

McCannell, Dean. *The Tourist: A New Theory of the Leisure Class.* Berkeley: U of California P, 1999.

McGran, Kevin and Ann Perry. "Theatre Ticket Deal a Smash Hit." *Toronto Star* 1 May 2003: B01.

Meethan, Kevin. *Tourism in Global Society: Place, Culture, Consumption.* New York: Palgrave, 2001.

Morgan, Nigel and Annette Pritchard. "Contextualizing destination branding." *Destination Branding: Creating the Unique Destination Proposition.* Ed. Nigel Morgan, Annette Pritchard, and Roger Pride. Oxford: Butterworth Heinemann, 2002.

Ooi, Can-Seng. *Cultural Tourism and Tourism Cultures.* Copenhagen: Copenhagen Business School, 2002.

Peter, John. "What's with you, Mrs Robinson?" *The Sunday Times* 9 April 2000: 17.

Sassen, Saskia and Frank Roost. "The City: Strategic Site for the Global Entertainment Industry." *The Tourist City.* Ed. Dennis R. Judd and Susan S. Fainstein. New Haven: Yale UP, 1999.

Taylor, Kate. "Art Groups Need to Tell Tax Payers a New Story." *The Globe and Mail* 21 March 2002: R1.

Wickstrom, Maurya. "Commodities, Mimesis, and The Lion King: Retail Theatre for the 1990s." *Theatre Journal* 51 (1999): 285–98.

Wynne, Derek and Justin O'Connor. "Consumption and Postmodern City." *Urban Studies* 35.5–6 (1998): 841–64.

Multicultural Text, Intercultural Performance: The Performance Ecology of Contemporary Toronto [1]

by Ric Knowles

In its promotional material the city of Toronto regularly makes two significant claims: to be the world's most multicultural city, and to be the third most active theatre centre in the English-speaking world. This chapter looks at the relationships between these claims, and positions theatrical activity within the city in relation to Canada's official multicultural policy. It articulates multicultural *texts*—the policies, documents, and official discourses of Canadian multiculturalism—against intercultural *performance*—the complex ecology of grassroots interculturalism that plays itself out among the many intercultural theatre companies within the city who attempt to construct culturally alternative communities and solidarities across difference.

This text versus performance binary, of course, problematically imitates understandings of dramatic scripts as "texts" that are, or fail to be, "realized" in performance, but I hope to complicate that relationship in three ways. First, I read the city's performance of the official multicultural script [2] through the work of W.B. Worthen and Robert Weimann, understanding the relationship between text and performance as mutually constitutive. For multiculturalism, as for a dramatic text, "performance is not determined by the text [...]: it strikes a much more interactive, performative relation between writing and the spaces, places, and behaviors that give it meaning" (Worthen 12). Intercultural performance in Toronto operates in relation to multicultural text as "a formative force, as an institutionalized power in itself, as a cultural practice, in its own right" (Weimann 4–5), and one that performs official multiculturalism in ways that are independently generative, instantiating the text in ways that constitute its social effect.

A second way in which I complicate the text/performance binary is to read the grassroots performance of the intercultural city as heterotopic (Foucault), as opposed to the utopian vision of the official script, defining heterotopias, in Kevin Hetherington's phrase, as "spaces of alternate ordering" (viii). [3] I suggest, too, that official multiculturalism's utopia is essentially idealist, as opposed to the messy materialisms of heterotopic practice.

Finally, I treat contemporary Toronto as a complex intercultural performance ecology, drawing on Baz Kershaw's articulation of performance as an ecosystem. Kershaw describes "the complicated and unavoidable inter-dependency between any element of a performance event and its environment," where "the smallest change of one element in some way, however minutely, effects change in all the rest" ("Oh" 36). He also suggests, significantly, that the health of an ecosystem is best judged by the diversity of its species (Kershaw, "Theatrical"). Like heterotopias, too, ecosystems are always in process, operate at the intersection of local and global environments, and in the contemporary world are always threatened by unfettered capitalism.

My purpose is to understand how individual gendered, raced, and classed subjectivities and community identities within the multicultural city are not just reflected in, or given voice by, but are *constituted through* performance. How does this processual, performative (re)construction of subjectivities relate to the "ethnic" communities of official multiculturalism? How do these performatively constituted subjectivities interact with one another in shifting coalitions? How do they relate to dominant understandings of the city's social space, which constitute the dominant culture as unified and monolithic, minoritized non-European cultures as "ethnic" enclaves?

Much has happened since Toronto theatre has been the subject of extended scholarly treatment, but perhaps the most significant development of the past two decades has been the emergence of a vibrant interdependent ecology of intercultural performance that crosses cultures and disciplines, challenges the hegemony of whiteness on the city's stages, and reflects the cultural differences that are visible and audible on the city's streets and streetcars. Some companies, such as the Filipino Carlos Bulosan Theatre, are dedicated to specific cultural communities. Others, such as the AfriCan Theatre Ensemble, Theatre Archipelago, and Rasik Arts, primarily perform work from cultural "homelands." Others still, such as Obsidian Theatre, b-current, fu-GEN Asian Canadian Theatre, Red Sky Performance, and Native Earth Performing Arts *constitute* internally diverse (and sometimes historically conflicted) cultural communities *as* "African Canadian," "Asian Canadian," and "Aboriginal," developing and performing new work that speaks across such differences. Finally, companies such as Cahoots Theatre Projects, Modern Times Stage Company, and the feminist Nightwood Theatre, are yet more broadly intercultural. None of these companies has its own space, each relying on quickly disappearing rental space or co-production with resident companies. And each mounts a limited season of one or two major productions per year. Most, however, are also crucially involved in developing new work at fringe and new play festivals such as SummerWorks, b-current's rock.paper.sistahs, Factory Theatre's intercultural CrossCurrents, and the AfriCanadian Playwrights Festival; and some of this work is starting to appear in the subscription seasons of the resident companies.

Multicultural Policy

Canada's multicultural policy is widely celebrated for its utopian vision and its potential use by marginalized groups and individuals to gain access to full participatory democracy. And there is no doubt that considerable Trudeau-era idealism clings to what was the world's first state-sanctioned multiculturalism policy. Indeed, in 2005

Caribbean Canadian sociologist Cecil Foster envisioned a realizable nation *"Where Race Does Not Matter"* emerging from Trudeau's "idealist dream" (ix). But it is important in acknowledging the idealist value of utopias to recall the historical dystopias that have emerged when such ideals have been imposed monologically, to historicize the emergence and development of the Canadian multicultural script since the 1960s, and to take into account the ways in which that script continues to shape the material conditions for intercultural performance in Toronto.

The federal policy "Multiculturalism within a Bilingual Framework" was introduced by Prime Minister Pierre Elliott Trudeau in 1971 as a response to concerns expressed by "ethnic minorities" about the establishment of the Royal Commission on Bilingualism and Biculturalism.[4] The commission was appointed in 1963 to determine how to develop Canadian nationhood based on equality between French and English "charter groups" with "other ethnic groups" taken into account only as a secondary issue. In this narrative, "official multiculturalism" emerges as an afterthought in the effort to contain the independence movement in Quebec. Within Toronto's arts, education, and theatre communities, this meant the availability of targeted arts funding for francophone or bilingual (English-French) work, but not for work from "othered" cultures.

A second determining context from which the 1971 policy emerged was the 1960s liberalization of Canada's immigration policies. The 1962 policy, formalized in the Immigration Act of 1967, initiated an idealist system that eschewed discrimination on the basis of race, national origin, or culture. The unspoken purpose of the policy change, however, was to bolster a dwindling labour force with cheap, easily policed bodies at a time of exuberant economic expansion. It had the effect, nevertheless, of opening Canada's borders for the first time to significant numbers of non-European immigrants, who came to be known as "visible minorities," and who settled disproportionately in the city of Toronto, where street life was transformed, and the possibilities for intercultural exchange increased dramatically.[5] It is possible, then, to see those policies as having produced the felt need to both exploit and "manage" diversity, particularly racial diversity, through means other than immigration. Enter multiculturalism.

A third context that leaves traces in Canada's multicultural practice is more symbolic than material. This was the need, following Canada's 1967 centenary, to establish a distinctive national identity, if only to differentiate Canadians from Americans. Canadian multiculturalism became a widely broadcast symbol, and Toronto became the poster city for Canadian identity as one "tolerant" of diversity—one of the policy's stated goals, but one that problematically positions "diversity" as non-Canadian —something "other," that "real" Canadians "generously" tolerate.

In its 1971 "White Paper" articulation, its 1982 entrenchment in the Charter of Rights and Freedoms, and its passage into law as Bill C-9, the focus of the multicultural script was on "preserv[ing]" the "cultural heritage" of people of diverse ethnicities and "advanc[ing] multiculturalism throughout Canada in harmony with the national commitment to the official languages of Canada" (Multiculturalism and

Citizenship Canada 13, 15).[6] This combined focus on the culturalist preservation of the heritage of the "other" and on containment within a dominant French-English charter-group has been the basis for the most salient critiques of the multicultural script. Neil Bissoondath attacks it for ghettoizing cultural communities through the rhetoric of preservation, resisting assimilation while controlling access to material and cultural capital and limiting cultural production to folkloric exhibitions and multicultural festivals. Himani Bannerji critiques the liberal discourse of "tolerance" embedded in the script as articulated by Charles Taylor, where a (white) liberal "we" is seen to "tolerate" "others" rather than to dissolve into a more inclusive multicultural entity (125–50). Sneja Gunew points to "state multiculturalism" as a bureaucratic tool for "managing" diversity. State multiculturalism, she argues, has been "framed by a liberal pluralism where cultural differences are paraded as apolitical [ahistorical and static] ethnic accessories" (Gunew 17), and where women are positioned without agency as the stolid bearers of the "ethnic" tradition.[7] Bannerji has scrutinized what she calls "capitalist state inspired multiculturalisms" (1) for their capacity to obscure "a hidden class struggle being conducted behind cultural-historical masks of 'authentic' identities." She also critiques the Canadian multicultural script's capacity to function "as an epistemology of occlusion which displaces the actual living subjects, their histories, cultures, and social relations, with ideological constructs of ethnicity" (11), while attributing various social and economic inequalities, together with racialized and gendered violences, not to systemic racism and sexism, but to untouchable "cultural differences." Smaro Kamboureli provides a nuanced reading of the Act itself, exposing its internal contradictions and its tendency, fuelled by veiled racist and assimilationist principles, towards the legitimation and commodification of ethnicity ("Scandalous" 96–106)—commodification that manifests itself within Toronto theatre as the display of exotic difference on mainstream stages for dominant-culture audiences.

For these and other critics, the central reference points for the multicultural script, against which a conflation of "visible minorities" can be defined, are the inscribed charter languages of French and (for Toronto) English,[8] and "a consolidated and hegemonic 'whiteness' as the encompassing sign for all forms of socio-economic and political privilege" (Gunew 19). Finally, and scandalously, "the 1971 policy does not mention First Nations peoples, and the 1988 Act specifically excludes them" (Kamboureli, "Making" 11), leaving the relationship between multiculturalism and indigeneity a vexed issue to this day, particularly in urban centres such as Toronto, with its significant off-reserve "urban Indian" population. Indeed, the only peoples with genuine claims to "founding" status in relation to the places now called Canada, are, in the multicultural script, "relegated," as Bannerji says, "to the status of footnotes" (101).

Performing the multicultural script: funding

Official performances of the multicultural script, as realizations of "the text" inscribed in official discourse, have borne out the concerns of its critics. One of the most deter-

minative official performances, the funding of arts practice, provides a salient example, one that intercultural performance practitioners in Toronto have been forced to
negotiate for decades. As sociologist Peter Li demonstrated in 1994, in the first two
decades following the implementation of multiculturalism, arts funding under the
policy produced separate and unequal support structures for "occidental" (365) and
minority arts. Throughout the 1970s and 1980s, artists from "the high-status art world
of mainly white Canadians" (Li 366) enjoyed a formal system of peer-reviewed
funding through the Canada Council for the Arts. Meanwhile, "the more nascent multicultural circle [was] sustained by Canada's official policy of multiculturalism
through the Government's direct funding and control of activities under [...] multicultural programs" designed to promote heritage activities among minoritized
cultures (366).

Not surprisingly, funding allocated throughout the 1970s and 1980s through the
federal Multiculturalism Directorate, available to individuals only if they were
"supported by recognized community [i.e., multicultural] organizations/groups or
institutions" (qtd. in Li 387), went almost exclusively to non-professional "national
and regional multicultural festivals, which involved folkloric dancing, ethnic theatre
performances, and craft exhibitions" (Li 378). In short, multiculturalism as performed
through arts funding practices kept othered cultures in their static, nostalgic, and
dehistoricized ethnic place, allowing dominant cultural expression to flourish within
an established Euro-American tradition. They created "the institutional framework
for reproducing minority art, culture, and heritage in forms and manners that are
consistent with maintaining the hegemony of the dominant group" (Li 369).

The effects of this for theatrical practice are clear, as Mayte Gómez demonstrated
in 1993. Locating her study within an analysis of official policies that anticipated Li,
Gómez examined Toronto's Cahoots Theatre Projects's 1993 "Lift Off" festival. She
found that universalist discourse encouraged by the multicultural script resisted interaction across genuine, shifting, materially, and historically located cultural or formal
difference within the city. Theatre that set out to simply realize the script, that is, reinforced rather than disrupted the dominant/other binary on which colonialism rests,
inscribing diversity rather than, and without, real difference. This has remained true,
as large "mainstream" companies in Toronto, complying with the multicultural script,
fill the "diversity slots" in their seasons with "ethnic" exotica without significantly
shifting their audience base or comfort level.

Arts funding practices shifted in the 1990s, as the Multiculturalism Directorate
was replaced in 1991 by the Department of Multiculturalism and Citizenship. This
was in turn split in 1993 between the new Department of Canadian Heritage and the
Department of Citizenship and Immigration, when a Secretary of State (for multiculturalism) was appointed at a junior level, not represented in Cabinet. The Department
of Canadian Heritage, moreover, was given responsibility, not simply for multiculturalism, but for an array of other areas including fitness and amateur sports, the parks
component of Environment Canada, and cultural broadcasting. In 1997–98, in
response to criticisms by the new right-wing Reform Party, the Liberal government

eliminated funding for "ethnocultural" groups on the grounds that multicultural funding, which in any case had been steadily shrinking, should be available to all, not just "ethnic," Canadians. One consequence of this, as Paolo Prosperi notes, was that "for ethnocultural organizations who were in the past the beneficiaries of core funding, those wanting to secure funding from [that] point forward [had] to do so on a project-by-project basis" (qtd. in Abu-Laban and Gabriel 114–15).

The binary system of providing arts funding to individuals and companies from the dominant cultures while funding "ethnic" groups through multicultural grants had nevertheless been broken, and artists from various cultural backgrounds, including First Nations, began to gain (limited) access to arts funding.[9] The shift improved the optics, but did not mark a substantive change. Canadian Heritage has continued to provide direct funding to projects from "othered" cultures, often privileging them in their folkloric guise and managing cultural and artistic expression directly. But the pot was diminished, with funding also made available to dominant-culture "heritage" projects. Funding from the arts councils, meanwhile, has perpetuated the inequity that the realignment seemed designed to mend, because along with the restructuring came not only the discontinuation of core funding for "ethnocultural" groups but also a virtual freeze on ongoing operating funding. Because of budget cuts and increased demand, operating funding, in effect if not explicit policy, was only available to already established companies. In Toronto this means that a handful of companies, most of whom have secure production venues, and all of whom are "white,"[10] remain on operating funding and control the theatre seasons and performance spaces on which "other" companies rely for co-productions or rental space. The "other" companies, meanwhile, must apply for one-off project grants from funding agencies that can and do claim to privilege "multicultural" ventures. The "multicultural" companies are thereby placed in dependency relationships to the "charter" anglo companies, which are *de facto* given the power to police what productions from the "ethnic" communities are staged, and which tend to favor work that is non-threatening to their largely middle-class anglo audiences. Meanwhile, "ethnic" companies are forced to compete with one another for small pools of one-time funding, threatening to fracture potential solidarities among them.

Finally, the federal government's performance of the multicultural script in the past decade has invoked an increasingly corporate version of the utopian vision, as politicians and bankers, using the slogan "multiculturalism means business," have argued for the "competitive advantage" of "internal globalization" in the new world economy.[11] The concerns this raises for those interested in the social-justice potential of multiculturalism have to do with how an economic emphasis on "productive diversity" turns attention away from anti-racism, how it impacts on minoritized groups whose home countries do not offer opportunities for trade, how it impacts on Aboriginal groups, and how it inflects issues of class and gender (Abu-Laban and Gabriel 117). In the delicate performance ecology of Toronto, meanwhile, the recent loss to developers of crucial venues for the city's intercultural companies has increased those companies' dependency on established theatres for inclusion.

Intercultural Practice

Intercultural practitioners in Toronto are forced to work with the official multicultural script because it directly shapes their material realities. Fortunately, however, that script is not monolithically prescriptive: the constitutive relationship between policy and practice, text and performance, is not unidirectional, and performance has its own independently generative regimes and practices. Within Toronto's performance ecology, interculturalism works dialogically to reconstitute the official script's social effects. As Toronto cultural critic Marlene NourbeSe Philip argues:

> Multiculturalism may have been a cynical ploy by Liberal politicians to address the balance of power in Canada, but the creativity and inventiveness of the people in being able to turn to their own advantage policies that may not have their interests at heart can never be underestimated. (38)

Some of these people are theatre workers who perform the official script in ways that ignore the folkloric enclaves into which they have been slotted, performing into being new diasporic subjectivities and establishing solidarities across acknowledged difference. Coalitions are being constructed around what Ella Shohat and Robert Stam call *"mutual and reciprocal relativization"* (359, emphasis in original), in order to counter both exclusionary practices from the outside and compensatory nostalgias from within specific communities. These coalitions are also reinserting Aboriginal peoples as central to Canadian multiculturalism in performance, without surrendering their Nations' status as "First." Finally, these companies, individually and collectively, have evinced a continuing capacity to get their work onto the city's stages by co-producing with one another and by inventive fundraising, allowing them to remain at once professional arts *and* "multicultural" organizations, speaking *as* artists out of specific cultural positions, in defiance of the exclusionary binaries of the official script. While alliances among these companies are proceeding *intra*nationally, meanwhile, theatre workers from various communities are attempting to establish broadly diasporic networks beyond the nation-state. There are three overlapping practices undertaken within and across Toronto's multicultural theatre companies as performative rewritings of the multicultural script: strategic reappropriation, diasporic transnationalism, and urban intraculturalism.

Strategic reappropriation

The most familiar of these strategies involves reappropriation by the colonized of the symbolic capital of the dominant culture, as canonical texts and forms are rewritten and reconfigured through difference. Thus a play such as Djanet Sears's *Harlem Duet*, a "prequel" to Shakespeare's *Othello* featuring Othello's first, Black wife, Billie, first produced in 1997 by Nightwood Theatre, not only engages in postcolonial "talking back" to empire, but also reverses Shakespeare's representation of Othello as an isolated character in an overwhelmingly white world (and naturalized European culture). Sears relocates the action to Harlem, center of African North American diasporic culture, where it is Shakespeare who is isolated and decentred, surrounded on the bookshelves by *African Mythology* and *Black Psychology,* and in the play by central moments from Black history.

Native Earth Performing Arts has also reappropriated Shakespeare, in *Death of a Chief,* their adaptation of *Julius Caesar,* which received three public workshops in 2005–06 and full productions at Buddies in Bad Times in Toronto and at the National Arts Centre in Ottawa in 2008. In *Harlem Duet* Sears had both claimed and rejected Shakespeare—"the Shakespeare's mine, but you can have it," says Billie, dividing the bookshelves at the dissolution of her marriage (52). The anticipated postcolonial critique in *Death of a Chief,* however, is replaced by an acceptance of the cultural authority and "universality" of Shakespeare, but one that simultaneously *lays claim* to that authority, and with it the right, in the words of artistic director Yvette Nolan, "*to say those words if they feel like it,*" in full consciousness that "language is power" (Nolan, "Death" 2, emphasis added). *Death of a Chief* uses Shakespeare for its own ends, analyzing through Shakespeare the post-contact poison that has infected Native communities since the beginnings of the colonial project. One of the goals of the workshops was to provide training often denied to Aboriginal actors; another was to deflect the pain of internal betrayals within the community, and of the public expos- ing of those betrayals, onto Shakespeare's exposition of the dysfunctions at the root of European history. But chief among the goals of *Death of a Chief* was to negotiate and perform into existence a Native community in Toronto, out of the many displaced nations that find themselves there. Each workshop began with a negotiation within the company about the ceremonial elements of ritual performance in their various cultural traditions. As Nolan says:

> when you put people in a room together, you end up with a discussion of what those traditions are, and who they've learned them from [...]. [W]hen we work on a project like *The Death of a Chief,* which has, at any given time, between eight and fifteen Aboriginal artists in the room. [...a]ll of those people bring their traditions to the room [...] and it works just like it says in the stories that it works, in that we sit and dis- cuss it until we figure out what everyone can live with. (Personal Interview)

Ultimately, "we created our own ritual," Nolan says (Personal Interview). It is impor- tant to notice here the ways in which Native Earth draws upon and respects traditional performance forms without engaging in the preservationist rhetoric of the multicul- tural script. These are respectful, but created and negotiated rituals, used to forge dias- poric urban identities across First Nations. The *Death of a Chief* workshops, then, have been processual—heterotopic—in intent. The hope is, according to Nolan, that "*if we can work it out in this play then maybe we can work it out in our lives too*" ("Death" 4, emphasis added).

A third mode of intercultural reappropriation is represented by the work of Modern Times Stage Company, which has also presented Shakespeare *(Hamlet,* 1999; *Macbeth,* 2005), along with classics from Persian culture but whose mandate under

Persian/Iranian Canadian artistic director Soheil Parsa is the blending of Eastern with Western forms and "the creation of culturally inclusive alternative theatre experiences" (Modern Times, "Company" 6). This blending results in productions that are determinedly modernist, but with a reappropriative twist. Their 2006 production of *bloom*, directed by Parsa, written by Argentinean Canadian Guillermo Verdecchia, and featuring a multicultural cast, began as an adaptation of T.S. Eliot's *The Wasteland*. Because of permission problems with the Eliot estate, the show was finally presented as having been "inspired by" Eliot's modernist epic. Like most Modern Times productions, *bloom* is most interesting for its intercultural appropriations of modernism itself, its skirting of the modernist-capitalist alignment over ownership, and its representing-with-a difference the high modernist appetite for the consumption of "other" cultures. Ultimately, the play productively misrepresents Eliot's own work as just one among the fragments that a significantly unsettled "we" "have shored against [our] ruins" in the savage, post-apocalyptic world in which the play is set (Eliot 50).

Diasporic transnationalism

In recent years, as Abu-Laban and Gabriel have argued, the multicultural script has moved increasingly towards "selling diversity," appropriating multiculturalism in the service of globalization. But they have also noted the capacity for strategic transnationalisms to perform globalization differently, rehearsing heterotopic modes of alternate ordering, pointing to "groups and individuals who contest policy changes and new directions," "actors" who "may themselves be part of new transnational networks and organizations that supercede national boundaries" (22).

The simplest theatrical expressions of this type of transnationalism have to do with maintaining connections with cultural "homelands." Companies such as the AfriCan Theatre Ensemble, Theatre Archipelago, and Rasik Arts have been dedicated to producing plays from their respective homelands and, in spite of some residual tendency to promote compensatory nostalgias, these companies have nevertheless introduced to Toronto major works from the international repertoire, contributing to the productive internationalization of Canadian multiculturalism, and introducing new performance forms to the city. They have also excited new diasporic awarenesses, in that the communities they performatively constitute cut across the boundaries of nation-states within their respective homelands. As Theatre Archipelago's artistic director Rhoma Spencer has said of her complex setting of the Jamaican play, *Fallen Angel and the Devil Concubine* in Toronto's mixed Parkdale district, "'the Caribbean' only *exists* in the diaspora," and can only be addressed there (Spencer, emphasis in original).

First Nations companies in Toronto such as Red Sky Performance, Native Earth, and Turtle Gals Performance Ensemble, in spite of Aboriginal peoples having been excluded by official multiculturalism, in spite of their having little purchase in the realm of global capital, and in spite of working within very different diasporic contexts, [12] have proven themselves to be expert at forging transnational connections with other Indigenous peoples. Since its founding in 2000 by Anishnaabe Artistic Director Sandra Laronde, Red Sky has worked out of Toronto with Indigenous artists from Canada, the United States, Mexico, Australia, and Mongolia to bring the traditional performance forms of a worldwide Aboriginal community into the realm of the modernist avant-garde. Red Sky is producing neither "issue plays," "authentic" Aboriginal performance (with all the colonialist pre-occupations with purity that implies), nor tourist shows, but contemporary dance/theatre productions that draw upon, develop, and juxtapose traditional Aboriginal performance forms from various Indigenous cultures. Their productions remain in repertory and tour Canada and internationally, creating work for Aboriginal performers, replacing racist stereotypes with representations of astonishing beauty and skill, and exploiting tactically (Certeau xix–xx, 34–39) the pieties of Canada's official multiculturalism in order to advance globally the cause of Aboriginal people in the arts.

Native Earth has also recently negotiated the discourses of globalization through collaborations with Indigenous peoples rather than national governments, but theirs is a transnationalism that circumvents the industrial model of production and diplomatic exchange through touring as "foreign relations," or free trade in commodified cultures. Rather than collaborations within a single production, Native Earth's "Honouring Theatre" project involved a repertory system of mounting and touring productions by Aboriginal companies from Canada, Australia, and New Zealand to all three countries over three years (2006–08). It involved forging strategic alliances, "establishing," as the tour's program puts it, "indigenous trade routes through the arts" that echo pre-contact trade routes among Indigenous nations (Native Earth, *Honouring*). This ambitious project staged Nolan's own play, *Annie Mae's Movement*, Injibarndi/Palku playwright David Milroy's memory play, *Windmill Baby*, and Samoan playwright Makerita Urale's text and movement piece, *Frangipani Perfume*. The companies included actors and directors from a wide range of Indigenous Nations from North America and the South Pacific.

Like Red Sky and Native Earth, Turtle Gals Performance Ensemble, founded in Toronto in 2000 by Jani Lauzon, Monique Mojica, and Michelle St. John, is concerned with exploring "a continuum of past, present, and future" and developing "non-linear multi-disciplinary theatre forms" out of Indigenous performance traditions (Turtle Gals, "Information"). And like Red Sky and Native Earth, their interest exceeds and explodes national boundaries to take in, in their case, the Indigenous peoples of the Americas. The form of Turtle Gals' work is hybrid, growing out of the performers' own mixed race, which also serves as the hemispheric and autobiographical content of their work. This, however, is autobiography in the broadest sense of the term: autobiography that includes the performers' blood memories of their hemispheric ancestors, disregarding the later-day borders of nation-states.

All of this—the autobiographical, the hybrid, the hemispheric, the traditional, and the contemporary, together with a deeply rooted sense of First Nations cultural memory—plays itself out in Turtle Gals' complex interdisciplinary productions. *The Scrubbing Project* is the company's signature piece and its most directly autobiographical show, dealing with the writer/performers' own hybridized identities, their internalized racism, and their experiences "living with genocide," as the play's darkly comic "support group" is called. But it also deals, as Anishnaabe scholar Jill Carter points out, with "recovery, remembrance, revitalization and reintegration of *all* Aboriginal peoples," regardless of their current national location (14, emphasis in original).

Urban intraculturalism

If Red Sky, Native Earth, and Turtle Gals have used strategic transnationalisms to complicate the dominance of globalization from First Nations perspectives, theatre companies across Toronto have developed a kind of co-operative intraculturalism-from-below in order to perform differently the corporate drive within the multicultural script towards what Royal Bank president John Cleghorn in 1995 called "internal globalization" (qtd. in Abu-Labal and Gabriel 105)—multiculturalism deployed as market advantage for Canada within the "home" nations of immigrant communities. By constructing a heterotopian space within the city, these companies might be thought of as adapting Rustom Bharucha's call for a grassroots theatrical *intra*culturalism in the face of prevailing utopian discourses of theatrical intercultur-alism that leave power within the hands of charismatic and well-funded Westerners such as Peter Brook, Ariane Mnouchkine, and Eugenio Barba. I am here following Mayte Gómez in applying Bharucha's concept of intraculturalism to Canada, and specifically to Toronto, as a "second world" settler/invader society (Slemon), thinking through interculturalism "from below," practiced "tactically" in relation to the mono-logical "strategies" of the dominant (de Certeau xix–xx, 34–39; see also McClintock, Mufti, and Shohat; Moss).

Toronto's intercultural performance ecology features a complex web of intercon-nections among individuals and companies working in solidarity across their acknowledged differences. Yvette Nolan, Artistic Director of Native Earth, calls this network "the brown caucus,"[13] and gives a sense of how it functions:

> The Native Earth office [in 2006] consists of two Aboriginal women, one Black woman, and one Asian woman, and we bring all our communities to the work. We always choose *other* in the work. When we choose direc-tors, designers, dramaturges, we always choose *other*. Even though Weesagechak [Begins to Dance] is an Aboriginal festival developing work by Aboriginal writers, we first choose *other* dramaturges, dra-maturges who are Aboriginal or Asian or queer. *Other* as in not white, not from the dominant culture, those who have a sense of self outside of the dominant culture. (Personal Interview, emphasis in original)

The geography of contemporary downtown Toronto facilitates working across difference. As urban planners Mohammed Qadeer and Sandeep Kumar found in 2006, the city's downtown is free of what they call "ethnic enclaves." Downtown neigh-borhoods are mixed. They flow into one another, allowing for the performance of

intercultural exchange and intercultural identities not pre-scripted by official multiculturalism. The offices of Toronto's intercultural theatre companies coexist and share
resources in locations like the Distillery District and 400 Richmond Street West (both
former industrial complexes now devoted to galleries and arts offices), and similar
buildings in the former garment district on Spadina Avenue. These companies also
share workshop and performance spaces at such places as the Great Hall, Factory
Theatre, and Theatre Passe Muraille, all on or near Queen Street West and close to the
office buildings of Spadina and Richmond Streets. When Nina Lee Aquino, artistic
director of fu-GEN Asian Canadian Theatre Company, was approached in late 2006
about taking up residency at the Richmond Hill Centre for the Performing Arts in the
largely Asian Canadian north Toronto suburb of Richmond Hill, she turned down the
otherwise attractive offer in fear of ghettoization: she was aware that the company's
real constituency was located within the performance ecology of the city's downtown
(Aquino). Similarly, South Asian Canadian writer-performer Anita Majumdar's popular one-person show, *Fish Eyes*, grounded in various forms of Indian classical dance,
was designed for the downtown core. Majumdar believes, moreover, that it reached its
diasporic South Asian Canadian community in part because it did not play the ghet-
toized suburban community centers of official multiculturalism (Majumdar). It has
reached its South Asian Canadian audience precisely because she resisted folkloric
imagery, and targeted established professional theatres. *Fish Eyes* proved itself downtown, where its success validated the show within its home community and where it
began to play its role in reconstituting that community as South Asian Canadian.

Native Earth's offices are in the Distillery District, next to the offices of
Nightwood, directly beneath those of Modern Times, and not far from the downtown
offices of fu-GEN and Obsidian Theatres. One of Native Earth's office staff until the
summer of 2006, Aquino is also Artistic Director of fu-GEN, playwright in residence
at Cahoots, director of Carlos Bulosan's 2007–08 production, and Artistic Producer of
CrossCurrents, the intercultural play development festival at Factory Theatre where
she is also Apprentice Artistic Director. And she is not unique. Second-generation
Chinese Canadian actor and playwright Keira Loughren is Artistic Producer, with
African Canadian Kimahli Powell, of SummerWorks, the city's vibrant and diverse
new-play festival. Powell is also the producer of b-current's rock.paper.sistahs festival
and a co-producer of Buddies in Bad Times's "art sexy" program. Djanet Sears, the
artistic director of the AfriCanadian Playwrights Festival, dramaturged Kuna-
Rappahannock playwright Monique Mojica's *Princess Pocahontas and the Blue Spots*.
Argentinean Canadian Guillermo Verdecchia has been artistic director of Cahoots,
has directed Filipino, Latino, First Nations, South Asian, and Korean Canadian plays,
and has collaborated as a writer with Egyptian Canadian Marcus Youssef and Iranian
Canadian Camyar Chai. In attendance at the 2006 fu-GEN fundraiser were the
artistic directors of Native Earth, Obsidian, Rasik Arts, Carlos Bulosan, Cahoots, and
b-current. And the list goes on. These theatre workers are cumulatively answering
Bannerji's call for the creation of solidarities, for opening up, in the face of racism,
Eurocentrism, ethnocentrism, and official multiculturalism, "a space for a broader
community among us" (158). They are creating a heterotopic space for alternate

ordering that is neither static, folkloric, nor merely symbolic, in which new social identities and social formations are performatively forged out of the crucible of traditional performance forms, the technologies of contemporary theatrical practice, and the daily work of negotiating across real and acknowledged social and cultural difference.

Conclusion

I have been able here to cite only a few examples of the ways in which the official multicultural script is being performed in contemporary Toronto, and how those performances change the nature of the city's complex intercultural performance ecology. What is key is that the companies I have been discussing, and others, do not set out merely to realize that script as prescriptive, as governmental bodies and "mainstream" theatre companies have done, nor do they simply resist its prescriptions and thereby reify its dominant position in a counterproductive binary logic. Rather, they work to reconstitute that script and its social effects by performing it strategically through the technologies of the traditional and contemporary performance practices to which they have access. Through strategic solidarities across acknowledged difference and a kind of intercultural performative excess, they continually rewrite, reconfigure, and restage multiculturalism in ways that are cumulatively heterotopic, moving "the world's most multicultural city" from below towards an ever-evolving mode of alternate ordering.

(2009)

Notes

¹ Research for this essay was funded by a grant from the Social Sciences and Humanities Research Council of Canada.

² By "the multicultural script" I mean the composite discourse of documents that have emerged since the 1971 White Paper instituted multiculturalism as a policy, including the 1988 Act, the 1996 review, and the annual reports that have accumulated over the last two decades.

³ I am indebted to Joanne Tompkins for drawing my attention to Hetherington.

⁴ Information about the history of multiculturalism here is derived primarily from Esses and Gardner and from Abu-Laban and Gabriel (105–28), but see also Berdichewsky, Bibby, Breton, Gwyn, and Reitz and Breton. Bannerji convincingly disputes the dominant view that the 1971 policy came about in response to "demand from below," arguing that it was in fact "an ideological elaboration from

above [...] which rearranged questions of social justice, of unemployment and racism, into issues of cultural diversity and focused on symbols of religion, on so-called tradition. Thus immigrants were ethnicized, culturalized and mapped into traditional/ethnic communities" (44–45).

5   See Bannerji (30). The editors of *Our Diverse Cities* provide statistics on immigration—almost half a million immigrants in the past quarter-century, 43 percent to Toronto, where almost 50 percent of the population is foreign born. They also indicate a significant increase in immigrants from Asia, Latin America, and Africa (Carter, Vachon et al. 1).

6   I am quoting clauses 3(1)a and 3(1)j of the Act from Multiculturalism and Citizenship Canada's *The Canadian Multiculturalism Act: A Guide for Canadians,* which functions as a kind of annotated "critical edition."

7   See also Bannerji, especially 151–74.

8   Gunew discusses "the somatic technology constituted by the learning of [standard] English" (63) as "a kind of virus inhabiting the body" (61).

9   In Toronto this came primarily from the Canada Council, the Ontario Art Council, and the Toronto Arts Council.

10   I use "white" here not as a category of race, but as indicating normalized access to power, privilege, and funding.

11   These phrases have recurred in political speeches since the 1990s. They are quoted here from a 1994 speech by Sheila Finestone in which they appear in rapid succession (qtd. in Abu-Laban and Gabriel 116).

12   Yvette Nolan has pointed out the ways in which Toronto's "Indian diaspora" represents a closing in rather than a dispersion, as Native peoples covering wide swaths of land were forced into unnaturally choked off and lifeless urban locations—like Toronto (Personal Interview).

13   Nolan is clear that she is not essentializing race. She includes among the "brown caucus" companies such as Mammalian Diving Reflex that are somatically "white," but determinedly "other."

Works Cited

Abu-Laban, Yasmeen and Christina Gabriel. *Selling Diversity: Immigration, Multiculturalism, Employment Equity, and Globalization.* Peterborough, ON: Broadview, 2002.

Aquino, Nina Lee. Personal Interview. Distillery District, Toronto. 22 October 2006.

Bannerji, Himani. *The Dark Side of the Nation: Essays on Multiculturalism, Nationalism, and Gender.* Toronto: Canadian Scholars, 2000.

Berdichewsky, Bernardo. *Racism, Ethnicity and Multiculturalism.* Vancouver: Future, 1994.

Bharucha, Rustom. *The Politics of Cultural Practice: Thinking Through Theatre in an Age of Globalization.* Hanover, NH: UP of New England, 2000.

———. *Theatre and the World: Performance and the Politics of Culture.* London: Routledge, 1993.

Bibby, Reginald W. *Mosaic Madness: The Poverty and Potential Life in Canada.* Toronto: Stoddart, 1990.

Bissoondath, Neil. *Selling Illusions: The Cult of Multiculturalism in Canada.* Toronto: Penguin, 1994.

Breton, Raymond. "Multiculturalism and Canadian Nation Building." *The Politics of Gender, Ethnicity and Language in Canada.* Ed. Alan Cairns and Cynthia Williams. Toronto: U of Toronto P, 1986. 27–66.

Carter, Jill. "Writing, Righting, 'Riting'— *The Scrubbing Project:* Re-Members a New 'Nation' and Reconfigures Ancient Ties." *alt.theatre: cultural diversity and the stage* 4.4 (2006): 13–17.

Carter, Tom, Marc Vachon, John Biles, Erin Tolley, and Jim Zamprelli. Introduction. *Our Diverse Cities: Challenges and Opportunities.* Special issue, *Canadian Journal of Urban Research* 15.2 Supplement (2006): i–viii.

Certeau, Michel de. *The Practice of Everyday Life.* Trans. Stephen Randall. Berkeley: U of California P, 1988.

Eliot, T. S. "The Wasteland." *The Complete Plays and Poems 1909–1950.* New York: Harcourt, Brace & World, 1971. 37–55.

Esses, Victoria M. and R.C. Gardner. "Multiculturalism in Canada: Context and Current Status." *Canadian Journal of Behavioural Science* 28.3 (1996): 145–60.

Foster, Cecil. *Where Race Does Not Matter.* Toronto: Penguin, 2005.

Foucault, Michel. "Of Other Spaces." *Diacritics* 16.1 (1986): 22–27.

Gómez, Mayte. "'Coming Together' in Lift Off! '93: Intercultural Theatre in Toronto and Canadian Multiculturalism." *Essays in Theatre/Études théâtrales* 13.1 (1991): 45–60.

Gwyn, Richard. *Nationalism Without Walls: The Unbearable Lightness of Being Canadian.* Toronto: McClelland & Stewart, 1995.

Gunew, Sneja. *Haunted Nations: The Colonial Dimensions of Multiculturalisms.* London: Routledge, 2004.

Hetherington, Kevin. *The Badlands of Modernity: Heterotopia and Social Ordering.* London: Routledge, 1997.

Kamboureli, Smaro. Introduction. *Making a Difference: Canadian Multicultural Literature.* Ed. Smaro Kamboureli. Toronto: Oxford UP, 1996. 1–16.

———. *Scandalous Bodies: Diasporic Literature in English Canada.* Toronto: Oxford UP, 2000.

Kershaw, Baz. "Oh for Unruly Audiences! Or, Patterns of Participation in Twentieth-Century Theatre." *Modern Drama* 42.2 (1998): 133–54.

———. "The Theatrical Biosphere and Ecologies of Performance." *New Theatre Quarterly* 16.2 (2000): 122–30.

Li, Peter. "A World Apart: The Multicultural World of Visible Minorities and the Art World of Canada." *Canadian Review of Sociology and Anthropology* 31.4 (1994): 365–91.

Majumdar, Anita. Personal Interview. Epicure Cafe, Toronto. 7 March 2007.

McClintock, Anne, Aamir Mufti, and Ella Shohat, eds. *Dangerous Liaisons: Gender, Nation, and Postcolonial Perspectives.* Minneapolis: U of Minnesota Press, 1997.

Modern Times Stage Company. *bloom.* By Guillermo Verdecchia, directed by Soheil Parsa. Program. 24 February–19 March 2006.

———. "Company Mandate." 13 November 2010. http://www.moderntimes stage.com/mandate.html.

Moss, Laura. *Is Canada Postcolonial: Unsettling Canadian Literature.* Waterloo: Wilfrid Laurier UP, 2003.

Multiculturalism and Citizenship Canada. *The Canadian Multiculturalism Act: A Guide for Canadians.* Ottawa: Minister of Supply and Services Canada, 1991.

Native Earth Performing Arts. *Honouring Theatre.* Program. Fall 2006.

Nolan, Yvette. "*The Death of a Chief:* An Interview with Yvette Nolan." Interview with Sorouja Moll. Native Earth Performing Arts Office, Distillery District, Toronto. 12 March 2006. *Canadian Adaptations of Shakespeare Project.* 7 July 2006. http://www.canadianshakespeares.ca/i_ynolan2.cfm.

———. Personal Interview. Native Earth Performing Arts Office, Distillery District, Toronto. 29 June 2006.

Philip, Marlene NourbeSe. "Signifying: Why the Media Have Fawned Over Bissoondath's Selling Illusions." *Border/Lines* 36 (1995): 4–11.

Qadeer, Mohammed and Sandeep Kumar. "Ethnic Enclaves and Social Cohesion." *Our Diverse Cities: Challenges and Opportunities.* Special issue, *Canadian Journal of Urban Research.* 15.2 Supplement (2006): 1–17.

Reitz, J.G. and Raymond Breton. *The Illusion of Difference: Realities of Ethnicity in Canada and the United States.* Toronto: C.D. Howe Institute, 1994.

Sears, Djanet. *Harlem Duet.* Winnipeg: Scirocco, 1997.

Shohat, Ella and Robert Starn. *Unthinking Eurocentrism: Multiculturalism and the Media.* London: Routledge, 1994.

Slemon, Stephen. "Resistance Theory for the Second World." *Postcolonial Studies Reader.* Ed. Bill Ashcroft, Gareth Griffiths, and Helen Tiffin. London: Routledge, 1995. 104–10.

Spencer, Rhoma. Interview with Andy Barry. "Metro Morning." CBC Radio, Toronto. 23 May 2006.

Turtle Gals Performance Ensemble. Information Sheet. Turtle Gals Performance Ensemble office files.

———. *The Scrubbing Project.* Unpublished playscript, 2005.

Weimann, Robert. *Author's Pen and Actor's Voice: Playing and Writing in Shakespeare's Theatre.* Ed. Helen Higbee and William West. Cambridge: Cambridge UP, 2000.

Worthen, W. B. *Shakespeare and the Force of Modern Performance.* Cambridge: Cambridge UP, 2003.

Evicted in—and from—Toronto:
Walker's *Beautiful City* at Factory Theatre

by J. Chris Westgate

Defined as a "pivotal year" in the career of George F. Walker, 1982 marks a noteworthy shift in Walker's dramaturgy. [1] During the 1970s, Walker's plays occurred in two phases: the early, absurdist-inspired works (*The Prince of Naples* and *Ambush at Tether's End*), followed by the later works that borrowed from and interrogated popular culture (*Sacktown Rag, Bagdad Saloon,* and *Beyond Mozambique*). [2] The plays of both phases were marked by existential and ontological questioning, and were seemingly intended to sow confusion and anxiety in audiences. In 1982, though, Walker workshopped at Cornell University an early version of *Better Living*, a play that would become the first of *The East End Plays* and inaugurate Walker's next phase. Ultimately six plays, including the major successes *Criminals in Love* (1984) and *Love and Anger* (1989), this collection marks a shift in subject and style in his dramaturgy. As Chris Johnson notes, "[i]n these plays, Walker turns for material to the working-class Toronto East End of his boyhood and adolescence, material which he had previously explored only in *Sacktown Rag*, and there only somewhat tentatively" (35). Walker characterizes his plays from this phase, when he was writing directly about Toronto during the 1980s, as becoming increasingly "generous," a term that suggests the growing accessibility of *The East End Plays*, all of which approach realism, if somewhat uncomfortably. Likewise, the generosity of his plays suggests something about a vision of the future. As Johnson argues, these plays do something rather un-Walker-like: they introduce not hope, "but what he has called 'possibility'" (82).

Importantly, this shift toward the last phase corresponds with an implicit reassessment of responsibility within Walker's dramaturgy. Before *The East End Plays*, his plays were mostly polemical: that is, they shook the foundations of beliefs, values, and assumptions in order to highlight the anxiety that Walker believed was everywhere in Canadian society. Probably the defining concern for Walker regardless of phase, anxiety—which is at once psychological, cultural, and existential—comes from "the question posed again and again by Walker's plays," as Johnson maintains: "Who controls the future?" (61). During the early phases, Walker's dramaturgy sought to induce this anxiety in audiences without advocating any means of confronting or overcoming it: the result was pure polemicism. Because of this, no doubt, Johnson concludes that "it's impossible to contain Walker's political views neatly within any political doctrine" (66). Johnson is certainly correct insofar as Walker cannot be pigeonholed through the traditional "isms" used to designate political drama—liberalism and conservatism, Marxism and feminism. Nevertheless, *The East End Plays* demonstrate an increasing awareness of the limits of polemicism: of the agitation that serves no end beyond itself and, paradoxically, may reinforce the status quo by fore-closing the possibility of praxis. More notably, these plays advocate a particular future, though, again, not in ways that would define them under any specific ideology. In other words, *The East End Plays* denote a shift in Walker's dramaturgy from the polemical to the political: by this, I mean that they advocate a future "beyond" anxi-ety, even though they remain skeptical of how easily that future can be realized. While this shift typifies many of the six plays that comprise *The East End Plays*, my argument addresses *Beautiful City*, the third of the plays to be produced, for two reasons. First, it best demonstrates how Walker's political concerns were distinctly spatialized at the time; second, the spatialized concerns evident in *Beautiful City* suggest the exigency of the shift from polemicism to politics: Toronto during the 1980s.

Interviewed in 1987, the year that *Beautiful City* debuted, Walker defines the nature of this anxious future in relation to the loss of his Toronto home: "It was like being evicted—from the city. Our house, the house my family and I were renting, was sold" (Conlogue, "Places"). Kept from buying the house because of rising property values, Walker relocated his family to New Brunswick, feeling that Toronto's "soul" had been given over, Faust-like, to developers for "glamor and glory" (Conlogue, "Places"). Walker's family was, of course, just one family to be victimized by the gen-trification of Toronto underway during this decade. Thanks to a city hall's mandate of urban growth, residential neighbourhoods across Toronto, but particularly those in or close to downtown, were rezoned and redeveloped.[3] Neighbourhoods of older—but not necessarily rundown—homes were razed and replaced with apartment complex-es, shopping plazas, and most unbecoming of all (for those anxious about this transformation of the built environment), condominiums that loomed above neigh-bourhoods as aesthetic blight and economic menace. Not entirely new to the 1980s, this growth mandate nevertheless had become increasingly powerful as a narrative of Toronto's future and was displacing working-class residents and, not incidentally, his-toric theaters. Becoming unmistakable—to Walker and others—was the correlation between Toronto's transformed built environment and the lifestyles endorsed therein. In fact, Jon Caulfield's *City Form and Everyday Life: Toronto's Gentrification and Critical Social Practice* documents attitudes of those living in Toronto during the time Walker's family was being evicted. Of particular importance to respondents in Caulfield's study was anxiety about the "disappearance of local communities" that was commensurate with, if not directly a consequence of, this growth mandate (Caulfield 203). Watching the gentrification of the city in the 1980s, Walker perhaps saw an extension of the displacement beleaguering working-class families like that of his own childhood as well as his wife and children: families evicted in—and from—Toronto.[4]

Certainly *Beautiful City*, written during the relocation to New Brunswick, derives from Walker's frustration about the abolition of a way of life in Toronto. But *Beautiful City* is about the future of Toronto, both in the play—which is peopled with develop-ers, architects, and social workers—and for Toronto audiences living through this crisis. Instead of attempting to induce anxiety, which was already evident to many liv-ing in Toronto, *Beautiful City* makes a distinctly political argument about the nature of this anxiety and how it relates to the future in and of the city. This argument begins from explicit recognition of the indelible link between urban forms and urban life, which is notable unto itself because it confronts the illusion of spatial neutrality that critical geography has fought to refute. Additionally, *Beautiful City* underscores how space or spatial forms are frequently contested epistemologically and ideologically. The built environment of Toronto becomes political because it is simultaneously the setting and stakes—to borrow the language of Henri Lefebvre—of the future of the city that Walker suggests was worth fighting for during the same 1987 interview. Walker makes an implicit argument about what kinds of urban forms and lifestyles should guide the future, while disclosing that these forms are always politicized. Specifically, there is value on community through place rather than place as commodity,[5] value evident in his remarks about how working-class residents reacted to Toronto's bullish property market in the 1980s: "I'm thinking of what my neighbors say when houses are flipped on their street. These are people who would no more flip a home than they would flip a child" (Conlogue, "Places"). His language here is telling: the buildings and neighbourhoods are more than property to those living in them; they are investments in the future. Walker's frustration is especially evident in his remark, "it's our generation that's doing it," that's responsible for the abolition of a way of life in the city (Conlogue, "Places").

If *Beautiful City* is about the future of Toronto, then it is a future contested through what I've defined elsewhere as sociospatial terms (Westgate 21–37). Beginning from the assumption that sociality and spatiality are thoroughly and often ideologically imbricated, sociospatial criticism considers the ways emplacement, geography, and urbanism influence the writing and reception of dramatic literature. While the term *sociospatial* derives from Ed Soja's *Thirdspace: Journeys to Los Angeles and Other Real-And-Imagined Places*, the methodology draws from numerous theorists on geography and urbanism, including Henri Lefebvre, Michel de Certeau, and, most significantly for Walker's play, David Harvey. In *Social Justice and the City*, Harvey defines a "geographical imagination" in distinctly political terms: "This imagination enables the individual to recognize the role of space and place in his own biography, to relate to the spaces he sees around him, and to recognize how transactions between individuals and between organizations are affected by the space that separates them" (24). To Harvey, self-definition and political agency are mediated by the spaces dividing and unifying individuals; and recognition of this geographical mediation is necessary for any sociopolitical change. Beginning from Harvey's theory, my argument considers how this geographical imagination informs the dramaturgy of *Beautiful City* and how it provides the scaffolding for the political ambitions of Walker's play.[6] Johnson provides intriguing information about the first point when he describes Walker's routine of going "for long walks in [his] home [city] ... watching, absorbing, thinking, then after a period of creative wandering, go[ing] home and writ[ing], quickly" (37). Walker's dramaturgy, in other words, emerges from observation and engagement with the city. Given the concerns evident in *Beautiful City*, it's likely that the play's argument about the future of Toronto emerged from this "creative wandering," which suggests recognition on Walker's part of how changes to the built environment resulted in corresponding changes to the lifestyles lived therein. Beyond reflecting the play's origins, this engagement with Toronto extends toward the play's advocacy of what might be defined as epistemological rediscovery of the city.

Like Michael McKinnie's recently published *City Stages*, then, this argument brings the "spatial turn" of drama criticism to Canadian studies in order to pursue insights into Walker's dramaturgy during this phase and *Beautiful City*'s 1987 production at the Factory Theatre. This production occurred at the Factory's new (and current) home at 125 Bathurst Street, a Victorian mansion converted into a theatre, after Factory was forced out of its original home in a former candle factory at 374 Dupont Street and experienced a decade-long itinerancy in Toronto. Prompting the eviction from 374 Dupont were a number of factors, including Factory's emphasis on developing new playwrights,[7] the administration of the theatre building, and changes to the infrastructure of Toronto during the mid-1970s—changes that foreshadowed what would happen during the 1980s. Importantly, *Beautiful City*, like most of *The East End Plays*, premiered at 125 Bathurst Street during the period when Factory Theatre was facing *another* crisis about economics and property values, a crisis that threatened the Factory—and other theatres in Toronto—with insolvency and foreclosure. Anxiety about the future of Toronto theatres was just as palpable as anxiety about the future of Toronto during the 1980s. In fact, Ken Gass, founder of Factory Theatre, was part of a "Committee of Concern" established in 1988 that became an insurgent voice against development in Toronto (McKinnie 112). In this time of uncertainty for Factory Theatre came Walker's *East End Plays*, including *Love and Anger*, which helped "rescue" the Factory with urgently needed box office revenues (Haff 78).[8] The word *rescue* has been frequently used in consideration of *The East End Plays*, but only in the literal, financial sense. Because of this, the term itself overlooks many of the key sociospatial elements of the production of these plays against the backdrop of economic and existential crisis, specifically, how *Beautiful City* conflated production and politics, theatre and community, real estate and cultural identity—all toward a renewed "geographical imagination" of Toronto.

I. Condominiums, Consumption, Community: The Future of the City

Never one for slow openings, Walker introduces the terms of *Beautiful City*'s argument from the first words. "This is the future," announces Tony Raft, gesturing toward a model of an apartment complex sitting on his desk and, implicitly, toward the glassy landscape of buildings and condominiums beyond the high-rise office (11). Three things emerge during this first scene that prove central to the play's sociospatial ambitions. The first is that, right now, the future of this city—not explicitly named Toronto, but most likely so—is in the hands of criminals like Raft, the nominal head of an American Mafia family right out of mob films. Drinking heavily and prone to bouts of melancholy and megalomania, Tony has been orchestrating the gentrification of the city for a decade. If this isn't enough to make audiences uncomfortable, then comes the second thing during Tony's conversation with Paul Gallagher, the lead architect working for the Raft family up until now. "Forget the Italian tiles in the bathrooms... Forget the Samurai kitchen, the generationally conceived bedrooms, the solarium, the atrium. Forget everything except the primary living space," says Tony in his staccato, mobster rhythms. "So ask yourself, are you going to be pleased... spending one and one half million dollars on what is essentially four bare eggshelled-surfaced goddamned walls?!" (12–13). What emerges here is how Tony conflates comfort, in this bricolage of styles, with consumption in ways that suggest much about the transformation of urban landscapes and the lifestyles circumscribed therein. In fact, Tony's development of apartment complexes has been driven by a distinctly *un*social premise about spatial organization: "Everything indoors. My motto is 'No more strangers in your life'" (16). The third thing? This is Walker's answer to this future of the city, which comes, in typical Walker fashion, through a joke. Immediately following Tony's opening announcement, Paul groans, "Shit" (11). Inspiring this response is the sudden pain in Paul's side, which could be appendicitis (except Paul remembers that he's already had his appendix removed), could be "just" anxiety (except Paul has to be hospitalized), and ultimately suggests the gist of Walker's opinion about the future of the city imagined by Tony. It is, simply put, shit.

Notably, this opening introduces anxiety in direct correlation to the future of this city. Described as *just* an anxiety attack by Tony, Paul's illness corresponds with Johnson's definition of anxiety (being psychological, cultural, and existential), though in distinctly spatialized terms: it is revulsion against the city imagined by Tony, even though Paul cannot make the connection consciously yet. But Tony can and has, as demonstrated by his remarks about the gentrification of the city: "When I first came to this city one of the first things I noticed was how much anxiety there was around me" (14), he says, implying that anxiety was not only the result of this gentrification but simultaneously the impetus for it. After glancing at Paul to see if he is still listening above his increasingly agonized groans, he adds, "The anxiety here is so deep and so widespread, it's like a natural resource. It can be used" (14). Not defined directly, the source of this anxiety can nevertheless be inferred through the new urban forms that Tony has wrought from this natural resource. The apartment complexes and condominiums already proliferated across the city endorse the middle class since they, most often, come at the expense of older, generally working-class neighborhoods. This reimagining of the built environment corresponds with an obfuscation of poverty and diversity, erased from downtown landscapes through gentrification. What is left is a city reconceived to endorse—at least what Tony believes to be—a middle-class "life-world," Caulfield's term describing the modes of encounters in and through space as part of a lifestyle (110). [9] This spatialized endorsement of a distinctly class-based sociality becomes even more evident with the waterfront mall that Tony intends as the next phase in the city's future. Influenced by Eaton Centre, no doubt, Tony's mall begins from the wonder that is doing "all your shopping indoors" and extends through having "dinner, or even a picnic or a roller coaster ride... and never get[ting] rained on" (*Beautiful City* 26). Implicit in this next phase are the defining assumptions of this middle-class lifeworld: enclosure of space and exclusion of those who may disrupt or disturb enjoyment of that space. But this mall is precursor to Tony's ultimate vision: "Tunnels. I'm going to connect all the major downtown living areas by tunnels," and he will give keys to those using the tunnels, so that it will be feasible to have no strangers in their lives (65).

However much seemingly framed by idiosyncrasy, Tony's future for this city reflected growing trends in North American urbanism during the 1980s. As Trevor Boddy concludes in "Underground and Overhead: Building the Analogous City," downtowns became increasingly threatened in this decade through the emergence of "raised pedestrian bridges" and "mazes of tunnels"—both putting pressure on concepts of public space—in cities as different as Montreal and Minneapolis, Dallas and Calgary (124). One good example is Calgary's Plus Fifteen system, "the world's largest off-the-ground pedestrian network," proposed originally in the 1960s (Boddy 141). Influenced by Le Corbusier's modernism, this structure funnels middle-class walkers through a network of enclosed, glassy corridors fifteen feet aboveground. Visually, this system confirms social stratification in the city, with the privileged walking through the corridors, plainly visible from below but avoiding streets and sidewalks—with their mixture of social classes and ethnic difference—altogether. More significant for *Beautiful City*, though, would be Montreal's tunnel system, which began with Place Ville Marie's underground shopping mall. Originally modest, this relocation of elements of the city underground became a platform of Mayor Jean Drapeau's renewal campaign, which intended to make PVM "the hub of downtown redevelopment, and helped negotiate tunnel connections to the Queen Elizabeth Hotel and to the major commuter train station" (Boddy 145). With shops connecting this underground route, it would become feasible to do one's shopping without ever confronting the harshness of Montreal weather or uncertainty of downtown streets. [10] This premise informed development of Toronto's PATH, which boasts some twenty-seven kilometers of shopping arcades underground, roughly the same amount of retail space as the West Edmonton Mall. [11] Watching the gentrification of Toronto, Walker perhaps saw in Montreal the next (il)logical stage in the transformation of the city. Most importantly, this transformation of cities across North America correlated with the shift from the democracy of downtowns to the quasi-feudalism of enclosed urbanism, precisely what Tony intends: "We have to keep this city under our control. This city has a radiant future. It needs people who believe in that future to be in charge" (47).

Already underway via turning residential neighborhoods into apartment complexes or condominiums, with the Raft family in charge for a decade, this transformation of urban forms produces two hazards to traditional lifestyles in *Beautiful City*. The first involves distortion of the family structure, in particular that of Michael Gallagher, Paul's brother. Another architect working for the Rafts, Michael comes to the forefront after Paul's illness leads to his vanishing from the middle-class world typified by Tony's high-rise office. During scene 6, with a model of the waterfront mall on the desk and the subject of conversation, Michael explains the pressures his family puts on him: "Do you know how many cars there are in my family. Five. Five cars. And they all have to be replaced every two years. The wife, the kids, they've come to expect it" (39). Implicit here is the play's attentiveness to the interplay of urban form and urban lifestyle: Michael's family demands more and more commodities precisely during the time that the built environment of the city is changing from supporting families to producing merchandise, convenience, and class consciousness. Michael's confession, "I'm terrified of my wife and kids. They're monsters of consumption," plainly suggests the link between the nature of his menacing family and Tony's shopping mall, which is sitting on the desk as a model (39). As David Harvey theorizes in *Spaces of Hope*, the shopping mall transforms not just the built environment but additionally the way that we define ourselves through that environment, in particular by confirming the value of "commodity culture, and endless capital accumulation" (168). More explicitly during this scene, Walker redefines the traditional family through contrast with the Mafia family of the Rafts, first through Tony's response to Michael's anxiety—"The thing is, never be worth more to them dead than alive. If you're going broke, first thing to do is cancel all your policies" (39)—and second when Tony, at his mother's behest, conscripts Michael into the Raft organization, which conflates criminal enterprise and urban development. In effect, Walker's play redefines the family in this "beautiful city" through crime and consumption, something underscored by Mary Raft: "Welcome to the family business" (43).

This redefinition represents a threat to the play's other family, that of Gina Mae Sabatini. A mother of five daughters, Gina Mae lives in an old house, presumably in an older residential neighborhood, and works at Bargain Harold's, a discount store giving the poor some "taste" of the good life (28). Not incidentally, she is also a practicing witch—one of the wonky [12] bits that typify Walker's plays—although her interactions in *Beautiful City* tend to be more sociological than mystical. Her eccentricity notwithstanding, Gina Mae represents a way of defining family and community through the way of inhabiting spaces, something that becomes clear when her home is blown up near the play's conclusion. Although he helped Tony and Stevie plant the bomb beneath her house, Michael runs in at the last minute with a warning. As everyone runs out, Gina Mae announces, "I was born here. This was my mother's house. My grandmother's house," before the stage goes black with the explosion (59). The destruction of this home is not limited to the loss of the building or even the possessions in it, but involves the destruction of what this kind of home represents in the urban landscape. This building is the source of history and genealogy, locating the Sabatini family for generations in a particular locale in the city, just the epistemological grounding that turns space into place. Additionally, the geography of the home itself represents stability against change: a nexus of memory, grounding, and identity for this family in ways that correspond with what Caulfield documented through his sociology of Toronto in the late 1980s. Defining respondents' attitudes about the downtown region was the feeling of living in a "community" or a "village," which suggests that they thought of their houses not as something that belongs to them (property) but instead as someplace where they belong (home) (Caulfield 169–70). One respondent noted the underpinnings of what others expressed: "The community feeling is based on seeing people day-by-day and sharing a common patch of city space with them" (Caulfield 173). This is what is threatened by the escalation of condominiums in the landscape—not to mention Tony's dystopian underground city— in *Beautiful City*. This, then, suggests the second consequence of the transformation of the built environment of the city: destruction not just of homes or neighbourhoods but of the lifeworlds[13] made possible by these urban forms.

Evident in Walker's dramaturgy, then, is an argument about the changes under-way to urban forms in Toronto and what such changes portend for those trying to live in this city. In many ways, Walker represents the anxiety felt by those evicted within and from the city during the 1980s, but this argument would be self-evident to those victimized by the changes. The question for Walker is this: how to confront those responsible, implicitly or explicitly, for those changes, and thus for this crisis? The answer comes with Paul, the architect whose sickness and recovery drive the plot of *Beautiful City*. Beyond metaphorically complementing the threat to the health of "family," which it indeed does, Paul's illness functions almost expressionistically: it conveys his body's instinctive revulsion against the urban forms developed or imagined by Tony. In the opening scene, with Tony rambling on about the eggshell-surfaced walls of the apartment complexes, Paul suddenly moans, "Something... ruptured! You gotta... get me to a hospital" (13). When the next scene opens onto Paul's hospital room, Walker foreshadows the play's argument through Paul's obser-vation, "Nothing seems connected except for those dreadful underground tunnels. And they all seem to lead to the morgue" (17). Thematically, the point proves clear enough: the loss of connection—later represented as social and familial—leads to dis-ease and death. More significantly, Paul's illness, the play suggests, is triggered by Tony's future of the city. In fact, Paul reaches this conclusion when Michael visits him in the hospital: "Too many years of listening to [Tony's] bullshit. It infected my body like a poison" (20). Introduced here, the motif of poisoning is linked with the Raft family and recurs throughout the play, suggesting concerns about contagion or cor-ruption. When Michael tells Paul about Tony wanting them to design the waterfront mall, this triggers another immunological response in Paul's body: "Shit. I'm dying here," he groans as he begins hemorrhaging (22). Borrowing from the initiation story, Walker relocates epiphany, or at least its beginnings, in the body rather than the mind. In this Gregor Samsa-like response,[14] the body registers and revolts against the urban metamorphosis underway in Tony's city (as well as Walker's Toronto)—a commentary that is simultaneously comic unto itself and yet critical of intellectualism.

The plot of *Beautiful City* that follows this scene corresponds with the following premise: the rediscovery of the city proves necessary for Paul's recovery. The first stage involves leaving the hospital for Bargain Harold's, where he meets Gina Mae and therefore distances himself, symbolically and geographically, from the world of the middle class. The next stage involves almost phenomenological rediscovery, as Gina Mae takes Paul into the city's streets and alleys and rummages through bags of garbage behind a restaurant. "I'd sure like to know what these people are throwing out," she says, digging shoulder-deep into bags with a determination that makes Paul nervous. "One person's garbage is another person's meal" (31). When he jokes that he wouldn't eat anything from the tables of this restaurant, much less what they throw out, Gina Mae's quip reveals the privileged assumptions framing Paul's experience of the city: "You'd eat it all right. If you were hungry enough" (31). Certainly critical of what Paul represents about the perspective of the middle class, this scene never becomes didactic because of the humorous premise guiding the argument. The problem confronting Paul is that he cannot consciously make the connection between the urban forms he has enabled or endorsed through his lifestyle and his strange illness. His mind lags comically far behind his body's disease, or dis-ease; consequently, he cannot understand the argument put forward during this scene in the alley, which begins from much the same premise underlying Harvey's "geographical imagination." Of particular interest is the assumption that interactions are mediated by the geographical and ideological distance between the middle class and the city's poor, who are forced to rummage through garbage for food. Bringing Paul to the alley becomes Gina Mae's (and Walker's) way of erasing something of this distance, first through proximity, just by their being in the alley, and second through experience: at one point Gina Mae produces stale bread and tastes it, which shocks Paul. The structure of *Beautiful City*, in fact, foregrounds this collapsing of distance for audiences: beginning with the high-rise office of Tony, the play moves down the socioeconomic ladder toward the city's alleys, where bags of garbage become an index of the city's stratification.

Of course, the middle class of Toronto was well aware of—and perhaps invested in—this stratification during the 1980s. Reminding audiences of it was not nearly as important as redefining the terms of this stratification, which is just what *Beautiful City* does through Paul's recovery. At the beginning of scene 5, Gina Mae justifies taking Paul into the alley with the promise that "a bit of life is going to unfold here in a while" (31). Soon thereafter, Gina Mae's brother-in-law Rolly and his son Stevie arrive, they argue about Rolly's feckless criminal endeavors, and Gina Mae threatens to turn Stevie into a crow. Once Rolly and Stevie leave, Paul demands, "That's real life?" Without any hint of irony, Gina Mae answers in terms that implicitly link Paul's understanding of "life" with the urban forms he inhabits: "Sure it is. Where the hell have you been living. This is what goes on!!" (37). Then Gina Mae announces "the simple ugly truth" that Paul has to confront before he can begin his recovery: "There's life right here on earth and you're not part of it!!" (38). During this scene, Walker stipulates a new definition of urban spaces, with the alley becoming associated with "life" and implicitly contrasted with other spaces in this city: namely, the apartment complexes and condominiums that Paul has designed and, no doubt, where he lives. This contrast is corroborated in scene 10, another scene located in an alley, when Gina Mae's daughter Jane talks about the condominiums that have been transfiguring the landscape: "Living in those things is like living away from... you know... life" (65). Made to Tony, who has been kidnapped by Gina Mae after the destruction of her home, Jane's criticism of the changes to the built environment falls on deaf ears because it is precisely this connection to "life" that Tony's future will mediate, if not eliminate altogether: "Life sucks," Tony tells her without irony. "People shouldn't have to go anywhere near it" (65). Already becoming the norm in this city (and in Toronto, at least to Walker), this future will reach its apotheosis in Tony's underground city, where everyone will have keys to the tunnels and little, if any, contact with strangers, and therefore be able to live far away from "life." Certainly, this last point is "the simple ugly truth" that Walker believes audiences must confront.

Not surprisingly, *Beautiful City's* rebuttal to this future emerges from the alleys. Once Mary Raft arrives with the ransom for Tony's release in scene 10, Gina Mae defines *her* future of the city through what she demands from the Raft family: "I want a community centre. I want two new parks. I want low cost housing. I want a shelter for the homeless and the mistreated… I want a throbbing, connecting, living, creative neighbourhood" that will provide "a nice little place for my daughter to live" (69). In this future, urban forms would be conducive, instead of hostile, to the meeting of strangers, to the feeling of community, and to the democratic freedoms sustained, both symbolically and literally, through public space. The built environment of Gina Mae's future, in other words, embraces what Boddy defines as the "messy vitality of the metropolitan condition, with its unpredictable intermingling of classes, races, and social and cultural forms" and resists the quasi-feudalism of the increasingly enclosed, filtered experience of the gentrified city (Boddy 126). Notably, the play ends without this future realized and the terms of its realization mediated by the mysterious police-woman Dian Black, who appears in the alley to blackmail Mary Raft into agreement with Gina Mae's demands—without, in other words, clear resolution. Nevertheless, this future reaffirms the interplay of urban forms and urban lifestyles evident elsewhere in the play, though in terms of recovery and rehabilitation rather than destruction and distortion. During scene 5, Gina Mae promised to "reconstruct" Rolly, to turn him "into a decent useful human being" (37). Grown more skeptical about this by the end, Gina Mae nonetheless agrees to help rehabilitate him, implying that her future of the city allows for petty criminals.[15] Also, Paul finds himself suddenly healed, with his strange illness having gone into remission, though he remains comically obtuse as to what made him so ill and what induced his recovery. During the conclusion, epiphany extends beyond the confines of the play (since neither Paul nor Tony is capable of epiphany) and confronts audiences first with approbation (for those endorsing the destruction of the city) but more significantly with responsibility (for reclaiming the future of the city)—both of which were framed as political during the production at Factory Theatre.

II. Theatre, Community, Toronto: Maintaining Factory Theatre

Like any political drama, *Beautiful City* requires some means of translating its argument beyond the stage if it is to be efficacious. For Walker, this means transforming anxiety first into recognition (about the value of communal urban forms) and then responsibility (for defending those forms against development). The troubles confronting Factory Theatre during this period suggested, intriguingly, the opportunity, means, and possibly exigency for both. Three years before the debut of *Beautiful City*, Bob White, the artistic director of Factory, described these troubles after the theatre bought Mulvey House, a Victorian mansion located at 125 Bathurst Street:

> Perhaps the fall of 1984 is not the best time to be raising large amounts of money for a new theatre… But we have no choice. We can't keep moving from theatre to theatre. If it isn't in the cards for Factory Theatre to survive, then it's time to confront that directly. How we do in main-

taining this new space will answer that question once and for all. (qtd. in Godfrey).

Two details emerge here that prove important to this argument, the first of which is White's reference to Factory's recently concluded itinerary. This began with Factory's eviction from 374 Dupont Street, the former candle factory that was the theatre's first home and that inspired its name. Closed by city inspectors in 1973 because Factory Theatre had "registered with the city as a drama school, not as a public performing space" when it was founded in 1970 and was never truly "up to code," Factory was evicted in—and from—the city (Johnston 98–99). In January 1974, it temporarily took up residence at the Bathurst Street United Church; then, during the following May, it moved into "another converted warehouse at 207 Adelaide Street East" (Johnston 100). Unable to find a permanent home due to skyrocketing property values in Toronto, Factory had to rent theatre space from other troupes, briefly, before moving on in the 1970s and early 1980s. Defining nearly a decade of Factory's history, this itinerancy was punctuated by its purchase of the building at 125 Bathurst Street, which remains the theatre's home today. But a burning question faced Factory Theatre at the time: was this punctuation a period or another ellipsis?

Although certainly a welcome decision, given the difficulty of attempting to produce theatre without a permanent home, purchasing this location nevertheless came with a host of financial pressures attendant with property ownership, in particular on account of the inflationary real estate market of Toronto during the 1980s. This leads to the second detail that frames *Beautiful City*'s original production at Factory Theatre: White's putting the survival of Factory in terms of its capability to "maintain" the space of 125 Bathurst Street. [16] The word, of course, denotes the financial need of renovating Mulvey House, a nineteenth-century Victorian mansion, toward the needs of a late twentieth-century theatre. Factory underwrote such renovations by selling debentures—loans from public investment that, notably, did not name the property as collateral ("Bay Street")—shortly after taking possession of the location. But "maintain" additionally conveys the almost political necessity of holding onto or, better yet, defending this space against the clamour of development and gentrification in Toronto. In other words, White implicitly spatializes the existential crisis confronting Factory Theatre during this time: the terms of its survival become imbricated with its ability first to renovate 125 Bathurst Street toward a financially solvent theatre, and, second to defend this space against the rising tide of development transforming Toronto. Though the second was clearly implicated in the first, it nevertheless suggests an almost ideological battle within Toronto's landscape, with Factory Theatre front and centre, about the nature of urban forms that will determine the future of this city. Defending 125 Bathurst Street, though, was rather thorny because "the widespread property-value inflation in Toronto's downtown real estate market through the 1980s," as McKinnie documents in *City Stages*, created a "whipsaw effect on theatre companies" (121). Central to the problem was the fact that "the types of buildings that could serve as performance spaces were usually in the commercial market, and theatre companies had difficulty competing for these spaces with profit-driven enterprises that could often pay higher rents" ("Bay Street"). Compounding this were "rising prices in the city's residential market," which encouraged landlords to convert "the buildings in which theatre organizations resided into condominiums" ("Bay Street"). Doubly threatened, then, Factory's mandate of maintaining 125 Bathurst Street involved simultaneously defending itself through stewardship of this space and, more implicitly, defending this space for theatre in Toronto through its stewardship.

The premieres of *The East End Plays*, including *Beautiful City*, were indelibly linked with Factory Theatre's mandate to maintain this space. The first production mounted at 125 Bathurst Street was *Criminals in Love* in November 1984, when pressures attendant with this property were becoming overwhelming. On opening night, "White confided to [Walker] that the theatre was on the brink," notes J. Kelly Nestruck. Walker recalled, "I guess [White had] had a couple, [and] he said to me, 'I gotta tell you, I hope this play goes, because if it doesn't this theatre is finished'" (Nestruck). To the relief of White and others at Factory Theatre, *Criminals in Love* became a commercial hit that garnered Walker another Chalmers Award and, as Johnson notes, "rescued Factory from financial crises" (36) with much needed revenue. Five years later, *Love and Anger* became an even bigger success and economically buoyed the theatre once again. Like Johnson, Nestruck discusses the productions of *The East End Plays* during this period in terms of rescuing Factory Theatre financially, a one-way exchange in which Walker's plays translate to revenues. In fact, Nestruck's argument is that Walker uncannily comes to the rescue whenever Factory Theatre is threatened by producing commercial hits, occasionally a string of them. Between *Criminals in Love* and *Love and Anger* came *Beautiful City* in 1987, when the theatre remained "on the brink" financially. Poorly reviewed [17] and not as successful as other plays, the production of *Beautiful City* was not ultimately about producing revenues for Factory Theatre. Despite this, *Beautiful City* was, perhaps, even more directly invested in the crisis confronting Factory at the time, though the terms of that investment had more to do with defending this theater's space than with rescuing the theater. In fact, including *Beautiful City* in the discussion of how Walker's plays contributed to Factory Theatre's efforts to survive during this period suggests that the terms of this discussion used by Nestruck and Johnson prove insufficient to account for the give-and-take between play and production. The production of *Beautiful City*, in other words, was more complex in how it related to Factory's maintaining 125 Bathurst Street, and more instructive about the shift in Walker's dramaturgy considered in my last section.

The interplay of play and production for *Beautiful City* begins with the building located at 125 Bathurst Street. Read diachronically, or with attention to temporal changes, the Victorian mansion known as Mulvey House suggests intriguing connotations for Walker's argument about Toronto. Built in 1860, the building had known a number of incarnations during its history: initially a private residence; then, following major renovations in 1910, the St. Mary's Arts and Literary Centre; and eventually Factory Theatre in 1984. [18] Contained within this building, in other words, was more than a century of history, with each phase endorsing or enabling particular lifeworlds in the city: a palimpsest of home, school for the arts, and theatre. This kind of urban form was precisely what was being lost during this period of development, with the rise of condominiums, apartment complexes, and shopping malls like the Eaton Centre in Toronto's downtown, one example of the postmodern architecture described by Frederic Jameson in *Postmodernism, or, The Cultural Logic of Late Capitalism*. Jameson's well-known argument is that the architecture of such buildings induces a confusion that is simultaneously empirical and epistemological because of the erasure of connections to history and the surrounding environment. This leaves onlookers unable to conceive of any coherent perspective regarding the building, the city, or even themselves. By contrast, the history encoded in Mulvey House (and, not incidentally, recited in newspapers when Factory took up residence there) [19] turns this building into a space where history and emplacement can be sensed and experienced. The same is true when reading this building synchronically, or with consideration of the relations among elements at a particular time. The façade of the building, dominated by two large doors facing Bathurst Street, suggests crowds of foot traffic slowly gathering on performance nights. [20] The building's façade, in other words, endorses a set of values about how this space should function in Toronto, specifically, as a gathering place for those living in 1980s Toronto.

Like Gina Mae's home in *Beautiful City*, then, Mulvey House serves as nexus of history, memory, and emplacement in the city and, for that matter, an exemplum of the play's concerns. Drawing from this visual and connotative significance of the building certainly helped translate the argument of *Beautiful City* beyond the dramatic world of Tony, Paul, and Gina Mae toward the infrastructure of Toronto by demonstrating the sort of urban forms necessary for what Jane and her mother describe as "life." The corollary of this premise, though, is equally noteworthy: *Beautiful City* perhaps actualized the latent values in 125 Bathurst Street during the production. The synchronic reading of Mulvey House would become apparent with crowds of theatregoers assembled outside the building, though this would be true for any production. The diachronic reading, on the other hand, may have emerged not just in concert with the production of *Beautiful City* but because of it. During the production, the play's concerns about the contested future of Toronto would have imbricated the space of 125 Bathurst Street literally (through advertising and marketing that stressed these concerns) and symbolically (through the conflicts brought to the stage). Because of *Beautiful City*, the space of 125 Bathurst Street became one venue to recognize and even resist the crisis of eviction in and from Toronto. This suggests another possibility among the "social meanings" that Marvin Carlson demonstrates theatre has taken on over the centuries: a space that endorses and enables communal gathering and reaffirmation of communalism, as in Toronto when community was being lost because of the mandate for urban growth (8). [21] Semiotically and symbolically, the building housing Factory Theatre offered what respondents to Caulfield's study lamented as being lost: "a common patch of city space" (173). Although not specifically included among the forms outlined as necessary for the city's future by Gina Mae, the details of Mulvey House suggest how at least this theatre corresponds with the premise guiding that future: "a throbbing, connecting, living, creative neighborhood" (George Walker 69).

Most intriguing about this interplay between play and production, however, is what is implied in this actualization of values *in* and *of* urban forms. Because of the way that *Beautiful City* may have imbued 125 Bathurst Street with its argument, the play may have conflated the values of this space with the values of the stewardship of this space. During its incarnation as a theatre, 125 Bathurst Street has been precisely the opposite of what Tony Raft advocated for his city: it was space where strangers could gather, meet one another, and foster the sense of community. Mulvey House, in other words, was not inherently valuable but instead valuable because of the way it was maintained. This conflation, first of all, underscores the ways that urban spaces are continually contested economically and ideologically, in this case in terms of the larger fight between development *and* community unfolding across Toronto during the 1980s. More specifically, this conflation contributed to Factory Theatre's mandate of maintaining 125 Bathurst Street since Factory's stewardship was exactly what was being threatened by the likes of Tony Raft. Admittedly caricatured, Raft nevertheless illustrates the nature of this threat confronting any number of Toronto's theatres at this time, including Toronto Workshop Productions (TWP). Like Factory Theatre, TWP had purchased a new home during the 1980s, this one located at 12 Alexander Street (less than three miles away and facing the same pressures as Factory Theatre). Confronted with insolvency, TWP became the subject of a "scheme" to have its building sold if it would support the developer's plan for rezoning the neighborhood for condominiums, [22] just after the production of *Beautiful City*. Having Raft onstage during this period was a way of illustrating the threat confronting Factory Theatre's stewardship of this space. The conflict was simultaneously literal and ideological: about the space that would be lost and the values in the construction of spaces. Threats to Factory Theatre, then, became threats to the space itself and, more importantly, to the continued existence of these *kinds of spaces* in Toronto. Through this conflation, in other words, the production of *Beautiful City* endorsed Factory Theatre's mandate to maintain this space.

Beyond this, *Beautiful City* extended this mandate toward Toronto during the 1980s. Produced three years into Factory Theatre's residency at 125 Bathurst Street and against the background of gentrification, Walker's play foregrounds eviction and displacement as conditions that were simultaneously geographical and existential for characters like Gina Mae and Jane (surrogates for the working class in Toronto). With the play's themes imbricating the production's locale, this no doubt brought renewed attention to Factory's decade-long itinerary that purchasing 125 Bathurst Street had concluded. Defined through the themes of *Beautiful City*, then, Factory Theatre becomes doubly metonymic regarding the ongoing crisis in Toronto. On the one hand, Factory had already been victimized by many of the same forces of development confronting the homes and neighbourhoods of Toronto during its itinerary; and therefore the theatre represented one part of the geographical and existential crisis represented in the play. On the other, Factory Theatre's locale and what that locale represented for Toronto were specifically in crisis despite the funds brought in by *Criminals in Love*; and therefore the space of 125 Bathurst Street stood in for what was occurring all across Toronto. Thus the production of *Beautiful City* defined Factory

Theatre as a flashpoint in the geographical imagination of Torontonians during the 1980s: it became a way of demonstrating and even politicizing the interplay among theatre, community, and city. This was particularly important in relation to the "other housing crisis," phrasing employed by theatre activists during this decade to conflate the plight of theatres with "public anxiety about the supply and cost of residential housing" (McKinnie 119). As McKinnie notes, "By using a popular political discourse about the need for affordable housing, advocates for theatre companies framed their predicament as an extension of a wider problem" (119). In effect, *Beautiful City* performed the same kind of framing, though in a more politicized form. Subsuming Factory's contested stewardship of 125 Bathurst Street, Walker's play presented the "simple ugly truth" about Toronto's future: if Factory failed to maintain this space, it would be another step toward the dismaying future imagined by Tony Raft.

In many ways, then, *Beautiful City* produced at Factory Theatre conflated the future of theatre in Toronto with the future of Toronto itself. Begun with White's acknowledgment of the need to "maintain" their new home at 125 Bathurst three years earlier and kept in the public consciousness through the debenture campaign, this conflation became increasingly clear with the advocacy of specific urban forms in Walker's play. This, then, suggests the second need for political drama noted at the opening of this section: taking responsibility. Supporting Factory Theatre, in whatever manner, allowed the community to become part of maintaining this space, literally the theatre located at 125 Bathurst and symbolically the future of Toronto's downtown, by turning the Factory Theatre's new home into a front in the ongoing battle against rezoning and redevelopment during the 1980s. Defending Factory Theatre was implicitly linked with defending the future of the city historically and culturally since Factory had been among the original alternative theatres that helped transform the landscape of Toronto a decade before. But this defence of Factory Theatre would have been even more noteworthy geographically—that is, concerning 125 Bathurst Street. Invited to take responsibility by Walker's play, audiences were confronted with the argument about and for maintaining specific urban forms, implicitly including the converted mansion-become-theater that needed to be maintained during this period. Maintaining Factory Theatre became a way of resisting development if, for no other reason, because it kept this space from being sold to developers (as was the fear about TWP) and turned into condominiums. Certainly, this was to the benefit of Factory Theatre, which was trying to survive an inflationary economy and booming real estate market. But it was perhaps to the benefit of the community, which was empowered with symbolic and real-world means for resisting the future of Toronto advocated by Tony Raft, a form of political agency emerging from the geographical imagination defined by Harvey. Maintaining Factory Theatre became a means of endorsing a future for how Toronto should be constructed, organized, and inhabited. Because of *Beautiful City*, in other words, Factory Theatre potentially became a bulwark against the gentrification and growth transforming Toronto's "soul" denounced in *Beautiful City*.

III. Conclusions

A number of conclusions emerging from consideration of the production bring this argument full circle. About the exigency of *Beautiful City*, it is tempting to conclude that Walker may have written the play not just with Toronto in mind (as he acknowledges in interviews) but, further, in recognition of the details of Factory Theatre's crisis. Knowing about this crisis before and during the writing of *Beautiful City*, Walker may have intended much of what has been suggested here. Since authorial intention is always difficult to pin down, however, I won't go any further than noting the intriguing possibility. Besides, there is more than enough commonality between the play's argument and the theatre's mandate during this period to support the conclusions put forward here. About the shift in Walker's dramaturgy from polemics and to politics, notably spatialized politics, plenty of evidence emerges from the play and from interviews. Driven by an increasingly geographical imagination during this decade (for whatever reason), Walker's dramaturgy in *Beautiful City* specifically and *The East End Plays* more generally centred more and more on epistemological rediscovery of the city—both in the structure of the plays and the ambition implicit in this structure. Beyond merely advocating Gina Mae's future for the city, *Beautiful City* concludes by thematizing negotiation through the *deus ex machina* ending, which suggests the audience's need to make sense of the ending imaginatively and, potentially, to take some responsibility for negotiating that future through the 1987 production at Factory Theatre. Because of this, the terms employed by Nestruck and Johnson in discussing the relationship of *The East End Plays* to Factory Theatre during the 1980s prove insufficient. They don't account for, and perhaps even erase, the distinctly spatialized concerns evident in the dramaturgy and, perhaps, the production itself: the argument about maintaining (defending) this space against the threat dramatized in *Beautiful City*. One final conclusion that emerges from this research relates to the question that followed the establishment of alternative theatres in the early 1970s: "Alternative to what?" [23] By the 1980s, this question could be answered almost as much culturally as artistically for Factory Theatre: an alternative to the future imagined by the Tony Rafts of the world—a future that George F. Walker considers, without qualms, to be shit.

(2009)

Notes

[1] Chris Johnson (17) describes this year as when Walker learned the "rules" of writing plays in ways that allowed him to evolve as playwright as well as the period when his subject and style were changing.

[2] See Haff (78–79) and Johnson (41–60) for more discussion of Walker's engagement with popular culture, especially the B movie.

[3] See Caulfield for discussion of the growth mandate in Toronto from the 1960s to the 1980s.

[4] Walker was born in a Cabbagetown neighbourhood that was bulldozed for the development of Regent Park. See Conlogue, "Places."

[5] Craig Stewart Walker locates this conflict within a larger nexus of Canadian socioeconomic and cultural identity.

[6] In this way, I'm building on Craig Stewart Walker's argument that *The East End Plays* fall within the tradition of City Comedies that goes back to the Renaissance.

[7] See Johnston (98–104) for a discussion of Factory Theatre's mandate and how it related to the theatre's difficulty in remaining solvent.

[8] "[Walker's] most recent play, *Love and Anger,* a 1989 Chalmers winner, became the longest running original play in Toronto theatrical history, entertaining more than 30,000 people over a six-month period since it opened Factory's 20th anniversary season in October, 1989. When it moved from Factory to the St Lawrence Centre on May 2, 1990 (again directed by Walker), *Love and Anger* became the first original Canadian play to be transferred directly from a non-profit to a commercial theater" (Haff 78).

[9] Caulfield uses this term to describe the interplay of urban forms and urban lifestyles, how one makes the other possible, very much like the sociospatial premise underlying Walker's dramaturgy.

[10] Notably, "new tunnels connected previously isolated segments" during the 1980s, and consequently, "east-west paths proliferated to the point where much of the corporate core of downtown Montreal could be traveled without ever venturing outside" (Boddy 146).

[11] Though development of the PATH began in earnest during the 1970s, it was during the 1980s that it became a city mandate to develop Toronto underground. See City for details.

[12] This term is used by Walker and by Walker's critics, particularly Johnson. It refers to elements of the plays that are neither realistic nor logical and often put pressure on the basic assumptions guiding the world, in this case that Gina Mae has the power to transform people into woodland creatures.

[13] This premise underlies many of the other *East End Plays,* where the focus of the play is the family structure, or lifeworlds of the play are threatened, implicitly, because of the changes underway to Toronto, though such connections may only become clear when the plays are read collectively.

[14] Samsa is the anti-hero of Franz Kafka's *The Metamorphosis* who, without explanation, one morning wakes as a gigantic insect. The story follows his bizarre alienation from family members and society after this metamorphosis—ed.

[15] But not, notably, Stevie, who must be driven to the airport and expelled from the city. This suggests that there are limits as to who can be rehabilitated and become contributing members of the city, as well as Walker's disdain, perhaps, for those without any sense of collective responsibility.

[16] Worth noting here is the counterargument to White's claims about purchasing 125 Bathurst Street: that becoming invested in real estate meant changing some of the mandate beyond "alternative" theatre in Toronto. McKinnie offers detailed discussion of this debate regarding Theatre Passe Muraille and Toronto Workshop Productions. See McKinnie 73–89, 92–114.

[17] Conlogue describes the production as "rich but incomplete," with particular complaints about White's direction not fulfilling the needs of Walker's play. See Conlogue ("Beautiful City"). Iris Winston had even more cynical remarks about regional productions that followed. See Winston.

[18] For details of this space, see Godfrey.

[19] See Godfrey; "Briefly."

[20] Significantly, this is completely symbolic, as patrons of Factory Theatre enter at the south end of the building on Adelaide Street, but the symbolism is certainly potent.

[21] Carlson describes theatre buildings serving as "a cultural monument, a site of display for a dominant social class, an emblem of depravity and vice, a center of political activism, a haven of retreat from the world of harsh reality" (8).

[22] See McKinnie's discussion of Toronto Workshop Productions in *City Stages*, 110–11.

[23] The question here emerges from the fact that the "alternative" theaters of Toronto quickly became almost "mainstream" in terms of popularity, leaving some question about the definition of these theatres. See Johnston 250–52.

Works Cited

"Bay Street Gives Theatre Opening Act." *The Globe and Mail* 5 July 1984: B7.

Boddy, Trevor. "Underground and Overhead: Building the Analogous City." *Variations on a Theme Park: The New American City and the End of Public Space.* Ed. Michael Sorkin. New York: Hill and Wang, 1992.

"Briefly Theatre Finds New Home in a Victorian Mansion." *The Globe and Mail* 5 July 1984: E3.

Carlson, Marvin. *Places of Performance: The Semiotics of Theatre Architecture.* Ithaca: Cornell UP, 1989.

Caulfield, Jon. *City Form and Everyday Life: Toronto's Gentrification and Critical Social Practice.* Toronto: U of Toronto P, 1994.

Certeau, Michel de. *The Practice of Everyday Life.* Trans. Steven Rendall. Berkeley: U of California P, 1984.

City of Toronto. "PATH Facts." 14 December 2010. http://www.toronto.ca/path/

Conlogue, Ray. "*Beautiful City*: Flaws Show in *Beautiful City*." *The Globe and Mail* 1 October 1987: D5.

———. "Places Written in the Heart: Walker Has Left the City but the City Hasn't Left Him." *The Globe and Mail* 19 September 1987: C1.

Godfrey, Stephen. "An Itinerant Theatre Puts Down Roots." *The Globe and Mail* 6 November 1984: M13.

Haff, Stephen. "Slashing the Pleasantly Vague: George F. Walker and the Word." *Theater* 22.3 (1991): 78–85.

Harvey, David. *Social Justice and the City.* London: Edward Arnold, 1973.

———. *Spaces of Hope.* Berkeley and Los Angeles: U of California P, 2000.

Jameson, Frederic. *Postmodernism, or, The Cultural Logic of Late Capitalism.* Durham, NC: Duke UP, 1991.

Johnson, Chris. *Essays on George F. Walker: Playing with Anxiety.* Winnipeg: Blizzard, 1999.

Johnston, Denis. *Up the Mainstream: The Rise of Toronto's Alternative Theatres, 1968–1975.* Toronto: U of Toronto P, 1991.

Lefebvre, Henri. *The Production of Space.* Trans. Donald Nicholson-Smith. Malden, Mass: Blackwell, 1991.

McKinnie, Michael. *City Stages: Theatre and Urban Space in a Global City.* Toronto: U of Toronto P, 2007.

Nestruck, J. Kelly. "Buddies in Bad and Good Times: George F. Walker and the Factory Theatre Remain Close after 35 Years." *National Post* 4 May 2005: AL3.

Soja, Edward. *Thirdspace: Journeys to Los Angeles and Other Real-And-Imagined Places.* Cambridge, Mass.: Blackwell, 1996.

Walker, Craig Stewart. "George F. Walker: Postmodern City Comedy." *The Buried Astrolabe: Canadian Dramatic Imagination and Western Tradition.* Montreal: McGill-Queen's UP, 2001. 264–354.

Walker, George F. *Beautiful City. The East End Plays: Part 2.* Burnaby, BC: Talonbooks, 1999. 9–78.

Westgate, J. Chris. "Toward a Rhetoric of Sociospatial Theater: José Rivera's Marisol." *Theatre Journal* 59.1 (2007): 21–37.

Winston, Iris. "Night Out in the Big City Proves to be a Yawner." *Ottawa Citizen* 19 March 1993: E7.

Building Utopia: Performance and the Fantasy of Urban Renewal in Contemporary Toronto

by Laura Levin and Kim Solga

When we set out to "stage" a city, whose vision of the city do we rehearse as "real" or "true"? Who benefits from that staging, and who pays the hidden costs? These questions are related to others that urban activists around the world have rightly asked for decades: who benefits and who suffers in the name of aggressive, developer-driven urban regeneration projects? But they are also much more profound. First, they require that we understand how such projects co-opt and redeploy the experiences of those they ultimately marginalize—the working class; low-profile, low-income arts and culture workers; inner-city ethnic minorities, often refugees or newly arrived migrants—as they attempt to reimagine the contemporary world-class city as fresh, hip, and, above all, "creative" (Florida). Second, they demand that we interrogate how performers and activists who set their work up *against* these inherently conservative regeneration practices address—or fail to address—the lives and experiences of those same citizens positioned, awkwardly, at both centre and margin of what we will call the "creative city" script.

Our case study in this exploration is the city we both call home, a city that has been, over the past five years, overwhelmed by the fantasy of creative redevelopment from both the top down and the bottom up. As official Toronto preens itself to take to the "world stage" in everything from sports and industry to arts and culture, it consistently markets an urban experience shaped by what Ric Knowles calls "diversity without difference": private, pay-to-enter venues masquerading as public space; complex webs of ethnic, religious, racial, and economic difference masquerading as a smiling multicultural mosaic. And yet, on the flip side of this official agenda, too many of the performer-activists working in counterpoint to the city's renewal efforts are busy generating their own versions of proprietary public space. They offer a provocative variation on the city's official themes, to be sure, but not a variation that comes close enough to thinking through how economic and social stratification subtly but insistently determines who gets to benefit from the dream of a utopic Toronto, and who gets shut out of the party.

Nights in the Global City

Toronto's current cultural renaissance emerges as a blend of official discourses produced and disseminated by city hall, often in conjunction with both higher levels of government (provincial and federal) and private enterprise, positioned alongside a grassroots movement driven by a combination of environmental and cycling activists, public space advocates, and arts professionals. Despite several differences, however, all of these groups share the stated desire to turn the city into a kind of urban utopia. The notion of "Torontopia" has its roots in the activist community, [1] but the overlap between those who work at city hall and those who work around and against it is considerable. Mayor David Miller and his like-minded left-wing counselors are known to be avid fans of the grassroots output, in particular the influential *Spacing* magazine, which focuses on public space issues in Toronto. In fact, we can hardly speak of competing discourses of renewal; the official and the grassroots scripts are really variant conversations working in productive tension with one another. And, perhaps not surprisingly given the broadly performative pedigrees of so many of their players (politicians and artists alike), most of the city's "utopian" initiatives consistently employ explicitly theatrical forms of urban dramaturgy as they attempt to reconfigure traditional models of public space and trigger new forms of civic engagement.

The largest and most pervasive of these initiatives sees public institutions working with both government and corporate sponsors to promote Toronto as a global city of the future, a place built by and for Torontonians but whose most important spectator is the *tourist*. Official Toronto has eagerly leapt aboard the "creative city" bandwagon, adopting the ready-made "urban-development script" (Peck 740) defined by economic development guru Richard Florida. Florida encourages planners to lure an increasingly powerful class of creative types (engineers, artists, musicians, designers, and knowledge professionals) to their cities, arguing that it is these creatives who hold the key to economic growth and effective urban branding. According to Florida—who was himself lured to Toronto in the summer of 2007 to take up the position of director of the University of Toronto's new Martin Prosperity Institute—members of the creative class look for a community with "abundant high-quality amenities and experiences, an openness to diversity of all kinds, and above all else the opportunity to validate their identities as creative people" (218). In Toronto, even before Florida's near-messianic in-person arrival, the arenas of culture, heritage, and the arts already had become zones for Florida-style creative self-actualization, ground zero of the city's branding as it seeks the elusive "world class" label. As Toronto's *The Creative City: A Workprint* reminds artists, it is "not enough to generate new ideas" (City of Toronto 16); they must also consider how these ideas can be turned into shows that the world "wants to see" (18). [2]

The creative city script encourages urban actors to engage in extreme makeovers, and Toronto is following through with its own creative city mandate in two related ways. First, the city has invested heavily in the physical renovation of its most important cultural institutions, with dollars not only for bricks and mortar but also for a glimpse of the world's most visible "starchitects" and the performance of creative allure and cultural fashionability they trail in their wake. Contemporary Toronto is paying close attention to the theatricality of its facades, revamping what Erving Goffman would call its front stage areas (107). The Art Gallery of Ontario (AGO) on Dundas Street West has just reopened after a full-scale renovation completed by Frank

Gehry³; around the corner, Will Alsop recently reworked the Ontario College of Art and Design, building a stunning, black and white "flying" tabletop held aloft by brightly colored crayon legs. Most controversially, Daniel Libeskind brought literally massive change to the Royal Ontario Museum (ROM), smashing a multistory glass and aluminum crystal into the side of the old museum's Bloor Street elevation. The napkin on which Libeskind reportedly sketched the original design is now the stuff of legend in Toronto, so much an icon of the creative city ethos and its parallel commitments to tourism and the arts that the infamous sketch has found its way on to the cocktail napkins in the museum's posh bar.

These architectural projects resonate with the hyperawareness of "spectacle and theatricality" that Paul Makeham finds in the creative city script, pointing to "a kind of urban planning which endorses not realism but façade, which models itself not on utilitarian ideas of traffic flow and pedestrian efficiency, but the stage set, the carnival, and the forum" (157). The "creative city," then, is finally about the spectacle, rather than the performative production, of public space. The ROM offers an ideal example of this agenda. The museum renovation promised to remake the city *for* the city, creating, as Libeskind claims, a "bold reawakening" of civic life. Accordingly, a significant part of the crystal was originally meant to be transparent so that passersby could see exhibits from the street. This plan was jettisoned thanks to cost overruns and technical difficulties—a reminder that money is made at the ROM inside the gates, not at street level, and that the renovation is only "for the city" insofar as the museum is making money. Nevertheless, the ROM's official "Renaissance" in spring 2007 played up Libeskind's vision of the museum as a public place: museum officials engineered a one-night-only free "architectural opening" that turned the crystal into a stage set (a free concert took place on platforms at its base) and invited the public inside at no cost throughout the night and into the following day. The free opening, held in conjunction with the city's first annual Luminato Festival, was the talk of the town, but it also neatly effaced the fact that it was many Torontonians' one chance to see the new ROM affordably, provided they were willing and able to line up through the night: regular adult admission is a steep CAD$20.⁴ The AGO, the Gardiner Museum of Ceramic Art (also newly renovated and anchored, like both the ROM and the AGO, by an upscale restaurant), and the brand-new Four Seasons Centre for the Performing Arts are all similarly private venues that masquerade as open civic space; in each case, substantial disposable income as well as a fair amount of leisure time mark the price of access to local culture.

In tandem with these infrastructure investments, Toronto is also promoting the notion of city space as public creative space through regular cultural festivals such as the high-profile, Scotiabank-sponsored Nuit Blanche (an annual all-night celebration of art that promotes mass use of the streets and public transit after hours), the 2006 Humanitas Festival (a celebration of ethnic diversity and global citizenship presented in concert with the city's "Live With Culture" campaign), and Winterlicious and Summerlicious (seasonal opportunities for Torontonians to try elite restaurants for a fixed, comparatively low cost). Many of these festivals include a number of free events and use special transit routes and scheduling to encourage attendance from across income brackets; at least on the surface, they appear far more committed than the museums to enabling an inclusive engagement with art and "culture" in genuinely public space. Nevertheless, like Renaissance ROM and other infrastructure refurbishments, they have until now primarily generated the façade of a Toronto alive with culture rather than investing seriously and for the long term in the cultivation of local artistic labor.[5]

The Luminato Festival, a largely private capital initiative supported with federal and provincial rather than civic government dollars, is perhaps the best example of a culturefest originally mapped on to Toronto's existing arts scene with an eye more to tourist promotion than to the support of local culture workers. Although Luminato's mission statement insists that it "embraces" collaborative projects among local, national, and international artists, and despite the promise that the 2009 edition of the festival will include more commissioned work and a "greater national presence" than ever before (Bradshaw), the festival's framework resolutely remains corporate first, arts second (Janet Price, its most visible face, is CEO, not artistic director). Unabashedly deploying Florida's creative city vocabulary, Luminato bills itself as a week-long event designed "not only [to] engage Torontonians with free shows but also [to] rebrand Toronto internationally, […] boost[ing] the whole province's [economic] fortunes" (Taylor). The payoff has been huge. In 2008, after only one year of operation, Luminato won CAD$22.5 million in provincial funding—money, journalist Kate Taylor astutely notes, made possible in large part by the political connections of its co-founders (high-profile business leaders Tony Gagliano and David Pecaut), and money that also represents a troubling politicization of the arts-granting process in Ontario. As Taylor points out, Luminato's windfall cut directly into the funds available for numerous other, lower-profile initiatives, including those funded by the Ontario Arts Council, an organization that serves up to 400 arts groups across the province with individual one-time grants. While the CEO of Toronto's Harbourfront Centre, Bill Boyle, told Taylor in May 2008 that Luminato will always prioritize its relationship with Toronto artists over its international ambitions, material evidence of this local-arts-first attitude has until very recently been hard to find.[6] Only a handful of original works were commissioned for the inaugural Luminato in 2007; for the most part, the heavily hyped event featured shows that were already running in the city. The festival was thus effectively laid on top of Toronto's existing performance and visual arts landscape, creating a parallel art-as-culture show that encouraged residents not familiar with the city's arts scene to imagine that all this work was new and, more importantly, was made possible by the festival and its intensively visible corporate sponsor, L'Oréal. Further, what *was* new seemed at times quite uncertain of its audience, of its locale, and of its relationship to the city's populations and their needs.

Back Home (2005), a devised piece about Aboriginal and migrant dispossession in contemporary Australia produced by Sydney's Urban Theatre Projects and cosponsored in Toronto by the Harbourfront New World Stage festival and Luminato 2007, offers a telling example of the latter's local disconnects. In its original Australian incarnation, *Back Home* begins with a bus tour through Sydney's Western suburbs; the tour ends in an anonymous backyard. The performance takes place there, set within the crushing intimacy of a "foreign" citizen's private space. The goal of this journey is to reorient spectators, to force them into collision with neighbourhoods in their own city about which they may carry dangerous assumptions and a host of trace colonial anxieties. In Toronto, this context was lost. Worse: it was manipulated as show, turning dispossession into entertainment and reproducing colonial hierarchies within the framework of performance space. The modified bus tour raced spectators along Queen's Quay and the Gardiner Expressway, two of Toronto's least evocative roadways, while a young (white) researcher read facts about Toronto's Aboriginal history from a piece of paper. His script and our movement generated noticeable misses: often he would gesture behind the bus, or point far from the road, toward some space "out there" where we might locate Toronto's First Nations past. Meanwhile, the living neighborhoods through which we were driving—many of them struggling with poverty and creeping gentrification among their migrant populations—remained unstoried, unmarked. The tour's final destination was a makeshift backyard—backyard as theatre set, not backyard as invasive (and invaded) public-private space—on the grounds of the Centre for Addiction and Mental Health (CAMH). The playing and viewing area was cut off from the rest of the CAMH grounds by a chain-link fence; uniformed security guards prevented passersby from "crashing" the show. As the sun set and lights came up in the residence rooms inside the centre, the distance between "us" in the bleachers and the anonymous "them" in their hospital rooms— indeed, the distance between the story on the stage and the real stories of dispossession and loss in contemporary west end Toronto—could not have seemed greater. Was this performance really for Toronto and Torontonians? Or was *Back Home* imported onto the CAMH grounds to enact a hollow celebration of Toronto's civic responsibility in another example of the city on display for a proverbial elsewhere, for the global tourist empowered to define us as "world class"?

Luminato, like Nuit Blanche and the city's other annual culturefests, is now firmly embedded in Toronto's civic imaginary, and Torontonians appear by most accounts to be enjoying the party atmosphere that goes hand-in-hand with a broadscale commitment to the arts, whatever the underlying politics. But the creative city is, very clearly, not all fun and games: at its core, it is a place that embraces diversity only to obscure the inequities, ambivalences, and outright hostilities true difference brings.[7] The creative city script is fueled by a "salad bar" approach to multiculturalism, promoted without a hint of irony on the Tourism Toronto website: "You know the feeling you get when you come across an amazing menu and want to order every dish? That's what it's like to be here."[8] The creative city actively ignores the fact that ethnically, racially, and socially charged bodies can never "inhabit" public space in neutral ways; they always, as Harvey Young observes, "structure" that space by appearing out of place within it. The creative city script and the "diversity without difference" paradigm on which it depends intentionally obfuscate the social and racial markers that determine the contours of true public space. In the process they disavow the two questions central to the larger project of urban renewal: (1) How do we determine what it means to be "from" a city, to be able to claim place as coeval with self, to be able to feel "in place" and at home here, not just during Nuit Blanche or Renaissance ROM but on any ordinary day or night?; and (2) Who claims the right to be gatekeeper, to decide which residents qualify as "authentically" Torontonian and thus entitled to a share of the spoils?

Toward a New Toronto

In the wake of Toronto's creative city branding and its often conservative politics, an alternative discourse of urban renewal has emerged, generated by a heterogeneous group of artists and activists who are working, sometimes individually and sometimes in ad hoc or established organizations, to imagine a different kind of public space in and for Toronto.[9] Propelled by an excitement about the city's future and a participatory aesthetic, these "Torontopians" seek to reactivate public space through a set of signature performance practices, all of which have certain features in common. They claim city space for citizens rather than for corporate interests; they are free and open to all; they privilege the use (and sometimes the guerrilla occupation) of public transit; they inhabit the streets at all hours of the day or night, turning them into safe zones for childlike play rather than dreaded places that provoke morbid, parental fear. Above all, they assert public ownership over civic space as a given and enact that ownership in peaceful protest against the large-scale usurpation of civic space by corporate interests.

Some of the most evocative and effective of these performance practices have come from the Toronto Public Space Committee (www.publicspace.ca). The TPSC is among the oldest and most well respected of the Torontopian organizations and one of the very few whose mandate is overtly political. Founded by cycling activist David Meslin, this nonprofit group works diligently to protect Toronto's skyline, sidewalks, freeways, and airspace against privatization and ad-creep. To achieve its goals the TPSC uses a wide range of strategies, including directly political means (lobbying city hall and deputing in front of city council via its "Billboard Battalion" network) as well as performative interventions such as "guerrilla gardening" (in which residents are encouraged to plant and maintain gardens in neglected or abandoned spaces, often in defiance of "No Trespassing" signs). Demonstrating well the push-pull the TPSC and related groups feel toward the official renewal works sponsored by City Hall, in 2005 Meslin launched City Idol, a political competition timed to culminate with the 2006 municipal election. City Idol encouraged would-be city counselors to express radical new ideas about the city's future while competing for the right to campaign as a bona fide, sponsored candidate in the election. Asking participants to make speeches and improvise in debates, City Idol provided a fresh kind of actor training: rehearsals for political office. These and other Torontopian performances are documented in countless photoblogs, in *Spacing* magazine, published quarterly since 2003, as well as in the Coach House essay collections *uTOpia: Towards a New Toronto* (McBride and Wilcox), and *GreenTOpia: Towards a Sustainable Toronto* (Wilcox, Palassio, and Dovercourt). In the pages of these texts you can read about ongoing community building, beautification, and environmental preservation projects and track the many ways the Torontopians "play" in public space. While few of these interventions match the political savvy of the TPSC, they share above all a belief in the socially liberating potential of creative play to transform the city from a place of alienation to a space for meaningful connection.

Torontopia is by no means a rebel movement; on the contrary, it has steadily been winning the accolades of Toronto's creative class, as well as of politicians and performance scholars. Fans celebrate the Torontopians as countercultural heroes for conjoining the spheres of theatre and the everyday and for asking spectators to engage with public space in unexpected ways. But amid the laudatory hype that almost universally greets this movement, questions as urgent as those ignored by the official creative city script have gone unasked. Which citizens, and which practices of urban citizenship, remain outside, even scorned by, the playful frame of civic celebration the Torontopians have laid atop the underused and underappreciated spaces of the city? How does their work implicitly sanction a particular, ultimately quite specific image of Toronto and what it means to be a Torontonian? If, as Jill Dolan argues in *Utopia in Performance* (2005), a utopia is an imagined space always partial and potentially exclusionary, what are the limits of Torontopia's alternative social imaginings, and what are some of the material consequences of the movement's failure to engage seriously those limits both in practice and in print?

Both of us identify as Torontonians, and we want to emphasize that we are both very committed to seeing the Torontopia movement flourish. We are also, however, committed to moving existing critical discourse about site-specific and urban dramaturgy in a more productively political direction—something we feel has been lacking in contemporary performance studies even as it thrives in fields like art history. As Miwon Kwon argues, the shift at the end of the 20th century away from site-specific public art as an autonomous, multifaceted critique of the political, economic, and social tensions bisecting public space and toward that art as a public or community "good" (what Kwon, following Suzanne Lacy, calls "new genre public art") enabled a coercive, if often unintentional, censorship of those individuals and practices that could not easily be integrated into the community's sense of itself and its public goals (Kwon 56–99; see also Lacy). New genre public art, as Kwon notes, has a long history in the making of "socially responsible and ethically sound public art" (82), but it also risks totalizing both the idea of "community" and the equally fraught notion of "the public good" on which it rests. The fractured and diverse Torontopian activities that mark our city's contemporary cultural landscape share the goal of civic disruption in the name of community building; they thus qualify as examples of "new genre public art" and, we believe, require a sustained critique of their methods, outcomes, and potential blindspots in order to move forward productively.

The "Walking Creature" and the "Talking Creature": Fissures in the Torontopian Script

As we have noted, many of the spaces marketed as public and universally accessible by the creative city are actually proprietary: they embed various restrictions to access that are downplayed in their promotion. The Torontopians are helpfully critical of this fantasy of "private-public" space, and they use their guerrilla-style site-specific performance practices to open up the city to the hidden stories and spaces the creative city rhetoric so easily ignores. And yet, much of what the Torontopians have thus far produced under the banner of reinvigorated public spacing is *also* a fantasy. It erects its own (quite significant) barriers to access, built upon unacknowledged assumptions about which spaces and citizens count and which don't—all well disguised by the discourses of fun, play, discovery, and political progressiveness that surround the projects themselves. These barriers are in many ways more meddlesome than those set up by mainstream creative city initiatives because they are not foremost about money, but hinge instead on class and gender issues that the Torontopians too often dismiss as insignificant to their agenda. Some of these issues are spotlighted by dramaturgical problems we've encountered in two different genres of Torontopian performance: the "walking creature" and the "talking creature."

The "walking creature" refers to a host of practices that attempt to perform an alternative urban script by walking the city counterdiscursively. These practices are among Torontopia's most popular: they include the *[murmur]* project, which plants recordings about pedestrian-level urban life around the city to be accessed by passersby on their cellphones; the Toronto Psychogeography Society, which hosts walks all over the city, both downtown and in the suburbs, for small and large numbers; "hidden Toronto" tours; parkour activities; and various forms of urban gaming. [10] The dominant critical frame that the walkers apply to their labor is that of *flâneurie*, tracing a history of performance practices from the surrealists to Walter Benjamin, to the Situationists, [11] to Michel de Certeau. Flâneurie, of course, is not a politically neutral practice (as some urban performance enthusiasts tend to forget); it is based on a host of often-invisible social privileges. In order to be able to walk the city differently, one needs at the very least a tremendous amount of spare time, if not money. Flâneurie is no less a fantasy of civic ownership and control than that theorized by Certeau as he famously gazed down on Manhattan from the top of the World Trade Center (91–92). Performed at street level by an individual who then reports his findings to like-minded friends, family, and readers, flâneurie obscures both the enabling conditions that drive its urban wanderings and the political conflict those wanderings encode. [12]

"Walking in the city" assumes unrestricted physical access, but for whom is walking differently not a simple option because walking in even the most conventional ways is a fraught endeavor? Kwon again:

> [T]he paradigm of nomadic selves and sites may be a glamorization of the trickster ethos that is in fact a reprisal of the ideology of "freedom of choice"—the choice to forget, the choice to reinvent, the choice to fictionalize, the choice to "belong" anywhere, everywhere, and nowhere. This choice, of course, does not belong to everyone equally. (165)

For many citizens, wandering the city can be a tall order indeed: those whose job or family commitments don't permit weeknight, or even weekend, excursions; those who live in the suburbs or exurbs without a car or without convenient links to public transit; those with physical disabilities; the homeless or dispossessed; women. Doreen

Massey, writing about gendered access to public space in Benjamin's Paris, argues: "the notion of a *flâneuse* is impossible precisely because of the one-way-ness and the directionality of the gaze. *Flâneurs* observed others; they were not observed themselves" (234). Scholars of women in urban space have repeatedly noted that the price of a woman's freedom to walk was, at the beginning of the modern period, a quite literal one: women were permitted to appear in public to shop or to sell; otherwise, their wanderings risked crossing a dangerous border, and risked male violence in retribution.[13] Walking in the city might seem substantially easier for women today, but the risks of being watched uncomfortably or even threatened physically remain. In an essay posted on the Toronto Psychogeography Society website and originally published in *Spacing* magazine, Anna Bowness makes this very observation—but only in passing (1). Her small reference to the "violence" and "fear" that might attend a woman attempting the role of flâneur remains the only reference to gendered problems of access—and one of the very few references to problems of access of any kind—that we have found in the published materials on walking creature practices in contemporary Toronto.

Perhaps more pervasive than gendered barriers, however, are the invisible social barriers that shape the walking creature in its most prominent incarnations. The *[murmur]* project appears on the surface to be fully public: all you need to engage with its narratives is a mobile phone and a few extra minutes on the way home from work or school. But in practice *[murmur]* can be an expensive undertaking, as Laura Levin (this article's coauthor) discovered when she took a class of her York University students downtown to experience the project. Many of Levin's students owned phones with significant restrictions on daytime minutes, forcing them to pay an "out of plan" fee each time they dialed one of the numbers on the *[murmur]* route; for some, the bill for calling up *[murmur]* amounted to more than they might pay for a comparable night at the theatre. The *[murmur]* project, the students quickly discovered, assumes an ideal spectator: a downtown dweller with a "city" calling plan to match her hip urban lifestyle.

The challenges Levin's students encountered with *[murmur]* raise one of the core questions we aim at this kind of work: For whom is it made, and who benefits from its psychic remapping of Toronto? More significantly, for a class critique: What is its relationship to those who already occupy the "hidden" or "invisible" city—the homeless and those who work on the streets? *Diplomatic Immunities: The End* (2007), a devised theatre piece by Mammalian Diving Reflex (MDR), offers a glimpse of Torontopia's engagement with truly grassroots street culture. As part of their advance preparation for this show, Mammalian Diving Reflex performers interviewed a sex worker from the Bloor and Lansdowne area in west end Toronto. While the questions they asked her were not markedly different from those they asked other interviewees, the tenor of the interview, and the documentary-style framing of the subject by the camera, all worked to index the sex worker as a metaphor for her (supposedly) rough-and-tumble neighborhood. The problem was not that MDR performers feared this woman: their spoken intention was to explode conventional middle-class fears of street culture. Rather, the problem was more insidious: their questions, and their camera, turned them easily into cultural tourists and the sex worker in their crosshairs into a piece of ethnographic research they could then handily transport home to their audiences. Like other "exotic" objects of the walking gaze, this woman was a prop, not a player, in Mammalian Diving Reflex's self-edifying excursion into the urban outlands.

The walking creature's claim to open access obscures the covert barriers that determine who is "free" to participate; it also hides a troublingly elitist class politics. The flâneur is a detached figure; his concern is primarily for the city as an aesthetic entity, not for those who appear within the landscape (except as intellectual, perhaps erotic, objects of his gaze). He walks to revive the hidden city; the city's bodies are folded into his apparently progressive watching (just as Mammalian Diving Reflex folded the Bloor and Lansdowne sex worker into their progressive politics of fear-no-street-walker). But as the modern flâneur walks away, what traces does he leave behind? One of the characteristics of contemporary Toronto flâneurie is its insistence that anyone can walk the city, anytime, but within this framework lies an unspoken alternative: that *not* to walk the city is to fail to appreciate the city properly, to fail to understand that remaking Toronto as an urban utopia requires a commitment from every citizen to learn to navigate the city better, more progressively. Not to walk the city, in other words, is *to fail the city politically*.[14] On this new map, those who rely on cars for work or food shopping register as social dinosaurs rather than as citizens with vehicle-specific needs (Glouberman 127–28); those who rely on cars as a result of physical or other disabilities do not register at all. By laying these ideological distinctions subtly atop the city's existing grid, the walking creature erects a political barrier between those who care enough to "do" Toronto differently and those who need to be saved by the culture warriors from their mundane, artless lives.

The class division between the creative haves and have-nots is nowhere more in evidence than in Toronto's Kensington Market, the city's most iconic Boho village. In 2004, activists and business owners in the Market established "Pedestrian Sundays," an initiative that turned Kensington into a street fair once a week in an attempt to prove that the city was more fun, and more socially productive, without cars. In his thoughtful analysis of PS Kensington, Misha Glouberman describes how the initiative's supporters promoted themselves as inherently progressive citizen-activists while dismissing the logistical concerns of many of the Market's shopkeepers. Glouberman points out that Pedestrian Sundays offered a business boost for café and bistro owners, but their effects on the grocery businesses that form the Market's backbone were "disastrous," chasing away customers who relied on cars for grocery transport (128). Just as *[murmur]* subtly implies an ideal, hip local listenership, "[t]he utopian vision of the Market imagined a population of healthy young people with the kinds of lives that don't require cars," excluding in the process the area's older, traditional users as less creative, less committed, lesser-class urbanites (128). Far from realizing a fresh and inclusive neighbourhood space, in Kensington Market pedestrianization threatens to mythologize the "community" as "counter-cultural," easily skipping over—and in some cases discounting altogether—the diverse histories and contributions of existing residents both to that community and to the Market's larger public good(s).

It similarly risks homogenizing that community as being opposed to a certain *kind* of capital ("canned foods and toilet paper" [129])—that which area activists deem too commercial or not trendy enough.

In the walking creature narrative, primarily male, primarily young, primarily able-bodied culture workers replace the maligned barons of capital, but the underclass remains largely the same; a handful walk the city differently, but the majority live on, unchanged. The "talking creature," meanwhile, faces related problems: under the banner of intimate interaction, it reproduces existing models of difference. We borrow the term "talking creature" from Darren O'Donnell, founder of performance company Mammalian Diving Reflex; the talking creature forms part of a larger model of urban engagement that O'Donnell calls "social acupuncture." O'Donnell is actively resistant to many of the Torontopian practices that fly in and around the creative city orbit. He argues that too much of this work has either been co-opted by the very machines of capital it set out to jam, or, more troublingly, has fallen prey to an aestheticization that lacks any real sense of politics. "I worry that we prefer fun and whimsy to rigorous social engagement," O'Donnell writes, arguing that we need to raise the "stakes" of our urban performance practices, "to start engaging with unease and discomfort" (23) in order for a more inclusive map of the city to emerge.

The talking creature O'Donnell proposes includes work as diverse as "Free Dance Lessons" (originated by Paige Gratland and Day Milman and offered nightly as part of Luminato 2008), the Toronto Public Space Committee's City Idol competition, and the Trampoline Hall lecture series curated by Sheila Heti. The program's mandate is simple: to reframe human engagement with the city by reframing our engagement with one another, slowly changing our relationships to the strangers who use the city alongside us. In some ways, the talking creature goes a step beyond the implicit voyeurism of the walking creature by insisting upon a different kind of urban inter-subjectivity; it also offers welcome resistance to the intensely heteronormative, fun-for-the-whole-family message of large-scale "Live With Culture" events like Renaissance ROM. During Nuit Blanche on 29 September 2007, for example, O'Donnell hosted *Slow Dance with Teacher*, a performance intervention at the Hart House Great Hall on the University of Toronto campus. *Slow Dance* was designed to foreground, interrogate, and reframe what O'Donnell describes as "that exciting and forbidden desire" that characterizes student-teacher interactions, certainly in North American cultural mythology if not always in practice (Houston 102). While *Slow Dance* purposefully rehearsed many of the self-conscious anxieties that circumscribe young peoples' (and, indeed, older peoples'!) experiences of their bodies in awkward social situations (Houston 105), it also offered an opportunity, at least in theory, to push past those anxieties and take personal risks, as participants danced with strangers in an intimate way (arms around waists, heads on shoulders) often reserved for interactions with loved ones. Performances like *Slow Dance* suggest the promise of O'Donnell's talking creature, its potential to enact, and to probe the limits of, the alternative family structures that operate in the city as essential support networks for those who have been displaced from the communities in which they grew up. In this sense, the talking creature implies inclusivity and perhaps even a sense of security for the very people inadvertently left behind by the walking creature model.

This is the promise. In practice, the talking creature too often relies on false intimacy and a fetishized authenticity to produce interactions between participants that are touted as edgy and risky but on closer inspection turn out to be at best quite conservative. *Diplomatic Immunities: The End*, Mammalian Diving Reflex's attempt to transport some of O'Donnell's street-level talking creature interactions back into the theatre, showcases the problems with which this model struggles. While O'Donnell has admitted that recreating spontaneous interactions on the stage is in some senses impossible (86), he aims in the *Diplomatic Immunities* series[15] to resolve the issue by "creat[ing] an entertainment event that [is] as close as possible to simply hanging out" (87). *Diplomatic Immunities: The End* relies for currency on this sense of "real" people onstage in constant interaction with "real" folks in the audience: although they are onstage and we in our seats, the lights and video cameras focus on us throughout the performance, while the performers, styled as "research artists," zero in on individual audience members in order to ask them questions. Twice during the show the performers invite spectators onstage and direct the remainder of the audience to ask them questions; no frame or limit is placed on what these questions might be.

Two significant dramaturgical problems hamper *Diplomatic Immunities*' claims to urban activism. First, the performers insist that this is *not* theatre, eliding their own representational strategies and the obviously rehearsed quality of their interactions among one another and with us. Not only does the show refuse to admit that performance is a core part of everyday human interaction both onstage and off, but its obsessive resistance to representation, along with its insatiable demand for "authentic" audience responses, creates a coercive atmosphere within the audience proper. As Glouberman (also a "research artist" in the *Diplomatic Immunities* cast) writes, "Part of the force of a utopian idea is that it can make you feel ashamed to disagree" (127). In *Diplomatic Immunities*, every audience member competes with every other, and with the performers, to appear as authentic, natural, and unrehearsed as possible; rather than encouraging our genuine interaction or promoting an interrogation of what is at stake in attempting to generate "genuine" human interaction in the first place, the show demands our virtuosity even as "performance" becomes the 500-pound gorilla in the room.

More troubling, though, is the way in which *Diplomatic Immunities* invests in a temporary and ultimately hollow intimacy, a false sense of collective care that preempts any genuine acts of ethical witness between and among performers and audience members. O'Donnell's goal is to produce a sense of shared community in the vein of Dolan's "utopian performative," but the question of who belongs within and who remains outside the bounds of this imagined community hangs in the air without ever being properly examined. (This is the same problem, of course, that plagued the production's video interview with the Bloor and Lansdowne sex worker.) The night we saw the show together, we found ourselves wondering: Does ethnographically introducing us to the "other" break down boundaries between discrete communities, or does it simply reinforce the surface spectacles of difference that are the basis of so many events hosted by official "multicultural" Toronto? The questions performers asked of audience members during the show were often painfully generic ("What is your greatest fear?"), and when audience members questioned one another the results were either banal ("Why would you lie to your mom?") or prying ("What colour is your underwear?"). The cast reminded audience members that they could refuse to answer any question with which they were uncomfortable (one of the hallmarks of O'Donnell's talking creature practice both onstage and in the street), but in the moment of performance this proved a superficial disclaimer. The peer pressure in the theatre was palpable: we at once craved and feared being called upon. Once on the spot, the refusal to respond seemed to bring with it a risk of greater humiliation. Following Claire Bishop, O'Donnell calls the Q&A model on which *Diplomatic Immunities* is built a "dialogical" intervention (29); he argues that this model encourages the appearance of class, racial, and gender difference within the event frame, demanding that participants take responsibility for the uncomfortable information their questions may bring to light (32). At *Diplomatic Immunities*, however, the friction real difference can produce seemed rarely in evidence, and the performers carefully managed any deviations from their invisible script.

Ironically, this management had the opposite effect of Dolan's utopian performative. The performers failed to generate a sense of shared responsibility for the stories they were caching because they seemed unaware of the kind of commitments that charge the space between actor and spectator in performance, and unaware too of their own power to control and manipulate those commitments. On the night we attended, during the first sequence in which an audience member (a man who, by process of elimination, had been determined to be "the most frightened person in the room") was invited onto the stage, another spectator managed to interrupt—and expose—the show's carefully contrived authenticity. A theatre student (as we soon learned), he raised his hand to ask the man onstage if he wanted company; he then came down to join him. This young student was obviously very eager to be part of the show, for professional as well as personal reasons: while onstage he told the story of auditioning for a popular Toronto director and even performed his impression of the director watching him in a moment that seemed oddly, and fittingly, like he was at the same time auditioning for O'Donnell and his cast by "playing himself" in their show. He then told the audience, "This is me. This is who I am," spinning his improv, with all sincerity, as a form of authentic selfhood—a trick anyone who has been to theatre school will recognize as a resolutely performative gesture designed to secure professional status. Ironically, this sequence energized the room in a way few of the other moments in the show managed to. Audience members, finally faced with the productive tension between performance as artistic labour and spectatorship as social responsibility on which all theatre pivots, were eager to hear, and to laugh at, the young man's story—to see an actor occupy the stage, and occupy it willingly. Rather than taking their cue from this opportunity, however, O'Donnell's performers quickly shut the young man down, anxiously denying the links between their show and the world of rehearsed theatre he had inadvertently established.

In a talkback discussion at the 2008 Canadian Association for Theatre Research conference in Vancouver, Andrew Houston suggested that the problems we identify with *Diplomatic Immunities: The End* can in large part be attributed to the venue in which it was presented: a working theatre. Social acupuncture, he argued, tends to work more effectively on the street—in, for example, *Slow Dance with Teacher* or O'Donnell's trademark *Haircuts by Children* (touring since 2006)—where spectatorial response can rarely be so easily managed. [16] While we concede that *Diplomatic Immunities: The End* provides in many ways a unique and to some extent erroneous snapshot of Mammalian Diving Reflex's larger body of work, we also want to insist on the ways in which it telescopes the ethical minefield in which that work *always* circulates. The problems we encountered in the theatre with *Diplomatic Immunities* are no less prevalent on the street. In fact, in the apparently "authentic" space outside the theatre, many of those problems are amplified. Because MDR always claim that they are not making performance, but are rather facilitating encounters in "real" space, they always implicitly deny the specific codes of ethical conduct that must link creator and spectator, and spectators one with another.

A performance like *Slow Dance with Teacher*, for example, encodes a specific kind of cultural transaction for which Mammalian Diving Reflex cannot fully account. Part of a group of physically intimate experiments with strangers in public space initiated by MDR (O'Donnell 68–72), the event asks participants to assume personal, embodied risk—risk that is implicitly greater for women than for men, and that may be greater yet for members of the LGBTQ community. Even more than *Diplomatic Immunities, Slow Dance with Teacher* thus invites the question central to the critique we undertake here: Who benefits? While the risk embedded in *Slow Dance* is understood to be part of what charges it with political vibrancy for all parties involved (see Houston), because the event never makes clear the level of responsibility the organizers and volunteer "performers" are willing to take for its ad hoc participants, this risk also limits in a very real way who can take part, and how. Given that these urban experiments are explicitly set up to ridicule bourgeois concerns for personal safety, and, in O'Donnell's words, to create "a clear divide between those who cho[o]se to participate and those who [don't]" (71), the experience of "authentic" discomfort can be extremely hard for participants (or for those who choose actively *not* to participate) to articulate. The talking creature's premise is that our culture of fear undermines agency in urban spaces, yet this model trades one form of socially enforced control for another. In the spaces of "play" constructed by MDR, failure to conform to the ideal of pleasurable and "unfettered" social interaction incurs ridicule, discomfort, and ostracization, the very tools that are employed to enforce more recognizable forms of authority in the larger public sphere.

Social acupuncture is an "at your own risk" activity; it implies in its rhetoric and its assumptions about audience agency that taking a risk is a fairly straightforward matter of leaping beyond one's own inhibitions. Risk taking, of course, does not take place in a vacuum and does not always function in counterpoint to an irrational culture of fear (which itself often stifles and inhibits risk-taking); a variety of complex lived experiences influence the meanings of intimate social interaction for any given subject. As a theory of urban innovation, then, MDR's version of the talking creature neatly sidesteps its creators' own social and ethical positionings, as well as their assumptions about the neutrality of public space, even as it frames participation in its signature events as a matter of personal courage.

Toronto's official creative city script relies for its potency on the illusion of widely available public space and the fantasy of a city for all; simultaneously, the city's urban performance activists seek to jam these contrivances and to resituate public space as *genuinely* for all—that is, for "real" people rather than corporate power players. And yet the question of who qualifies as "real" in this *other* newly imagined, phantasmatically inclusive community hovers on the edges of Torontopian playfulness, provoking a series of questions about the costs of material as well as cultural growth, and about who Torontopia, like Toronto's official "Live With Culture" story, leaves behind. So how, then, do we avoid rehearsing more of the same in urban performance activism? Where are the practices that will generate the kinds of disquieting encounters with difference that we need in order to spark real shifts in the way we understand the shape of our city and the creative work of its many inhabitants? As we approach our own ending, we are all too aware that performance criticism embeds its own, unspoken privileges: we have been privileged to pull this work apart, but have not yet taken upon ourselves the challenge, the struggle, the responsibility to create an alternative. In closing, then, we would like to point in just one possible new direction and call for performances that take up the non-celebratory: that focus on what is frustrating, fraught, even at times genuinely dangerous about being in the city; that refuse to glorify the urban playground and take note, instead, of those for whom the city is not simply about play, but is also about work, about safety issues, and about struggle. Kwon calls this work "collective artistic praxis"; it makes a virtue of opposition, builds art from real conflict and collision rather than insisting on a consensus over what constitutes community values, morally, aesthetically, and politically (154). This work does not mean asking superficial questions of one another; rather, it means asking difficult, at times truly upsetting, questions of ourselves and of our work.

(2009)

Notes

[1] Jason McBride and Alana Wilcox's popular 2005 anthology *uTOpia: Towards a New Toronto* offers a wealth of history about and social context for the now-ubiquitous term "Torontopia."

[2] For a broader discussion of performance and creative city politics, see Levin, "TO."

3 Gehry grew up in the Grange neighborhood that surrounds the AGO, a fact that allowed the gallery to trumpet his natural fit for the renovation, never mind the obvious international power of his brand. Gehry was not just swooping in to lend his allure to the city, in other words; the gallery and the media could image him as a hometown boy, literally embodying Toronto's world-class status and de facto creative city power.

4 This seems to be a trend in museum post-renovation reopenings: when MoMA reopened in New York a few years ago, there was much controversy over the new admission price of US$20. The ROM's website (Royal) prominently advertises its "half price" Friday nights (from 4:30 PM to 9:30 PM), but conceals among the fine print the fact that every Wednesday, from 4:30 PM to 5:30 PM, admission to the permanent galleries is (briefly) free.

5 For a critique of the relationship among the art, artists, and communities that comprised the 2008 edition of Nuit Blanche, see Levin and Solga.

6 In September 2008 Luminato committed CAD$50,000 to a new grant program, Incubate, developed by the festival in conjunction with the Toronto Arts Council. The one-year pilot project, valued at a total of CAD$100,000, offers musical arts workers the opportunity to apply for one-time awards of up to CAD$10,000. This is a welcome development, and suggests that future Luminato events may do better at integrating lower-profile local artists.

7 Shortly after arriving in town, Richard Florida inadvertently provided a great example of how central "diversity without difference" is to his "creative city" script. Followed by *The Globe and Mail* reporter Peter Scowen to the city's Kensington Market neighbourhood, a zone in which older immigrants, young professionals, students, artists, potheads, and environmental activists—not to mention tourists—jostle cheek-by-jowl, Florida remarked on the unique flavor of a place located at "the intersection of immigrant and hippie." Asked to comment on the challenge of preserving such a mixed-use enclave, Florida argued that "the uses can change, the character of a storefront can change, Italians can replace Jews, Jews can replace Indians, a hippie can replace a Chinese entrepreneur, an upscale clothing shop can replace that kind of guitar shop, [but] the tragedy is when the neighbourhood is cleared—when they come in with the federal bulldozers and just say, 'We're going to knock it down and put in high-rise condominium towers'" (Scowen M3). Florida's remarks betrayed not only his ignorance of the place in which he found himself, but also his failure to appreciate the serious matter ethnic and class differences make behind the pleasurable façade of diversity in the creative city. Not only are parts of Kensington Market already gentrified, in some cases at the expense of longtime shop owners, but his conflation of cultures (Italian/Indian/Chinese/Jew) and classes (upscale clothing shop/downmarket guitar store) spoke to his failure to appreciate the local tensions that shape the Market today.

8 Luminato's mission statement offers a similarly banal take on "diversity": "Toronto is one of the most multicultural cities in the world. Luminato embraces and cele-

brates the cultural diversity of the city, and recognizes that creativity flourishes when cultures join together in a spirit of tolerance and respect" (Luminato).

⁹ Toronto has an urban play movement that is diverse and ever changing; it encompasses everything from local walking groups, lecture series, and community gardening organizations to parkouristes, urban explorers (such as the late cult hero Ninjalicious [www.infiltration.org]), and large-scale social events hosted by well-established play groups. We can cite here only some of its most visible representatives. In addition to the Toronto Public Space Committee and the editorial and writing staff of *Spacing* magazine, see the work of Shawn Micallef, a *Spacing* editor, author of its regular "Toronto Flâneur" column, head of the Toronto Psychogeography Society (www.psychogeography.ca/blog), and founding creator of the *[murmur]* public performance project, now in seven cities (http://murmur-toronto.ca). Also worthy of note: the Trampoline Hall lecture series (www.trampolinehall.net), a favorite among the city's young culturati, and Newmindspace (www.newmindspace.com), defined as "interactive public art, creative cultural interventions and urban bliss dissemination" by founders Lori Kufner and Kevin Bracken.

¹⁰ Parkour, which comes from the French word *parcours* meaning a route or journey, is a form of creative running which treats the urban terrain as playground or obstacle course. *Traceurs*, those who practice parkour, respond to city spaces through nimble and gymnastic movements—for example, vaulting urban structures, leaping from building to building, and swinging on bars or walls. For an in-depth discussion of parkour as performance, see Ortuzar.

¹¹ The Situationists were a group of French intellectuals in the 1960s and 70s, who believed that the key to resisting the colonization of urban space by "the spectacle" (the commoditization of human relations), was to experiment with the spatial conventions of everyday life. One form of urban resistance that they explored—and which has influenced a number of Toronto artists—was "psychogeography," defined by Situationist Guy Debord as "study of the precise laws and specific effects of the geographical environment, consciously organized or not, on the emotions and behavior of individuals" ("Introduction"). Psychogeography included what Debord called a "dérive" or "drift," where individuals wander aimlessly in the city, surrendering to "the attractions of the terrain and the encounters they find there" ("Theory" 22). The point of these drifts was to uncover the capitalist logics and contradictions that govern urban space and the possibility of moving through the city in a way that interrupts capitalist systems.

¹² In "Walking in the City," Michel de Certeau contrasts two views of urban space. The first is the city from above, the city seen from the 110th floor of the World Trade Center, which shows an impersonal landscape of skyscrapers—in his words, a "stage of concrete, steel and glass" (91). For Certeau, this view represents an omniscient, distanced, and totalizing gaze, a perspective adopted "by the space planner urbanist, city planner or cartographer" (93). The second view is the city from below, a city experienced by individuals through their daily movements through it and practices

within it. Reminiscent of other celebrations of walking by the Situationists and Torontopians, Certeau celebrates walking within this second city as a utopian, poetic practice: "they are walkers, Wandersmänner, whose bodies follow the thicks and thins of an urban 'text' they write without being able to read it. These practitioners make use of spaces that cannot be seen; their knowledge of them is as blind as that of lovers in each other's arms" (93).

[13] In addition to Massey, see Friedberg and Rabinovitz.

[14] For an excellent example of overtly polemical writing about the relationship between political progressiveness and walking the city, see Wrights & Sites.

[15] Mammalian Diving Reflex has taken its "research" work for *Diplomatic Immunities*—part of its larger project of "social acupuncture"—around the world, and in late 2007 produced a show in Lahore called *Diplomatic Immunities: The Scars of Pakistan. Diplomatic Immunities: The End* remains the company's flagship production of this work.

[16] *Haircuts by Children*, for example, is simply what the title says: an opportunity for adults to have their hair cut, in a supervised environment, by children with only minimal prior training.

Works Cited

Benjamin, Walter. "On Some Motifs in Baudelaire." *Illuminations.* Ed. Hannah Arendt. New York: Schocken, 1968. 155–200.

Bishop, Claire. "Antagonism and Relational Aesthetics." *October* 110 (2004): 51–79.

Bowness, Anna. "Walking and literature make sense together." 20 June 2007. www.psychogeography.ca/pdf/anna.pdf.

Bradshaw, James. "More commissions, greater national presence at Luminato." *The Globe and Mail* 17 February 2009: R2.

Certeau, Michel de. "Walking in the City." *The Practice of Everyday Life.* Trans. Steven Rendall. Berkeley: U of California P, 1984. 91–110.

City of Toronto. *The Creative City: A Workprint.* 2001. Official Website of the City of Toronto. Toronto Culture Division. 18 September 2008. www.toronto.ca/culture/brochures/ brochure_culture_workprint.pdf.

Debord, Guy. "Introduction to a Critique of Urban Geography." *Critical Geographies: A Collection of Readings.* Ed. Harald Bauder and Salvatore Engel-Di Mauro. Kelowna, BC: Praxis (e)Press, 2008. 23–32.

————. "Theory of the Dérive." *Theory of the Dérive and Other Situationist Writings on the City.* Ed. Libero Andreotti and Xavier Costa. Barcelona: Museu d'Art Contemporani de Barcelona, 1996. 22–27.

Dolan, Jill. *Utopia in Performance: Finding Hope at the Theater.* Ann Arbor: U of Michigan P, 2005.

Florida, Richard. *The Rise of the Creative Class: And How It's Transforming Work, Leisure, and Everyday Life.* New York: Basic Books, 2002.

Friedberg, Anne. *Window Shopping: Cinema and the Postmodern.* Berkeley: U of California P, 1993.

Glouberman, Misha. "No Place Like Kensington." *uTOpia: Towards a New Toronto.* Ed. Jason McBride and Alana Wilcox. Toronto: Coach House, 2005. 126–30.

Goffman, Erving. *The Presentation of Self in Everyday Life.* New York: Doubleday/Anchor, 1959.

Houston, Andrew. "*Slow Dance with Teacher:* Innocence After Experience." *Canadian Theatre Review* 133 (2008): 102–06.

Knowles, Ric. "Building Utopia." ATHE Annual Conference. New Orleans. 28 July 2007. Respondent.

Kwon, Miwon. *One Place After Another: Site-Specific Art and Locational Identity.* Cambridge: MIT P, 2004.

Lacy, Suzanne, ed. *Mapping the Terrain: New Genre Public Art.* Seattle: Bay P, 1995.

Levin, Laura. "TO Live With Culture: Torontopia and the Urban Creativity Script." *Space and the Geographies of Theatre.* Ed. Michael McKinnie. Toronto: Playwrights Canada, 2007. 201–17.

Levin, Laura and Kim Solga. "Zombies in Condoland." *Canadian Theatre Review* 138 (2009): 48–52.

Libeskind, Daniel. "Concept Sketch of the ROM." n.d. Royal Ontario Museum. 20 June 2007. www.rom.on.ca/crystal/napkin.php?view=3.

Luminato. "About Luminato." Luminato Website. 2008. 3 April 2009. www.luminato.com/festival/eng/mainabout.php.

Makeham, Paul. "Performing the City." *Theatre Research International* 30.2 (2005): 150–60.

Mammalian Diving Reflex. *Diplomatic Immunities: The End.* Conceived and dir. Darren O'Donnell. Performed by Mammalian Diving Reflex at Buddies in Bad Times Theatre, Toronto, 24 February 2007.

Massey, Doreen. *Space, Place, and Gender.* Minneapolis: U of Minnesota P, 1994.

McBride, Jason and Alana Wilcox, eds. *uTOpia: Towards a New Toronto*. Toronto: Coach House, 2005.

O'Donnell, Darren. *Social Acupuncture: A Guide to Suicide, Performance, and Utopia*. Toronto: Coach House, 2006.

Ortuzar, Jimena. "Parkour or l'art du déplacement: A Kinetic Urban Utopia." *TDR: The Drama Review* 53.3 (2009): 54–66.

Peck, Jamie. "Struggling with the Creative Class." *International Journal of Urban and Regional Research* 29.4 (2005): 740–70.

Rabinovitz, Lauren. *For the Love of Pleasure: Women, Movies, and Culture in Turn-of-the-Century Chicago*. New Brunswick: Rutgers UP, 1998.

Royal Ontario Museum. Royal Ontario Museum. www.rom.on.ca. 3 April 2009.

Scowen, Peter. "At the Intersection of Immigrant and Hippie." *The Globe and Mail* 10 November 2007: M3.

Taylor, Kate. "From Zero to $22.5-million in 2 Years." *The Globe and Mail* 24 May 2008: R12.

Toronto Public Space Committee. n.d. 20 June 2007. www.publicspace.ca.

Tourism Toronto. "Toronto 101: Why Toronto?" 2006. 20 June 2007. www.toronto-tourism.com/Visitor/Toronto101/WhyToronto.htm.

Urban Theatre Projects. *Back Home*. Dir. Alicia Talbot. Prod. Urban Theatre Projects (Sydney, Australia), Harbourfront New World Stage, and the Luminato Festival. Centre for Addiction and Mental Health, Toronto, 9 June 2007.

Wilcox, Alana, Christina Palassio, and Jonny Dovercourt, eds. *GreenTOpia: Towards a Sustainable Toronto*. Toronto: Coach House, 2007.

Wrights & Sites. "A Manifesto for a New Walking Culture: 'Dealing with the City.'" *Performance Research* 11.2 (2006): 115–22.

Young, Harvey. "Fresh Print Series 3: Space." Post-panel discussion. ATHE Annual Conference. New Orleans. 29 July 2007.

Decolonizing the *Gathering Place*: *Chocolate Woman* Dreams a *Gathering House* in Toronto

by Jill Carter

> Aboriginal literature and creative arts need to be expanded and infused with their unique Indigenous vision. [...] We must not mistake enthusiastic reception by the white middle-class as a measure of literary or artistic success of Aboriginal artists. Popularity may mean the Aboriginal work harmonizes with the archaic racial stereotypes of Eurocentric society. If it does not, then most white readers are likely to disbelieve and discredit the creative work. (Adams 115)

The late Anishinaabe activist and educator Rodney Bobiwash likens the Greater Toronto Area (GTA), before the arrival of the Europeans, to the bustling coastal cities of the ancient Mediterranean (7). A key site of "trade and commerce," cultural exchange and ceremonial praxis, the GTA was a flourishing centre of Indigenous activity and syncretism thousands of years before the Old World stumbled into the "New" (Bobiwash 7).

Now, as then, the GTA continues to be a catch-basin into which many bloodlines flow. And it remains, for various reasons, the Gathering Place for Indigenous Peoples from across the globe. For citizens of the Algonquian and Iroquoian nations—the nations who had begun stewarding this area 2,500 years before contact (Bobiwash 8)—these reasons are complex and varied. Historically, Aboriginal people who relocated from untenable reserve lands to cities, who fought for Canada in two world wars, or who dared to pursue higher education were forced, by the Canadian government, to give up their treaty rights (Obonsawin and Howard-Bobiwash 28; Sanderson 3). Despite Bill C-31, many of their descendants continue on without either Status under the Indian Act or the rights, privileges, and basic respect accorded to other municipal citizens. Similarly, adoptees and survivors of the residential schools (though they may have retained Status) were often unable to return to their home communities. For many of these people, Toronto the Gathering Place was the place of their exile; for others, Toronto was a place of escape in which they learned to maneuver the margins in shadowy silence.

Throughout the latter part of the twentieth century, Aboriginal people across Canada pushed back against the forces that had silenced them and began to seize the platforms from which to speak for themselves in every realm of community and national life. In 1951, the First Nations pursued and won the right to openly fulfill ancient metaphysical responsibilities in ceremonial praxis, and the Indian Act was amended to lift a ban that had been in effect for almost a century. Nine years later, Aboriginal people won the right to exercise their political voice in the Canadian electoral process without divesting themselves of their treaty rights. Then, in 1967, Chief Dan George took the stage in the Vancouver premiere of Ukrainian-Canadian playwright George Ryga's *The Ecstasy of Rita Joe*, which is commonly recognized as *the* vehicle that gave Aboriginal people our first opportunity to voice our concerns to the Canadian public on the national stage. Almost one generation later, in 1985, Cree concert musician and playwright Tomson Highway was Artistic Director of Native Earth Performing Arts (NEPA) in Toronto. When his *The Rez Sisters* exploded onto the Toronto stage, audiences were energized, and critics were effusive. So powerful was this piece—so profound was its *affect* on both Native and non-Native audiences—that Toronto, this hub of Canadian theatre, claimed for itself the (unofficial) title of Canada's *Native* theatre capital. The renaissance was well underway. And NEPA stood at its centre—a contemporary Gathering House in the belly of the beast.

Today, Toronto's NEPA is the eldest of five Aboriginal theatre companies in Canada and, of these, generally presumed to possess the most robust infrastructure (Crean 32). Despite a dearth of resources (including the absence of a dedicated space), it has facilitated the development of two generations of Aboriginal playwrights and shaped the contemporary audiences' appreciation for early Native playwrights by remounting canonical works of particular aesthetic or historic import. More recently, under the direction of Algonquian playwright/director Yvette Nolan, NEPA has engineered intricate cultural bridges with its production of Spy Dénommé-Welch and Catherine Magowan's *Giiwedin*, the latest in a handful of operas composed by First Nations artists, and with *Death of a Chief*, Native Earth's interrogation of Band politics through its adaptation of Shakespeare's *Julius Caesar*.

Together, NEPA and Toronto's Centre for Indigenous Theatre, which has been training First Nations theatre practitioners since 1972, have drawn Aboriginal artists from every nation to this ancient Gathering Place. Here, with each new production in borrowed space, they transform commercial sites of spectacle into contemporary Gathering Houses in which histories may be remembered and recounted, stories and cultural praxis may be exchanged, languages may be revived and transmitted, and dislocated exiles might be drawn in from the margins to locate themselves with Indigenous communities.

I am one of these exiles, born in the margins of the Gathering Place. A woman of mixed heritage—Anishinaabe and Ashkenazi—I am a child of exiles, escapees, and survivors. And like those who came before me, I am a survivor. I am a survivor of a terrible story—one that orphaned my grandmother, broke my grandfather, and tore the family they created apart. Stories write pogroms. Stories build residential schools. Stories spirit children away from their mothers. Stories kill or they heal. I learned a story that told me I was not even human. In my secret heart, I believed it. Nonetheless, I went looking for a new story.

I came to the theatre to discover myself as a "human being." I looked to the theatre to teach me my life's worth and to teach me to articulate my humanity. I looked to the theatre to save me from my despair and to try, through this medium, to transfigure a salvaged wreck into a life well lived. What is theatre? What do we want from it—as audiences or as artists? How has this medium served contemporary Native peoples? How *could* it serve us?

Since 1967, when Ryga's *Ecstasy* inspired questions around what story was being told and who was telling it, Native theatre artists have been posing and responding to ever-evolving questions around the stories we tell in the contemporary Gathering House. In the late 1980s, Tomson Highway's *Dry Lips Oughta Move to Kapuskasing* elicited questions and contention around what sort of stories we *ought* to tell (Crean 30). And in this generation, it seems that the crucial question being asked by Aboriginal theatre practitioners in the Gathering Place (and beyond) is this: now that Aboriginal people have taken back our right to speak, is anybody actually listening (Nolan, qtd. in Dempsey 25)?

Certainly, Yvette Nolan is not the only Aboriginal artist who is preoccupied by this question; the very fact that it is being posed at all attests to the sophistication and, I would add, *commercialization* of Aboriginal theatre in Toronto and other major cities across Canada. Our artists are producing stunning works, and the companies that invest so much to nurture their development and then to bring them to the public, quite naturally, want to attract that public. Indeed, as Okanagan writer Jeanette Armstrong observes, "It's like a split in the road. The decision to try to survive, to get to present the work and find an audience leads to other decisions and compromises" (qtd. in Crean 31).

But in our scramble to be competitive—to convince a diverse population of urban theatregoers to invest their limited time and funds in our productions instead of our competitors'—are Aboriginal theatre artists being diverted from equally pressing questions? Now that Native theatre practitioners have settled the issue of who speaks and what stories need to be told, many are still faced with a dilemma: to *whom* are they telling these stories—particularly in megacities like the GTA where there are greater concentrations of non-Native people (and hence, potential theatre patrons) than Aboriginal people? *How* will they communicate their central messages? What forms will they employ to contain the stories they tell?

Throughout his 2003 Massey Lectures, Cherokee scholar and novelist Thomas King illustrates the extent to which the content of the stories we tell contains and *directs* the lives of those who tell Story and of those about whom Story is told: "The truth, about stories," King declares, "is that that's all we are" (2). But the power of Story, as King goes on to demonstrate, does not rest upon content alone. What we tell is important, to be sure. But *how* we tell is crucial to the integrity of Story, because form profoundly affects content for good or ill. Via a rigorous comparison between the Judeo-Christian account of Creation and (his own adaptation of) the Haudenosaunee origin story, King ultimately proves that while "the truth about stories is that that's all we are," the truth about form is that that's all the story is. At the end of the day, human attitudes, behaviours, and cosmo-visions are ultimately shaped by narrative form—the *how* of the telling (King 1–29).

To *whom* do Aboriginal theatre practitioners wish to relate Story? Is our first challenge, as Susan Crean articulates it, the challenge of "relating an aboriginal worldview to an outside (and largely non-aboriginal) audience" (31)? If this becomes the primary object in the crafting of Native theatre, is there a danger that we might increasingly begin to adopt narrative forms and dramaturgical structures that speak most potently to an audience of others and so distort our own content in the process?

Several years ago, I was working with a young Mohawk student (whom I will call "Jack") at the University of Toronto. Jack had a story he wanted to tell; he had begun to visit an elder in his community—a residential school survivor, a decorated war veteran, a vital knowledge holder, a man battling Alzheimer's and struggling to share his story before it was lost forever. Jack wanted to tell the story of his relationship with this afflicted elder; he wanted to faithfully record and transmit the story this man was trying to tell. He wanted to communicate the powerful and oft-times surreal moments when time, space, and identity are conflated—those moments when a simple cup of tea would carry actor and witness to a war zone half a world and half a century away. To this end, he had entered a program for young Native playwrights through which he would receive mentorship from a professionally recognized director/dramaturg and a staged reading of his fledgling script. He had been assigned his mentor—an individual who enjoys considerable commercial success as both a playwright and performer; they met and worked together. And then Jack stopped writing his story.

Shortly after he had left that program, he asked me if I would work with him. When I asked him why he had stopped writing in the first place, he showed me the formula his mentor had given him to follow—a formula for a "well-made play": three acts. Two characters with conflicting wants. Exposition. Climax. Denouement. Once Jack began to communicate his story to me and articulate the reasons he had for telling it; once he began to embody moments of his encounters with the elder and key moments in the elder's story, it became apparent that forcing *this* story into the framework his mentor had prescribed would have killed it. When I presented him with other possibilities—alternate containers through which the story could be performed—Jack became more hopeful and decided to continue his oral history project.

Recently, Monique Mojica was told by a key figure in the Native theatre community that her current project under development, *Chocolate Woman Dreams the Milky Way*, is *not* theatre. Such incidents call to mind some troubling questions: Have we, in the urban Aboriginal theatre community, come to believe a deadly story that has been written about us? For years, the experts have been telling us that our nations have no aesthetic principles or narrative frameworks that are applicable to crafting theatre; even today, critics are still disseminating the message that Aboriginal artists must borrow, adapt, and bend themselves to "fit" into "alien" Western forms to take the stage

(Crean 31). Have those who control arts funding and so determine who can take the stage imposed their ideas of what makes good theatre (or what counts as theatre, at all) upon our artists who live and work in the city? Certainly, our artists should exercise their freedom to work within whatever form they believe will best serve the story they are telling. NEPA's *Death of a Chief* (2008), which filters Band politics through a Shakespearean lens and the colonizer's republic through an Aboriginal lens, and its 2010 premiere of the opera *Giiwedin*, a lush pageant of linguistic and aesthetic syncretism, attest to the positive effects of developing cross-cultural forms.

However, space must be carved for both: Aboriginal artists should not be silenced or paralyzed by any notion that Western theatrical principles provide the *only* paradigms through which their stories can be realized. We have alternatives. Our ancestors in every nation have left for us the aesthetic and processual models that are, by their very design, structural frameworks for the "communitist" projects Jace Weaver calls upon to heal "the grief and sense of exile felt by Native communities and the pained individuals in them" (43).

Indeed, companies like Kaha:wi Dance Theatre, Earth in Motion, and De-ba-jeh-mu-jig are manifesting such models in their works. These companies create relevant, contemporary works that look back even as they move their artists forward, and that are informed by the aesthetic principles and cosmologies of the Nations from which their founders emerge. But while these companies often visit the Gathering Place with their productions, they are based in and work from their communities. Indeed, it is from within strong communities, where artists are steeped in their language and culture, that they are able to access and to work from "their cultural source[s], through indigenous 'creative structures'" (Favel Starr 70).

Native artists living and working in Toronto, by contrast, seem always to be in the process of "nation-building," as it were. As Yvette Nolan explains, Native theatre in Toronto emerges out of the synthesis of myriad cultural sources and expresses itself through hybrid creative structures:

> [W]henever we do anything, we have to start with some kind of ceremony. So we're always inventing ceremonies. Pan-Indian ceremonies, right? When we have an elder, it's generally not an elder from this neck of the woods; it's whoever's elder is around. And certainly, as we, as Native people, try to rebuild a bridge between ourselves and our histories, pasts, cultures, we're reclaiming stuff that is not ours. (qtd. in Knowles 57)

The works, then, that emerge from these structures are perforce informed (in form as well as content) by the conditions of colonization (Nolan, qtd. in Dempsey 25) – conditions beyond which the work cannot transport us and conditions beyond which we, the artists in the Gathering Place, cannot carry the work.

But what about the "stuff" that *is* ours—stuff that has, at great personal cost, been preserved by those who came before us, stuff like language that may be one generation from extinction? If, as Yvette Nolan asserts in reference to the stories we perform for Toronto audiences, "There is no such thing as *post*-colonization at this point" (qtd. in Dempsey 25, emphasis added), ought we not, then, to more strenuously consider the extent to which urban Aboriginal theatre can contribute to the greater project of *de*-colonization? Such projects require spaces in which to unfold. Their artists require "rooms of their own" within the larger Gathering House. In such rooms they might develop methodologies through which to craft stories that will move them and their audiences beyond the grief and enervation of exile into expectant, vigorous communitism.

"What Do I Have That Isn't Broken?": Performance as Intervention

Monique Mojica's *Chocolate Woman Dreams the Milky Way* is just such a communitist project. Emerging from a series of collaborative investigations undertaken by the *Chocolate Woman* Collective, it presents an intricate weave of elemental feminine forces belonging to Haudenosaunee, Powhatan, and Kuna cosmologies in heated interaction with the personal history of a woman who is genetically linked to and personally directed by these cosmologies. Time, space, identity, and cosmology coalesce as Sky Woman, *Olowaili* (the Morning Star for whom Mojica was named), the *Nis Bundor* (Daughters from the Stars), and Mojica plummet towards new worlds to begin the tasks of creation and recreation—recuperating what was seemingly lost, dis-covering what has always been present. Here, the eternal feminine agents in the creation of Haudenosaunee, Powhatan, and Kuna worlds are bound in the time and place of the play's unfolding with a Kuna-Rappahannock mortal of the twenty-first century through the *kwage* (core) of an essential action undertaken by all: the action of free-fall, a descent into hitherto unknown worlds where life begins anew. *Chocolate Woman Dreams the Milky Way* is, in Mojica's words, "performance as intervention" (Personal). And in its making and unfolding, it facilitates the return of the Indigenous human to self.

The first phase of the project began at Equity Showcase in November 2007 with Mojica (Kuna-Rappahannock, Writer/Performer), Floyd Favel (Cree, Director), Oswaldo DeLeón Kantule (Kuna, Cultural Advisor/Designer) and Erika Iserhoff (Cree, Co-Designer).[1] The project began in a time of personal crisis for Mojica. And it started with two urgent questions: "How do I save my own life? What do I have that isn't broken" (Phase One)? Since 2007, *Chocolate Woman* has evolved into a complex weave within which eight characters speak through two performers: Monique Mojica and Gloria Miguel (Mojica's mother and co-founder of Spiderwoman Theater, North America's longest-running Native theatre company and longest-running feminist theatre collective). The *Chocolate Woman* Collective has grown into a company of twelve artists who are now preparing themselves for *Chocolate Woman*'s last developmental phase, which will immediately precede its Toronto premiere in spring 2011.

Chocolate Woman is a crucial project at this time and in this place: Mojica has, despite many obstacles, successfully carved out space in which to erect a Kuna Gathering House within the larger "Gathering House" that houses Aboriginal theatre practitioners in Toronto. Indeed, this may prove to be one of the most important projects to emerge from the Toronto theatre scene in the early twenty-first century, as it is a key chapter in the larger project of decolonization. Throughout *Chocolate Woman's* gestation, its artists have been driven by a foundational question: "what happens when Native artists privilege nation-specific performance principles, aesthetic structures and Indigenous Knowledge (IK) and how does this transform contemporary performance" (Mojica, Personal)? As its artists have investigated this question in their creative labours, the *Chocolate Woman* Collective has established a solid framework of decolonizing methodologies, which can be realized in a repeatable series of practical steps that ultimately could be adopted and adapted by Indigenous artists from myriad nations in the creation of their own nation-specific works.

The *Chocolate Woman* Collective has developed a process whereby fragments of historical memory may be recovered, reconstituted, and re-inscribed as a holistic entity, and it is communicated through the relationship between multiple "archives" expressing themselves in multiple dimensions.[2] Rooted in the stories contained by the *mola* (textile art) of the Kuna people and in the narrative framework of the pictographic writings that notate Kuna medicine chants, *Chocolate Woman* explores the relationship between the iconic (pictographic) image in two dimensions and the three dimensional performative body, which embodies that image, moving it through time and space. Ultimately, this theatrical project, in its creation and in its performed realization, puts two decades of rigorous research into Native Performance Culture (NpC) to the test.

Native Performance Culture (NpC) is a term that has been coined by Floyd Favel[3] to represent the research that he has undertaken (with Mojica, Spiderwoman Theater, and Indigenous theatre practitioners from around the world) into the development of nation-specific techniques for the crafting of contemporary Native theatre that will "preserve the heart of our ceremonial life, by never revealing or showing it, yet be revitalized and transformed by it" (Favel Starr 71). Through rigorous examination of traditional dance, song, textile, oratory, and ceremony in a nation-specific context, they have been able "to identify performance principles and use these principles as starting points for contemporary work" (Mojica, Personal). Indeed, it is out of these investigations and principles that the construction of performance, set design, and script dramaturgy find their "structural base" (Mojica, Personal).

I characterize the first developmental stage of *Chocolate Woman* as an initiation into "apprenticeship" for the project leader. To connect herself with what has not been broken or lost and to reconnect with her community of origin (a community she had not yet visited), Mojica and the rest of the collective became the students of our cultural advisor and designer, contemporary Kuna artist Oswaldo DeLeón Kantule.[4]

Kantule's set—stunning in its simplicity—facilitated Mojica's exploration of the relationship between the living body and the inscribed image, allowing her, as Favel says, to "test the application of the pictographic method as a basis for telling stories" (Phase One). Hearkening back to the mola designs and pictographs with which he has grown up, Kantule painted three—eventually a fourth was added—glorious silks (each measuring fifteen feet in length) to represent *Muu Bilii* (Mother Ocean), *Puna Siagua* (Chocolate Woman) and *Nis Bundor* (the Daughters from the Stars). Like the single hammock that cradled Mojica's body and allowed her to plummet safely through worlds or to hover in prayerful reflection between earth and sky, these silks functioned as characters/co-performers in the piece rather than as furnishings or decoration. Before the silks came to be, Kantule recounted creation stories, putting Kuna words into our mouths, and interpreting pictographs that document traditional healing chants. Later, as Mojica began to retell these stories, weaving personal and familial history into the larger Kuna mythos, Kantule began (in the rehearsal studio as she spoke) to paint her "co-performers," thickening the layers of relationship and reciprocity. Just as Mojica's coming-to-be traces itself back to the elemental female agents of Kuna creation, so the silken goddesses on *Chocolate Woman*'s stage have been shaped, formed and adorned (in part) on the breath of this mortal descendant. Ancestor and descendant, spirit and flesh, eternal and mortal—they have spoken (and they speak) each other into being.

Traditionally in Kuna Yala, a ritual apprentice first learns the healing chants from the ritual specialist, not the text. Only after the apprentice has learned the chant *by rote*, reproducing his teacher's every gesture and tonal shift, will he be permitted to see the pictographic notation—a mnemonic device—and to painstakingly copy each character that belongs to the medicine chant he has been learning. Finally, the apprentice is ready to analyze and interpret the original characters (inscribed by an ancestral ritual specialist) and to ask questions around specific points or deeper meanings belonging to a single pictograph, a pictographic grouping, or the text entire (Severi 252). Working this way with Kantule, Mojica first explored the weave of Kuna creation to locate herself therein—the names she has been given, the Kuna words and vocal stylings she heard around the kitchen table as a child, and the intersection of events and lessons of her own life with those belonging to the cosmic female agents of Kuna creation and natural law. Then, to her astonishment (and to the astonishment of all), she found that her own body was "speaking" in pictographs. And when Favel instructed her to script the stories she was retelling and newly creating, she found herself having to create pictographs to properly capture all levels of the work (Carter, "*Chocolate*" 173). Out of this phase these discoveries and principles have emerged:

> 1. A vibrant and evolving relationship exists between the living body and its inscription—an *organic intertextuality*—the dis-covery and manifestation of which is facilitated by disciplined and rigorous exercise of traditional pedagogical models and aesthetic principle;

> 2. Application of these traditional models and principles through a series of rigorous exercises effects an *intervention* upon the contemporary Indigenous body. The work that emerges from such exercises might be deemed a "healing chant," for in its creation, the creatrix has begun the process of dislodging the *dis-ease* of colonization from her body, and in its transmission, this work produces effects like healing on its witnesses;

3. There are four aesthetic principles (identified and articulated by Kantule) that govern traditional aesthetic expression in Kuna Yala. These principles also govern the creation of *Chocolate Woman*. They are:

  a. Duality & Repetition: Kuna aesthetic and cultural praxis are based upon the reflection and celebration of the duality of Baba-Nana (the Mother-Father);

  b. Abstraction: abstract geometric designs protect the integrity of traditional designs and pictographs;

  c. Metaphor: as Kuna tradition has it, the spirits with and about whom mortals communicate make high demands on orators, as does the human community that witnesses these verbal gymnastics. Speech acts that unfold in the Gathering House are characterized by lush conceits; these challenge listeners to decode their meaning and dis-cover hidden connections, and they provide delight as these conceits are suspended and expanded. As well, deeper meanings (not meant for all) are encoded in the verdant metaphors, the true meaning of which can only be grasped by the specialist;

  d. Multidimensionality: reflects the eight levels of Kuna reality. As Kuna cosmology has it, there are eight layers of reality—four above and four below the finite, material realm we occupy.

4. Finally, Mojica, who had already begun to work with *Duleguya* (Kuna language) found that in order to advance in this work, she had to increase her proficiency in the language.

Between the first and second studio investigations, Mojica and Kantule continued their research in Kantule's London, Ontario studio by immersing themselves in Kuna oral tradition and its expression through the mola and the pictographic notations, and by interrogating the relationship of these to Kantule's contemporary work. Next, Mojica, Kantule, and Erika Iserhoff travelled to Kuna Yala where Mojica connected with her grandfather's community and family on the island of Nargana, met contemporary Kuna artists from many communities, visited participated in Gathering House Ceremonies and obtained permission from the Gathering House Chiefs to apply traditional aesthetic processes to and include Kuna creation stories in this project. Several months later, Mojica returned to Kuna Yala alone. At this time, she began to work in earnest with several of the Kuna artists she had met on her first trip. Some of these artists have joined the *Chocolate Woman* Collective, and in spring 2011, they will journey to Toronto for *Chocolate Woman's* fourth and final developmental phase and premiere.

The second developmental phase of *Chocolate Woman Dreams the Milky Way* took place in Toronto, and a public presentation was staged at the anitafrika Studio on 28 March 2009. Now, the performative mola began to thicken. Ric Knowles joined the company as dramaturg. Gloria Miguel also joined the company to embody the ancient grandmothers of earth (*Napguana* and *Ibe Don*), Water (*Muu Bilii*) and Sky (Mother Night). *Chocolate Woman*'s spare but vibrant "landscape" began to expand and thicken as the set took on layers or *Galus* (realms of spirit) and as specific layers of the process were identified and articulated. Floyd Favel, for instance, initiated the second developmental phase by articulating a "work plan" that had organically asserted itself during the first developmental phase:

(i)   The performer generates the story out of improvisation;
(ii) the performer then abstracts the story, basing her abstraction on Kuna verb motifs in the literary text;
(iii) she becomes a living pictograph or a "living mola moving"; she then notates the internal action of her work, which presents itself as an "action pictograph"; this resembles a dance notation;
(iv) ultimately, every performer will have her own internal score, documented in pictographs from which to work. (Phase Two)

It was in this stage and out of this processual framework that Knowles and Mojica developed a complex dramaturgical layer, which unfolds in eight stages. They developed a dramaturgy through which the language of *Chocolate Woman*'s interwoven stories will be distilled to isolate and intensify their core efficacy and further abstracted to protect the ceremonial traditions out of which they emerge. Their model thus far unfolds in this way:

1. The performer generates her text in English.
2. She notates it as a pictographic text (on the stage and on the page).
3. She translates the text to Spanish (as her Kuna advisor is most proficient in Spanish and Kuna, while she is most proficient in English and Spanish).
4. Her advisor (Kantule) translates the Spanish text to Kuna (specifically, into the language of ceremonial oration).
5. Kantule then renders a literal translation of the Kuna text he has generated back into Spanish.
6. The performer (Mojica) renders a literal translation of this Spanish text back into English.
7. Mojica then embodies the new "script."
8. From this, a new pictographic score may be generated. (Phase Two)

Through this process, then, a "purple mola" becomes a "mola stained the colour of purple corn." Similarly, a specific place name, the use of which might identify certain individuals and expose them to danger, becomes "the foot of the hills with the golden heart"; and the "White House" becomes "the domed house in the East."

Between the second and the third phase, the research continued. Mojica and Kantule explored the Anthropological Archives at the National Museum of the American Indian in Washington, DC. Here, they encountered "Igwanigdibippi's Map." (Igwanigdibippi is the late grandfather of José Colman; Colman will direct the

Toronto premiere of *Chocolate Woman* in 2011). In 1924, Igwanigdibippi visited the US to solicit political and military support for the Kuna people who were being oppressed by the Panamanian authorities. During that summer, at the behest of his host Richard O. Marsh, Igwanigdibippi mapped out the territory, history, cosmology, and political situation of the Kuna people (who were poised to revolt) in rich colours on a long sheet of butcher paper.

This document exemplifies the four aesthetic principles identified by Kantule in the earliest stage of *Chocolate Woman*'s development, including explicit and deliberate layering, accomplished by sewing smaller painted representations of specific histori-cal moments or contemporary events onto the larger work. Hence, it provides a perfect model of "a traditional art form adapted as a contemporary narrative" (Mojica, "Creating"). Indeed, during the third phase of investigations, conducted at the anitafrika Studio in Toronto during the first two weeks of November 2009, Igwanigdibippi's map became *the* model for script notation. Mojica abandoned the spiral notebooks in which she had originally recorded her pictographic score and began to notate the "script" on long scrolls of newsprint, which may (in some form) be layered into one or more of the *Galus* belonging to *Chocolate Woman*'s sacred topography. The third phase was concluded by an open studio during which members from the Toronto arts community were invited to observe the company's process.

Chocolate Woman Issues a Challenge…

The questions and challenges that *Chocolate Woman Dreams the Milky Way* calls forth are as complex as the work itself and the aesthetic principles that direct it. For the dra-maturg, there may be questions around script editing and privileging of (in this case) Kuna principles and cosmology over what may seem to "work" from the standpoint of a mainstream theatre professional. For instance, the story of a jealous mother, who sought to prevent her four sons from leaving her to establish families of their own by administering potions that would cause them to be repulsed by women, was (in *Chocolate Woman*'s second phase) erased from a larger creation story to tighten the narrative and quicken the pace of the scene. The origin story to which this jealous mother belongs goes on to recount how these brothers then became repulsed by their own mother, eventually isolated themselves outside of their village, and were visited by the four Daughters from the Stars, one of whom stayed behind to teach the people how to live properly and how to properly express mourning (Mojica, *Chocolate Woman*). While this omission may have "worked" from a theatrical standpoint, it compromised the spirit and intent of the original narrative. Ultimately, this jealous mother was reinstated to her rightful place in the story, because, as Kantule explained, her inclusion was necessary to place the four brothers within family (Phase Two). For a Kuna auditor, this placement is essential if one is to truly grasp the *kwage* of this foundational narrative.

Along with editing and dramaturgical challenges, this project will ultimately issue a challenge to those who receive the play. First, the publishing world: how will the "play text" ultimately manifest itself? Can/will contemporary publishers and book-sellers embrace and accommodate themselves to new formats? Then there is the challenge to audience reception. This issue has manifested itself on several occasions during the development of *Chocolate Woman*. In Toronto during an open studio at anitafrika (Phase Three), and then on 21 June 2010 during a lecture-demonstration at the Martin E. Segal Theatre Center (CUNY), several non-Native audience members expressed outrage, because they "did not understand" the work presented. As discussions progressed, it became clear that many people in the audience had come to the event with very definite ideas about what they "knew" about Native people (or what they thought they knew). These audience members wanted to see their assumptions played back to them and affirmed by Mojica's work. They had come expecting to witness a bitter testament to the "awesome" power of colonization—cut, of course, with a healthy dose of "Native humour." They did not know what to make of a piece that, in its very form and content, was powered not by the devastation wrought by the agents of colonization but by teachings and aesthetic principles emerging from cultural wellsprings absolutely *unknown* by them and absolutely uninfluenced by colonial disruption.

Apart from these challenges, this project problematizes the very infrastructure of the contemporary *theatron* itself with the presence of a physically challenged Elder on stage (See Carter, "Shaking"). The difficulties we experienced as we tried to locate and book rehearsal and performance spaces that would accommodate both the design of the production and the physical needs of a performer with limited mobility (Miguel) have certainly caused me to rethink my own hitherto unquestioning acceptance of any and all claims to building "accessibility"—at least, in Toronto. How might the physical spaces in which our stories unfold have to be reconfigured to adapt themselves to the aging body? What shifts in our own internal Gathering Houses—in our own assumptions, expectations, and attitudes—as performers, audiences, theatre operators, and funders be required in order to accommodate both the aging body and the creative and aesthetic processes that differ so markedly from the theatrical conventions, which we have come to accept as sacrosanct and inviolable?

Finally, other questions remain: will this process and its principles provide a workable processual model that may be adapted to the aesthetic principles, linguistic patterns, and cosmologies of other Indigenous nations? If so, what possibilities are contained herein? In our lifetimes, will we witness a revolutionary shift in the concept of "entertainment"? Will we witness the transfiguration of the commercial entertainment factories into spaces of healing and lasting communitas?

The *Chocolate Woman* Collective believes—as do I—that it will be so. But this new story has yet to unfold. This ancient space of happy meetings and inter-First-National exchange is a colonized space where, for far too long now, Aboriginal people have been treated as interlopers on our own lands. The physical, social, governmental, and (anti-)spiritual infrastructures of this redesigned Gathering Place contain the Aboriginal exile and direct almost every aspect of his/her life. Should the stories we tell in our Gathering House be similarly contained and directed? Should the projects we envision, nurture, and produce be initiated in response to the approbation of granting agencies or the need to attract audiences? "Bums in seats" are necessary. But in and of themselves, they are not enough. Box office receipts may sustain the corporate body (the theatre company); alone, however, they will not dislodge the dis-ease of colonization that afflicts every one of the 100,000 Aboriginal people that inhabit the "new" Gathering Place.

Elsewhere and in other realms of life, the people have awakened. Our communities are exercising their autonomy, contesting the violation of treaties, and moving towards self-governance. Our nations are reviving their languages and lifeways, re-writing their histories, and re-righting pedagogies. Here, then, in this Gathering House that we have constructed, it is not for us to cavil over what theatre *is* or *what forms it should assume*. It is fitting that a Gathering House built to serve many nations be equipped with many "rooms." In one, we may engineer bridges and broker cultural exchanges between Indigenous nations and between the Native and settler populations. In a second, we might construct platforms upon which the marginalized take centre stage to speak back to the oppressor. In a third, we might rewrite and re-right misaligned histories so that we might properly introduce ourselves to those with whom we share our lands. In another, we might grind our own lenses through which to read anew canonical Western works and interpret them with fresh eyes. In yet another, we may initiate a return home to our cultural sources and so write into being the theatrical experiences that stir recollection, that inspire hope, and that foster survivance in the spaces where many nations gather.

(2011)

Notes

[1] The *Chocolate Woman* Collective relocated to Guelph for final rehearsals, and the work-to-date was performed at the Macdonald Stewart Art Centre (University of Guelph) 21 November 2007. In this and subsequent phases of the work, I have served as company scribe: my role has been to notate text (as it was being generated) and to document the process. For spring 2011, I have accepted the position of assistant director.

[2] The primary source of these archives is Kuna tradition. The Kuna people are one of four Indigenous groups in Panama; they belong to the sovereign nation Kuna Yala, a series of islands off the coast of Panama. Each of these islands houses one community, and each is governed by its own *Sahilas* (Chiefs). At the geographic centre and spiritual heart of each island community is a Gathering House. Here, oral history and news of the day are orated by two Gathering House Chiefs, the primary orator and his respondent. As they speak, the women layer the community Story

into ornately crafted molas and men weave it into their baskets. Here, too, names are bestowed, puberty rites are celebrated, and illness is treated. The Gathering House *contains* every aspect of Kuna existence: it is the site of Kuna Story, its unfolding, its recounting, its aesthetic representation, and its communal memory.

3 For the final phase of the project, Floyd Favel will be unable to serve as director; instead, Kuna theatre practitioner José Colman will assume that role. While *Chocolate Woman*'s developmental stages are explicitly informed by Favel's "curriculum"—by the exercises that he has developed within his model for Native Performance Culture (NpC)—the process that emerges from the final developmental phase may perhaps grow into something very different.

4 Oswaldo DeLeón Kantule is the great-grandson of Nele Kantule who was one of the leaders of the Kuna uprising of 1925. In this year, the Kuna people pushed back against the oppressive Panamanian government, which outlawed Kuna customs and practices, including the wearing of traditional dress. Women who defied this ban and wore their colourful molas were jailed and physically and/or sexually assaulted by the Panamanian police. In 1925, the Kuna people, supported by the US government, staged their revolution and won their sovereignty.

Today, Kantule's father Tomàs DeLeón is a *Sahila* (Gathering House Chief) on the island of Ustupu. As a *Sahila*, this Elder carries the responsibilities of governance, passing on oral history, and bestowing names on Kuna individuals. Tomàs DeLeón is also an *Inadulele* responsible for identifying and gathering healing medicines and singing the healing chants.

Works Cited

Adams, Howard. *Tortured People: The Politics of Colonization*. Penticton: Theytus, 1999.

Bobiwash, Rodney A. "The History of Native People in the Toronto Area: A Historical Overview." Sanderson and Howard-Bobiwash 5–24.

Carter, Jill. "*Chocolate Woman* Dreams an Organic Dramaturgy: Blocking Notations for the Indigenous Soul." *Canadian Woman Studies/Les Cahiers de la Femme* 26.3, 4: 169–76.

———. "Shaking the Paluwala Tree: Fashioning Internal Gathering Houses and Refashioning the Spaces of Popular Entertainment through Contemporary Investigations into Native Performance Culture (NpC)." *alt.theatre: cultural diversity and the stage* 6.4 (2009): 8–13.

Crean, Susan. "Riel's Prophecy: The New Confidence of Aboriginal Theatre." *The Walrus* 5.3 (April 2008): 30–33.

Dempsey, Shawna. "Yvette Nolan Takes Centre Stage." *Herizons* (Fall 2009): 22–25.

Favel Starr, Floyd. "The Artificial Tree: Native Performance Culture Research, 1991–1996." *Aboriginal Drama and Theatre.* Ed. Rob Appleford. Toronto: Playwrights Canada, 2005. 69–73.

King, Thomas. *The Truth About Stories: A Native Narrative.* Toronto: House of Anansi P, 2003.

Knowles, Ric. "The Death of a Chief: Watching for Adaptation; or, How I Learned to Stop Worrying and Love the Bard." *Shakespeare Bulletin* 25.3 (2007): 53–65.

Mojica, Monique. *Chocolate Woman Dreams the Milky Way.* Play in Development. Unpublished.

———. "Creating Indigenous Dramaturgy: *Chocolate Woman Dreams the Milky Way* (Monique Mojica and Artists, Canada/US/Panama)." Martin E. Segal Theatre Center. The City University New York. 21 June 2010.

———. Personal Communication. Ongoing throughout *Chocolate Woman* project. Toronto, 2007 December 2010.

Obonsawin, Roger and Heather Howard-Bobiwash, "The Native Canadian Centre of Toronto: The Meeting Place for the Toronto Native Community for 35 Years." Sanderson and Howard-Bobiwash 25–59.

Phase One, Communication in rehearsals for *Chocolate Woman.* 5–16 November 2007 (Equity Showcase, Toronto). 19–21 November 2007 (Macdonald Stewart Art Centre, U of Guelph). Public Presentation: 21 November 2007.

Phase Two, Communication in rehearsals for *Chocolate Woman.* 16–27 March 2009 (anitafrika Studio, Toronto). Public Presentation: 27 March 2009.

Phase Three, Communication in rehearsals for *Chocolate Woman.* 3–20 November 2009 (anitafrika Studio, Toronto). Public Presentation: 20 November 2009.

Sanderson, Frances. "Introducing the 'Meeting Place.'" Sanderson and Howard-Bobiwash. 1–4.

Sanderson, Frances and Heather Howard-Bobiwash, eds. *The Meeting Place: Aboriginal Life in Toronto.* Toronto: The Native Canadian Centre, 1997.

Severi, Carlo. "Kuna Picture-Writing: A Study in Iconography and Memory." *The Art of Being Kuna: Layers of Meaning among the Kuna of Panama.* Ed. Mari Lyn Salvador. Los Angeles: UCLA Fowler Museum of Cultural History, 1997. 245–72.

Weaver, Jace. *That the People Might Live: Native American Literature and Native American Community.* New York: Oxford UP, 1997.

The Foster Children of Buddies:
Queer Women at 12 Alexander

by Moynan King

Queer women construct new performances from a sense and knowledge of difference. Over the past hundred years, the image of the lesbian woman has evolved from psychotic aberration to cultural minority, but the queer female artist is a woman always in flux. She remains "other" even within alternative and politically identified institutions such as women's theatres and gay theatres. The necessity and the compulsion to will ourselves, perform ourselves, and experiment ourselves into being makes for an exciting, changeable, and creative mode of self-presentation. Women artists in Canada embody the indomitable spirit of the artistic impulse. The drive and passion to press our desires to the surface, to resurface again and again from our marginalized and unstable positions in the arts hemisphere, is our reality and our legacy. [1]

This paper is a brief survey of the fluctuating presence and work of queer women artists at Buddies in Bad Times Theatre, North America's largest gay and lesbian theatre company, from the move to 12 Alexander Street in 1994 to the end of the 2009–2010 season. In this short history, I will highlight some of the plays and performance events created by queer women that have been instrumental in shaping the company itself and the queer community in Toronto. While a number of excellent critical essays have taken up the importance of Buddies in Toronto's alternative theatre scene and its wider cultural ecology, these works focus almost exclusively on plays staged by men and/or the artistic mandates of its highly visible male artistic directors. I want to tell a different story here, one that is perhaps more challenging to reconstruct because queer women's work often gets less press, less stage time, and less money. In writing this story, I aim to paint a fuller picture of Buddies as a centre for queer culture in Toronto and reflect upon material structures that have simultaneously contributed to the development of queer women's work and also reproduced its structural marginality.

Background

Buddies in Bad Times Theatre was founded in 1979 by Sky Gilbert as part of a group of artist-run theatre companies collectively called The Theatre Centre, which included Nightwood Theatre, Necessary Angel Theatre, AKA Performance Interface, and Theatre Autumn Leaf. In that same year, Buddies and Nightwood (Toronto's Feminist Theatre under the direction of Cynthia Grant) started the Rhubarb! Festival of new works, [2] signalling their commitment to the development of emerging artists. While the goal of Rhubarb! and the initial mandate of Buddies was to foster experimental work that challenged professional mainstream theatre, it became more politicized throughout the 1980s, particularly through its 4-Play Festival which commissioned four gay and lesbian plays. As Robert Wallace has argued, "[w]ith 4-Play, Buddies officially came out as a theatre company openly engaged in the production of work by and about lesbians and gay men" (110). In 1991, Buddies moved to the small 100-seat theatre on George Street where it established itself as an independent and definitively "queer" company. Some of the queer women's work there included plays by Marcy Rogers and Audrey (now Alec) Butler, sexually based performance events and workshops by Shannon Bell and Irene Miloslavsky, a lesbian literary salon hosted by Suzie Richter, and, within the context of Rhubarb!, the early works of emerging lesbian talents such as Ann-Marie MacDonald and Diane Flacks.

In 1994, Buddies in Bad Times Theatre moved uptown to the newly renovated theatre at 12 Alexander Street in a U-Haul containing all the worldly possessions of the company along with its small staff, big dreams, and fresh queer identity. For activists, artists, and academics in the 1990s, the word "queer" filled a semantic gap in our beds, in our bars, in our universities, and in our theatres. Queer spoke of expanding the limits of gay, bi, dyke, trans, etc., and of reclaiming a term that was previously linked to pathologization and insult. Buddies became synonymous with queer, and queer said normative and deviant be damned. Queer challenged sexual essentialism and put desire at the centre of theatrical exploration. In his "Queer Manifesto," Sky Gilbert, Buddies' founding artistic director, reflects the spirit of Buddies in his challenge to monolithic understandings of sexuality:

> There is Sex and there are Multiple Nameless Sexualities and who cares what they are called and yes contrary to Popular Opinion YOU DO HAVE A BODY AND THE TWO SPIRITED GOD WHO RUNS THIS DAMN UNIVERSE MADE IT FOR YOUR PLEASURE BECAUSE SHE'S SOMETHING OF A WHORE HERSELF. (*A Nice Place* 89).

The queer women (the lezzies, the bis, the trannies, and others) whose work intersected with Buddies in the 1990s were motivated by an urgent need to speak out of the authenticity of their lived experiences and the heat of their desires, which are the source and inspiration of their work. It is worth noting that it wasn't until 1986 that the Ontario Human Rights Code prohibited discrimination on the basis of sexual orientation. The groundswell of queer women's performance in the 1990s emerged in response to this shift in society at large, as queer women began to be seen as agents of their own destiny rather than sufferers of mental disorders. These were the days of radical queerness at Buddies, when the term "queer" meant not only flouting the norms of Toronto's "professional" theatres by turning to avant-garde methods, but also transforming the very idea of avant-garde theatre by re-imagining it as a sexual aesthetic.

Buddies' location in Toronto—social and physical—was instrumental in the development of queer women's performance work. Buddies' move to an established theatre venue in a historic building (12 Alexander had previously housed the left-wing theatre company Toronto Workshop Productions), provided a provocative and seemingly stable locus for the abandonment of heteronormativity and the emergence of a new aesthetic sensibility at the centre of the cultural discourse called queer. More importantly, Buddies' enthusiastic and explicit alignment with identity politics activism made it an attractive venue for queer female artists.

1994–1997

The move to 12 Alexandra Street portended great things for queer women's drama. At the very outset, women's drama was prominently featured in the season. Sonja Mills's *Dyke City*, staged in 1994, was the first lesbian play produced at the new venue. It was given a five-week run in the cabaret space at Buddies after a wildly successful presentation in the previous year's 4-Play Festival. Mills's play grabs lesbian stereotypes by the throat and spins them into a hilarious and subversive force. It cracks open a door on the secret society of lesbianism using an established comedic framework.

Dyke City is structured as a conventional situation comedy but with content that is pure queer. At the centre of this sitcom is Frances (played by Kathryn Haggis); she is the quintessential dyke, the dyke that embodies the messy potential of unabashed deviance. There is no straight in her, and the defiant clarity of her desires removes any conceptual haze from her identity. Frances embodies—without apology, hesitation, or shame—the type of lesbian that is not recuperable by mainstream society: a woman whose sexuality is unmediated by male desire and fantasy. Frances is joined by a cast of other characters that fill out the comic world of the play. The character of Jane (originally played by Eileen O'Toole and later replaced by Sarah Stanley) is the nice, downtrodden lesbian whose faith in serial monogamy is an exercise in serial suffering. And the character Madeline, who I played in this production, is the bisexual slut who creates conflict for her lover Frances by having sex with men. Frances would prefer a neat hermetic social world entirely populated by lesbians, yet she often finds herself dating women who either sleep with men, or eventually leave her for a man:

> My ex-lover Debra left me for a man. And Cheryl left me for a man. Katherine was fucking a man while we were together, and we were monogamous! And Debra, a different Debra, not Debra Debra, I dumped her, but she's with a man now. Faith, Alison. I've got eight or ten of them! My friends joke around with me about it sometimes. About how I am single handedly turning the dyke community into a bunch of hasbians. (Mills 5)

Mills, like other pioneers of Toronto women's queer theatre, exploited the forced and incongruous logic of comedy to challenge social structures and offer new images of women. Performer and writer Ann Holloway argues that the strength of the play can be attributed to a highly political mixing of genres: "*Dyke City* goes further than a sitcom can ever go, and this is because the more provocative style of stand-up comedy is implicitly contained within it. Frances keeps a running commentary going throughout the action—she has a metaphoric microphone in her hand when she satirizes feminist sexual politics that position the lesbian as deviant" (236). Mills's candid and unapologetic approach to sexuality can be summed up in Fran's admonition to Jane: "You can't politically correctify your feelings Janey" (Mills 9).

The first three seasons of Buddies at 12 Alexander presented a number of revolutionary plays by queer women including, also by Mills, *101 Things Lesbians do in Bed*, which frustrates the voyeuristic appeal of lesbianism by conveying instead the absurdity and monotony of domesticity; Sarah Stanley's *Gutter & Chains*, an avant-garde bathroom encounter between a fag and a dyke; and my play, *Bathory*, a darkly comic portrayal of Elizabeth Bathory, the 17th-century mass murderess inspired by the trials of Karla Homolka and society's predisposition to always see woman as a victim. *Bathory* grappled with this problem of representation and acknowledged that the route to power was paved with responsibility. It insisted on women's acceptance of our disastrous failings and our common humanity.

In addition to fostering a number of important plays by queer women, the move to Alexander Street brought several experimental performance events that helped to build a sense of queer community. One of these events was Strange Sisters, an annual lesbian cabaret extravaganza that had been running for seven years prior to the move to Alexander Street. Originally created by Suzie Richter, Alec Butler, and others, *Strange Sisters* was a Sapphic celebration which, in the true spirit of cabaret, featured a variety of different kinds of acts—everything from readings, to bands, to skits, and strippers—all by, for, and about queer women. The 1994 edition featured, among others, Diane Flacks, Jane Farrow, TJ Bryan, Carole Pope, Deb Pearce, and the inaugural performance of The Boychoir of Lesbos. The Boychoir was a group of women, dressed like an Anglican boys' choir singing a mix of traditional church music and re-arranged pop songs. Certainly, the Boychoir act was intended, at some level, as parody in the grand tradition of drag. But it was also approached as a fiercely authentic form of expression (and we could actually sing!). As Boychoir founder Tristan Whiston put it:

> We took it very seriously once we went into rehearsal or into performance. We got into character and the "boys" did not know what was funny—we never tried to "be" funny—we tried to be serious and the more serious we were the funnier it was. At some point our boy characters merged—we all had boy names and characters and I think we all just enjoyed letting them out to play. (Personal Interview)

This simultaneous interplay of performativity and performance, embodied in Whiston's idea of "letting them out to play," is a definitive quality of queer women's representations of self on stage and in everyday life. Nina Rapi in *Acts of Passion* asks: "Is 'the real' any more real than its representation? Real to whom? The writer, the performer, those represented, or the audience? Can fantasy be said to be more real than reality, especially when it is repeatedly and ritualistically enacted in everyday situations, for example, with the masquerade of femininity" (1). For some members of the Boychoir, most notably its Head Boy, Tristan Whiston, the culturally sanctioned imperative of femininity imposed on the female body was more fantastical—less real—than the manicured image of an Anglican choirboy with his neat short haircut and uniform robe.

Queer events at Buddies in this era had a significant impact on the men and women who attached themselves to this identity and had the effect of bringing them together as a more complex and expansive community. Inspired by this, the new location of Buddies uptown, and the absence of local performance events during Toronto Pride,[3] I created something called Cheap Queers, a three day pre-Pride event featuring over 50 queer and queer-friendly performers. The event was organized collaboratively by members of the queer community, who came together to form the collective, the Hardworkin' Homosexuals. Mariko Tamaki recounts her experience:

> Clearly, while other events had given me a safe space to perform, Cheap Queers, a carnival of chaos, had given me a challenge. The result was the difference between getting applause, which means only, really, that you've finished reading, and getting a loud, rip roaring Cheap Queers' audience bellow of appreciation, which means you've succeeded, which means you've survived... And watching the riotous applause that was earned by fellow performers, who took the stage to let loose a variety of queer apparitions [made] me want to push the bar, to experiment... (273).

The conceptual identity of *being* a Cheap Queer is now imbedded in the Toronto performance community. The event was part of a burgeoning queer performance culture that would develop over the next few years and include the emergence of groups such as the Greater Toronto Drag King Society (founded by Joy LaChica and Rose Perry), Pretty Porky and Pissed Off (founded by Allyson Mitchell, Mariko Tamaki, and others), and popular dyke comedians Elvira Kurt and Maggie Casella. The irreverent and diverse performances of these and other artists suggested that queer women were not so much seeking the traditional "safe" space of feminist performance, where a shared political viewpoint is often required, but rather a risky space, a space for real experimentation and self-expression, where debate is encouraged and differing views are expressed loudly and without timidity.

The women at Buddies contributed to the construction of the meaning of queer through their performances both on and off stage. From Deb Pearce's Mann Murray, a female to female drag act that parodied the feminine masquerade, to Suzie Richter's act of sporting a five o'clock shadow at the No Frills, queer women found multiple sites and styles for questioning gender essentialism.

1997–2002

In 1997 Buddies in Bad Times went through a major administrative shift. For a good read on these events and times, I refer you to Sky Gilbert's *Ejaculations from the Charm Factory* (255–71). The short version is that Sky, along with General Manager Tim

Jones, left Buddies, and Sarah Stanley, who had been appointed artistic director, took over the reins of the financially troubled and administratively traumatized company.

Sarah's term as artistic director was short (1997–1999) and plagued with financial stress. A few notable plays by queer women were presented at Buddies during her tenure, including Diane Flacks's *Random Acts* (1997), the hilarious, touching, and virtuoso one-woman play about chaos, order, and the uncanny interconnectedness of all things, and Rose Cullis's *Baal* (produced by Mercury Theatre, 1998), inspired by Brecht's play of the same name, about the life and times of a lesbian rock 'n roll singer who pursues a fierce and lawless independence. By and large, however, locally grown women's performance did not fare well, and it was often marginalized in relation to mainstage shows written by men. Most queer women's work came in the form of rentals (*Baal* and Savoy Howe's *Doohmanow: Looking for a Fight*, 1998), co-productions (*Random Acts*), and one-off events such as Strange Sisters, a reading by international literary superstar Jeanette Winterson, and Carole Pope's *Diva Show*. Sonja Mills's *Dyke City*, which grew to a nine-part series, continued through to 1999, but now, rather than being presented as plays with substantial runs, they were presented as one-time only events—low-budget, high-return productions in the main space. The creators and performers were paid next to nothing and the shows were presented only once to as many people as could be packed into the theatre.

The financial stress of the late 1990s created an inadvertent alteration of the production mandate and methodology at Buddies. Women's work was now sometimes developed—but rarely fully produced—by the company as it had been previously in Sky's model. And when Sarah left the company and was replaced by David Oiye as artistic director, there were no longer any women employed in an artistic capacity at the company. As Buddies stepped into the new millennium, the representation of queer women at the theatre had become an arm's-length affair and, by then, the company had weakened its vital connection to the more innovative queer women's performance practices.

This period did see the continuation of Strange Sisters (Cheap Queers by now had moved to a venue in the west end of Toronto), the production of a gay musical, *When We Were Singing*, by Dorothy Dietrich from Vancouver, and the presentation of *Frankie*, Mary Ellen MacLean's one-woman show from Halifax. In 2002, Jim LeFrancois was appointed artistic producer and a shift in mandate and methodology began. At this point, the Scandelles, headed by Sasha Von Bon Bon and Kitty Neptune, forged a strong partnership with the company, producing their own brand of burlesque, which inflected the aesthetics of the traditional form (social satire, bawdy humour, striptease) with an experimental queer sensibility. In their words, "Think Hedwig meets Showgirls meets the Dadaists—with a pinch of Carol Burnett" (Scandelles). This association would span the next eight years and see the development of a number of full-length burlesque style shows including *Under the Mink* (2007), *Who's Your Dada* (2008), and *Neon Nightz* (2009).

2003–2010

In 2003, I was invited to join the company as Associate Artist. My job was to reconnect the queer women's performance community and its audience with the theatre. I felt that the best way to start rebuilding these bridges was to create a new model for the presentation of queer women's performance, a model that was as experimental, expansive, and as inclusive as the practices of the artists it would present.

That was the basic premise with which I entered my new contract and approached the creation of Hysteria: A Festival of Women, which became an important venue for the presentation of performance work by queer women artists from Toronto and throughout Canada. The idea was to create a forum for the exchange of ideas and art, to both support and showcase women artists. For Buddies, it meant generating a hub of queer women's performance from which they could draw when developing material for mainstage productions.

Buddies and Nightwood had come together to create a women's theatre festival. My vision insisted on a multi-disciplinary format that responded to the work and needs of female artists. Performance practice was changing along with the queer community. Gender identities had continued to shift along with the growing spirit of queer culture, which now embraced transsexual and transgendered identities as distinct and significant gender categories. These developments were taking place alongside the advent of new and accessible technologies, which in turn were shaping the growth of multi-disciplinary and interdisciplinary practices. All of these cultural and aesthetic changes were at the centre of the work that was being developed in Hysteria. In selecting and curating material for the festival, we understood that between the fully-realized play and the five-minute cabaret act there was a whole world of performance potential. In creating a structure for a festival that wanted to open up, rather than dictate, what could be understood as theatre, we (co-festival directors Kelly Thornton and I) took a long look at the work we saw emerging in the women's performance community and let that inform the shape and feel of the festival. Performance spots ran anywhere from three minutes to six hours and they opened uncharted spaces within Buddies' programming, as well as within the physical space of the theatre itself.

Originally produced in conjunction with Nightwood Theatre (they dropped out of the project in 2004),[4] the Hysteria festival aimed to address the scarcity of women's work on Toronto stages (and Buddies' stage more specifically). Ironically, however, the festival has both ameliorated and compounded the problem by creating the optics of supporting and developing a vast amount of women's work without spending much money on each production and without giving these artists any time or space for development.[5] Nonetheless, Hysteria created a unique environment for generating multiple representations of "woman."[6] The first call for submissions to the 2003 festival resulted in over three hundred artist submissions. This is a remarkable figure that demonstrates the formidable presence of women in the arts despite minimal opportunities provided to women within the funded arts organizations.

In its five installments over six years (2003–2009) the festival saw an explosion of work by women. In *Sex Addicts and Home Repairs*, Dayna McLeod played a live host interacting with pre-recorded characters in a parodic subversion of reality TV. My collaboration with Trixie and Beever led to the creation of *Walk-In Clinic*, a performance installation dedicated to the treatment of the effects of feminist rage, which put the audience at the centre of the work and explored the performative nature of healing. Edwige Jean-Pierre launched her Toronto performance career through Hysteria with her darkly comic, off-beat monologues *Even Darkness* and *Lick and Seal*. Rhoma Spencer brought us an insightful, historical glimpse of Mary Fields in *Two Gun Mary*, based on the true story of a 19th-century slave girl who defied her social and gender status with her unique (and well-armed) rise to fame in a white man's world. And Lesbians On Ecstasy, the Montreal-based rock band, gave us the workshop presentation of their groundbreaking new rock opera *Amphitheatre of Homosexuality*. These examples represent a mere suggestion of the over one hundred queer women's performances that took the stage at Buddies during the first five installments of Hysteria. The bonds forged at the festival often created opportunities, networks, and new partnerships for its artists. Many artists represented at Hysteria went on to perform at other events including festivals in Toronto, Montreal, Winnipeg, and New York. Hysteria was also instrumental in developing several shows that were subsequently presented on their own at Buddies. These include: Ann Holloway's *Kinstonia: Dialect Perverso*, the Scandelles's *Under the Mink* (2007), d'bi young's *organ-eye-zed crime* (2006), Nathalie Claude's *The Salon Automaton: a play for three automatons and one flesh and blood actress* (2009), and my full-scale interactive performance installation *The Beauty Salon* (2008). Ivan Coyote's *You Are Here* was originally scheduled for a cabaret run in 2009 but was cancelled in the January of that year.[7]

Hysteria, the female malady, is a condition about which everything (and nothing) has been said. The body of the hysteric is a question to which there is no adequate answer. She never "is"; she is in the process of always becoming. Hysteria is also a word used to express the ways in which females do not behave properly. In the spirit of reclaiming the hysteric's embrace of self-invention and female disobedience, Hysteria gave the stage a veritable flood of images, images that expressed the queer body-in-process and asked questions about the historical silences surrounding those bodies.

Over the past decade, Buddies has been a catalyst for queer women's performance activity in Toronto. It is interesting to note, however, that most of these shows have been presented within festivals like Rhubarb!—e.g., Hope Thompson's *Green* (2004) and *Hospital Green* (2005), queer adaptations of the femme fatale of film noir, and Lex Vaughn's *Graham and Diane*, a comic exploration of the split personality of a closeted lesbian and her hypersexual ventriloquist's dummy (2009)—or as one-off events like *Anne Made Me Gay* (2008), a homage to the ginger-bushed islander on her 100th anniversary.

The 2009–2010 season brought a bold interruption to the history of programming at Buddies with the presentation of an almost exclusively female season. The Scandelles, who had been presenting their work regularly at 12 Alexander for the previous eight years (often self-producing), were given the coveted season opening slot for a full production of their show *Neon Nightz*, and Nathalie Claude's *The Salon Automaton* was translated and presented in association with Momentum Theatre from Montreal. The impetus behind this women's focused programming came from a desire to address historical inequities brought to light by the Canada Council for the Arts report "Adding it Up: The Status of Women in Canadian Theatre," [8] which showed that the vast majority of the plays appearing on the Canadian stage are written by men. However the placement of this season between artistic directorships at Buddies (and therefore between artistic visions for the company) marks it as an interruption rather than a sign of more significant changes to the theatre's mandate. By the beginning of this transitional season, Artistic Director David Oiye had left the company and at mid-season Brendan Healy took over as incoming artistic director. Interestingly, women's theatre productions provided a much-needed stopgap as the company, at the end of the 2008–2009 season, had found itself, once again, financially and administratively challenged.

When the 2009 Hysteria festival was over, my contract with Buddies ended. The future of Hysteria is uncertain at this point. Looking at the 2010–2011 season, the first under the artistic directorship of Healy, the prospects for performance by women "look" good as the season features two major shows by Canadian women playwrights. But if you pay close attention to the description of the season line-up, you'll notice that the company has produced an optics of equal representation without necessarily supplying the requisite financial support. On its website, Buddies states that it "welcomes" Sonja Mills's *The Birds* (i.e., it is a rental not receiving any financial or developmental support from the company) and "presents" Evalyn Parry's *Spin* in association with Outspoke Productions (which in this case means a generous in-kind contribution of space, publicity, and production crew but the artist is otherwise responsible for securing her own funding) (Buddies in Bad Times, "Season"). As critics attempt to come to terms with the history and future of women's representation on stage, this material context is too important to be ignored. All too often, women are content to bear the costs of their own productions while propping up the illusion that their work is being fully supported. Only time will tell whether this practice will continue at Buddies, or whether we will see a fuller commitment (in space, time, and resources) to women's work at the theatre.

Looking forward

Jess Dobkin's *Everything I've Got*, recently presented at Buddies' Rhubarb! Festival (2010), embodies and sums up a number of the particular challenges and opportunities encountered by queer women today as they make and perform work in Toronto. The queer body, and in particular Jess's body, is the primary site of investigation in this work: her body is the stage. As audience members, we watch her rigorously investigate what can be put into the body (dildos, butt plugs, googly eyes, or a second head) and what comes out of it (saliva, babies, props, blood, or clowns). On one level, Jess's inquiry illustrates the spirit of experimentation and self-invention that is present in the queer women's performances that have taken place at Buddies since its inception. Like the performers that came before her, Jess is fearless in testing out the boundaries of artistic creation, even the most private boundaries of the body. Yet we can also see in this same investigation urgent questions arising about the bounded spaces of women's artistic creation. She is literally giving us "everything she's got," a powerful exploration of the artist's lived experience of "too many ideas and not enough time." Could her examination of too many ideas and not enough time be read as an extension of the 300+ women who are clamouring to get into Hysteria and other festivals like it—in other words, those women who are competing against one another for the increasingly scarce resources of time and space in which to perform? In this sense, Jess's piece could be said to talk back to the marginalization of queer women's work. "If a performance falls in the forest," she asks, "…does it count" (Dobkin 10). Certainly the very history of the staging of Jess's show at Buddies—originally scheduled to be produced in the mainstage season and then diverted at the last minute into Rhubarb!—raises questions about the centrality of women's work in the company's mandate when it is so easily programmed or reprogrammed into low profile (and less desirable) season slots. I have entitled this paper "The Foster Children of Buddies," not because I think that queer women's work is less loved than that of its male counterparts, but to emphasize the fact that its structural marginality, it's changeable and temporary place in the house that is 12 Alexander, is an important part of its ongoing reality and its legacy.

Perhaps there are no obvious answers to these systemic problems and thinking through these issues is made all the more complicated by the fact that many women have played and continue to play roles in shaping the programming of theatres like Buddies. Still, it is time that we ask: what do theatres need to do to ensure that women's work is not marginalized, or more importantly, viewed as easily marginalizable—the kind of work that can take up less space and be produced for less pay? How can artistic directors and theatre administrators acknowledge these material structures and rethink queer women's position within them? To answer these questions, we must draw strength from the legacy of performers who have come before, driving their desires to the surface despite their marginalized and unstable positions in the art hemisphere and fearlessly assuming positions of power on stages like the one they helped forge at Buddies.

(2011)

Notes

1   This legacy will be explored further in a forthcoming issue of *Canadian Theatre Review*, to be published in winter 2012, which will focus on queer women's performance.

2   For more information on the emergence and development of Rhubarb!, along with selected texts from the festival from 1979–1998, see Boni.

3   The absence of local performance events at Toronto Pride 1994 is hard to imagine in 2010 when Pride lasts ten days and performance events are many and varied, including drag shows, community celebrations, large cabaret events, queer youth presentations, and performative dyke activism (e.g., the 2010 *Take Back the Dyke* event organized by Jess Dobkin and Alex Tigchelaar).

4   Nightwood left the festival because it felt that it overtaxed the small company's resources and the company was in the process of streamlining its mandate.

5   Hysteria festival artists were paid an honorarium. They did not rehearse or develop the work in the space outside of a very limited tech rehearsal on the day of their performance.

6   Since its inception in 1996, the Edgy Women Festival in Montreal (founded by Miriam Ginestier) has been another active site for developing multidisciplinary women's performance work and queer representations of women. Edgy Women is a smaller festival presented annually at a variety of venues.

7   Ivan Coyote's show was scheduled for a two-week run in the spring of 2009 but was cancelled because of financial difficulty. Coyote's show was not the only one cancelled that season; the final production of Ed Roy's *Gay for Pay* also fell prey to this reduction in programming, but *You are Here* was the only lesbian show scheduled that season outside the cabarets and one-off performance events, and it was hardly a big budget affair with only two performers and fairly basic technical demands.

8   For the full report see Burton.

Works Cited

Boni, Franco, ed. *Rhubarb-O-Rama*. Winnipeg: Blizzard, 1998.

Buddies in Bad Times Theatre. "Season Overview." 14 December 2010. http://www.buddiesinbadtimes.com/season.cfm.

Burton, Rebecca. "Adding It Up—The Status of Women in Canadian Theatre: A Report on the Phase One Findings of Equity in Canadian Theatre: The Women's Initiative." October 2006. *Professional Association of Canadian Theatres*. 26 October 2006. 14 December 2010. www.playwrightsguild.ca/pgc/news_docs/womens.pdf.

Dobkin, Jess. *Everything I've Got*. Unpublished, 2010.

Gilbert, Sky. *Ejaculations from the Charm Factory*. Toronto: ECW, 2000.

———. *A Nice Place to Visit*. Toronto: ECW, 2009.

Holloway, Ann. "Potluck Feminism—Where's the Meat": Sonja Mills's Comedy of Resistance." *Queer Theatre in Canada*. Ed. Rosalind Kerr. Toronto: Playwrights Canada, 2007. 232–37.

Mills, Sonja. *Dyke City*. Unpublished, 1994.

Rapi, Nina. "Introduction." *Acts of Passion*. Ed. Nina Rapi and Maya Chowdhry. Binghamton, NY: Haworth P, 1998. 1–8.

Tamaki, Mariko. "Cheap Queers." *Queer Theatre in Canada*. Ed. Rosalind Kerr. Toronto: Playwrights Canada, 2007: 271–74.

Scandelles, The. "About Us." *The Scandelles*. 14 November 2010. http://www.thescandelles.com/aboutus.htm.

Wallace, Robert. "Theorizing a Queer Theatre: Buddies in Bad Times." *Contemporary Issues in Canadian Drama*. Ed. Per Brask. Winnipeg: Blizzard, 1995. 136–59.

Whiston, Tristan. Personal Interview. 4 October 2010.

Suggested Further Reading

Akin, Philip, Nina Lee Aquino, Ric Knowles, Holly Lewis, and Yvette Nolan. "Cultural Exchange/Theatrical Practice: Five Questions from FOOT." *alt theatre: cultural diversity and the stage* 6.1 (2008): 18–27.

Aquino, Nina Lee. Interview with Ric Knowles. "'Between Home There and Home Here': An Interview with Nina Lee Aquino." *Canadian Theatre Review* 125 (2006): 75–82.

Bain, Alison. "Creativ* Suburbs: Cultural 'Popcorn' Pioneering in Multi-purpose Spaces." Edensor et al. 63–74.

Beaupre, Therese. "Video Cabaret: Form as Protest." *Canadian Theatre Review* 26 (1980): 44–57.

Boni, Franco, ed. *Rhubarb-O-Rama! Plays and Playwrights from the Rhubarb Festival*. Toronto: Blizzard, 1998.

Boyd, Shaun Ray and Sarah B. Hood (with Jean Yoon, Lonette McKee, Jason Sherman, and Colin Taylor). "The Voyage of *Show Boat*." *Theatrum* 35 (1993): 18–24.

Breon, Robin. "Noises Off-Right: Theatre in the Toronto Region." *Canadian Theatre Review* 93 (1997): 16–26.

———. "'Show Boat': The Past Revisits the Present." *Canadian Theatre Review* 79/80 (1994): 70–79.

Bryden, Ronald. "Toronto Theatre: *Mademoiselle est Partie*." *Canadian Forum* (August 1978): 7–11.

Burgess, David. "When Cowboys are Ranchers." *Canadian Theatre Review* 51 (Summer 1987): 36–43.

Burrows, Malcolm. "Marketing the Megahits." *Canadian Theatre Review* 61 (1989): 5–12.

Card, Raymond. "Drama in Toronto: The Forgotten Years 1919–1939." *The English Quarterly* 6.1 (1973): 67–81.

Carson, Neil. *Harlequin in Hogtown: George Luscombe and Toronto Workshop Productions*. Toronto: U of Toronto P, 1995.

Carter, Jill. "Shaking the Paluwala Tree: Fashioning Internal Gathering Houses and Re-Fashioning the Spaces of Popular Entertainment through Contemporary

Investigations into 'Native Performance Culture (NpC).'" *alt.theatre: cultural diversity and the stage* 6.4 (2009): 8–13.

———. "Writing, Righting, 'Riting': The Scrubbing Project Re-members a New 'Nation' and Reconfigures Ancient Ties." *alt.theatre: cultural diversity and the stage* 4.4 (2006): 13–17.

Cashman, Cheryl. "Toronto's Zanies." *Canadian Theatre Review* 67 (1991): 22–31.

Doyle-Marshall, William. "Obsidian Theatre: Regathering the Diaspora." *Performing Arts & Entertainment in Canada* 33.2 (2000): 35–38.

Duchesne, Scott. "'A Golf Club for the Golden Age': English Canadian Theatre Historiography and the Strange Case of Roy Mitchell." *Theatre Research in Canada* 18.2 (1997): 131–47.

Eaket, Chris. "Project [murmur] and the Performativity of Space." *Theatre Research in Canada* 29.1 (2008): 29–50.

Edensor, Tim, Deborah Leslie, Steve Millington, and Norma Rantisi, eds. *Spaces of Vernacular Creativity: Rethinking the Cultural Economy.* New York: Routledge, 2009.

Filewod, Alan. *Collective Encounters: Documentary Theatre in English Canada.* U of Toronto P, 1987.

———. "Performing a People's Canada: Theatrical Radicalism in the 1950s." *Essays in Theatre* 21.1 & 2 (2002–03): 99–118.

———. "Receiving Aboriginality: Tomson Highway and the Crisis of Cultural Authenticity." *Theatre Journal* 46.3 (1994): 363–73.

———. "The Spectacular Nation of Garth Drabinsky." *Performing Canada: The Nation Enacted in the Imagined Theatre.* Kamloops: U College of the Cariboo, 2002. 83–100.

Friedlander, Mira. "Growing Pains: The Changing Face of Toronto Theatre." *Theatrum Magazine* (February/March 1995): 14–17.

Gallagher, Kathleen. *The Theatre of Urban: Youth and Schooling in Dangerous Times.* Toronto: U of Toronto P, 2007.

Gass, Ken, "Toronto's Alternates: Changing Realities." *Canadian Theatre Review* 21 (1979): 127–35.

Gaysek, Fred. "Celebrating Shadowland." *Canadian Theatre Review* 58 (1989): 21–26.

Gilbert, Sky. *Ejaculations from the Charm Factory.* Toronto: ECW, 2000.

———. "Inside the Rhubarb! Festival." *Canadian Theatre Review* 49 (1986): 40.

Householder, Johanna and Tanya Mars. *Caught in the Act: An Anthology of Performance Art by Canadian Women.* Toronto: YYZ, 2004.

Illidge, Paul. *The Glass Cage: The Crest Theatre Story.* Toronto: McArthur, 2004.

Gómez, Mayte. "'Coming Together' in Lift Off! '93: Intercultural Theatre in Toronto and Canadian Multiculturalism." Knowles and Mündel 30–43.

———. "Healing the Border Wound: *Fronteras Americanas* and the Future of Canadian Multiculturalism." McKinnie, *Space* 91–123.

Grant, Cynthia. "Notes from the Front Line." *Canadian Theatre Review* 43 (1985): 44–51.

Hadfield, D.A. *Re: Producing Women's Dramatic History: The Politics of Playing in Toronto.* Vancouver: Talonbooks, 2007.

Hale, Amanda. "Ballrooms and Boardroom Tables." *Canadian Theatre Review* 53 (1987): 29–32.

Halferty, J. Paul. "Queer and Now: The Queer Signifier at Buddies in Bad Times Theatre." *Theatre Research in Canada* 27.1 (2006): 123–54.

Henry, Jeff. "Black Theatre in Montreal and Toronto in the Sixties and Seventies: The Struggle for Recognition." *Canadian Theatre Review* 118 (2004): 29–33.

Houston, Andrew. "An Environmental Engagement with Theatre and Life: An Interview with Richard Rose." *Canadian Theatre Review* 126 (2006): 53–57.

Hubbard, Lorraine D. "Black Theatre Canada: A Decade of Struggle." *Polyphony* 5.2 (1983): 57–66.

Jackson, Peter. "The Politics of the Streets: a Geography of Caribana." *Political Geography* 11.2 (1992): 130–51.

James, Sheila. "South Asian Women: Creating Theatre of Resilience and Resistance." *Canadian Theatre Review* 94 (1998): 45–54.

Johnston, Denis W. *Up The Mainstream: The Rise of Toronto's Alternative Theatres, 1968–1975.* Toronto: U of Toronto P, 1991.

Johnston, Kirsty. "Performing an Asylum: *Tripping Time* and *La Pazzia*." *Theatre Topics* 18.1 (2008): 55–67.

Kareda, Urjo. Interview by Deborah Cottreau. "Writing for a Playwright's Theatre: Urjo Kareda on dramaturgy at Tarragon." *Canadian Theatre Review* 87 (1996): 5–8.

Kinch, Martin. "Canadian Theatre: In For the Long Haul." *This Magazine* 10.5–6 (November–December 1976): 3–8.

Knowles, Ric. "Performing Intercultural Memory in the Diasporic Present: The Case of Toronto." Knowles and Mündel 167–83.

———. "Reading Material: Transfers, Remounts, and the Production of Meaning in Contemporary Toronto Drama and Theatre." McKinnie, *Space* 59–90.

———. *Reading the Material Theatre.* Cambridge: Cambridge UP, 2004. 129–47.

———. "Red Sky, Native Earth: Performing Toronto's 'Indian diaspora.'" *Essays in Theatre* 21.1 & 2 (2002): 119–40.

Knowles, Ric and Ingrid Mündel, eds. *"Ethnic," Multicultural, and Intercultural Theatre.* Toronto: Playwrights Canada, 2009.

Knowles, Ric and Jennifer Fletcher. "Towards a Materialist Performance Analysis: The Case of Tarragon Theatre." *The Performance Text.* Ed. Domenico Pietropaolo. Toronto: Legas, 1999. 205–26.

Koustas, Jane. "From 'Homespun' to 'Awesome': Translated Quebec Theatre in Toronto." *Essays on Modern Quebec Theatre.* Ed. Joseph Donahue Jr. and Jonathan Weiss. East Lansing: Michigan State UP, 81–107.

Levin, Laura. "TO Live with Culture: Torontopia and the Urban Creativity Script." McKinnie, *Space* 201–17.

Levin, Laura and Kim Solga. "Zombies in Condoland." *Canadian Theatre Review* 138 (2009): 48–52.

Mallet, Gina. "The St. Lawrence Centre: Toronto's Persistent Problem." Wallace, *Toronto* 25–32.

McKinnie, Michael. *City Stages: Theatre and Urban Space in a Global City.* Toronto: U of Toronto P, 2007.

———, ed. *Space and the Geographies of Theatre.* Toronto: Playwrights Canada, 2007.

McClean, Heather. "The Politics of Creative Performance in Public Space: Towards a Critical Geography of Toronto Case Studies." Edensor et al. 200–13.

O'Donnell, Darren. *Social Acupuncture: A guide to suicide, performance and utopia.* Toronto: Coach House, 2006.

Philip, M. NourbeSe. *Showing Grit: Showboating North of the 44th Parallel.* Toronto: Poui, 1993.

Rubin, Don, ed. *Canadian Theatre History: Selected Readings.* Toronto: Playwrights Canada, 2004.

———. "Sleepy Tunes in Toronto." *Canadian Theatre Review* 20 (1978): 93–95.

———. "The Toronto Movement." Wallace, *Toronto* 8–17.

Rudakoff, Judith, ed. *Dangerous Traditions: A Passe Muraille Anthology.* Winnipeg: Blizzard, 1992.

Saddlemyer, Ann and Richard Plant, eds. *Later Stages: Essays in Ontario Theatre from World War I to the 1970s.* Toronto: U of Toronto P, 1997.

Scott, Shelley. *Nightwood Theatre: A Woman's Work is Always Done.* Edmonton: Athabasca UP, 2010.

Shiller, Romy. "Drag King Invasion: Taking Back the Throne." *Canadian Theatre Review* 86 (1996): 24–28.

Smith, Patricia Keeney. "Living With Risk: Toronto's New Alternate Theatre." Wallace, *Toronto* 33–52.

Souchotte, Sandra. "Toronto Free Theatre." *Canadian Theatre Review* 14 (1977): 33–38.

Stuart, Ross. "A Circle Without a Centre: The Predicament of Toronto's Theatre Space." Wallace, *Toronto* 18–32.

Tator, Carol, Frances Henry, and Winston Mattis. *Challenging Racism in the Arts.* Toronto: U of Toronto P, 1998.

Usmiani, Renate. *Second Stage: The Alternative Theatre Movement in Canada.* Vancouver: U of British Columbia P, 1983.

Verdecchia, Guillermo. "*Léo* at the Tarragon: Naturalizing the Coup." *Theatre Research in Canada* 30.1–2 (2009): 111–28.

———. "Seven Things About Cahoots Theatre Projects." Knowles and Mündel 106–14.

Wagner, Anton, ed. *Establishing Our Boundaries: English-Canadian Theatre Criticism.* U of Toronto P, 1999.

Walden, Keith. *Becoming Modern in Toronto: The Industrial Exhibition and the Shaping of Late Victorian Culture.* Toronto: U of Toronto P, 1997.

Wallace, Robert, ed. *Producing Marginality: Theatre and Criticism in Canada.* Saskatoon: Fifth House, 1990.

———. "Survival Tactics: Size, Space and Subjectivity in Recent Toronto Theatre." *Essays in Theatre* 10.1 (1991): 5–15.

———. "Theorizing a Queer Theatre: Buddies in Bad Times." McKinnie, *Space* 104–23.

———. *Toronto Theatre Today. Canadian Theatre Review* 38 (1983).

Wilcox, Alana and Jason McBride, eds. *uTOpia: Towards a New Toronto.* Toronto: Coach House, 2005.

Wilcox, Alana, Christina Palassio and Johnny Dovercourt, eds. *The State of the Arts: Living with Culture in Toronto.* Toronto: Coach House, 2006.

Wilson, Ann. "Reaching Out: Soulpepper, Youth and the 'Classics.'" *Canadian Theatre Review* 106 (2001): 29.

Yoon, Jean. "Chinese Theatre in Canada: The Bigger Picture." Knowles and Mündel 94–103.

Notes on Contributors

Susan Bennett is University Professor in the Department of English at the University of Calgary. Her essay, "Toronto's Spectacular Stage," was originally prepared as a research contribution to the multidisciplinary "Culture of Cities" project investigating Toronto, Montreal, Dublin, and Berlin, based at York University from 2000–2006.

Jill Carter (Anishinaabe/Ashkenazi) is an avid theatre practitioner who has worked as a performer, director, dramaturg, and instructor for almost two decades. She is a recent alumna of the Graduate Centre for Study of Drama at the University of Toronto where she has just completed her doctorate. Currently, she teaches in the Aboriginal Studies Department and the Transitional Year Programme at the University of Toronto.

Alan Filewod is Professor of Theatre Studies at the University of Guelph. His books include *Collective Encounters: Documentary Theatre in English Canada* (1987), *Performing "Canada": The Nation Enacted in the Imagined Theatre* (2002), and, with David Watt, *Workers' Playtime: Theatre and the Labour Movement since 1970* (2001), and the forthcoming (2012) *Eight Men Speak: A Critical Edition.*

Amanda Hale is a writer and educator who divides her time between Toronto and British Columbia. She worked in Toronto theatre during the 1980s and co-founded the Company of Sirens. Her fourth novel will be published in Spring 2011. Currently she teaches creative writing at University of Toronto Continuing Ed. www.amanda-hale.com.

Moynan King is an award-winning theatre and performance artist. She is the author of five plays and, as an actor, has more than forty professional film, theatre, and TV credits. Her solo and collaborative performance works have been presented across Canada and the US. She was an Associate Artist at Buddies from 2003–2009.

Ric Knowles is Professor of Theatre Studies at the University of Guelph. His most recent authored book is *Theatre & Interculturalism* (Palgrave, 2010). He is general editor of Critical Perspectives on Canadian Theatre in English, and in 2009 was awarded the Excellence in Editing: Sustained Achievement award by the Association for Theatre in Higher Education. He also works professionally as a dramaturge. His current scholarly and professional work focuses on intercultural performance.

Laura Levin is Associate Professor of Theatre at York University. She is the editor of *Conversations Across Borders* (Seagull) and *Theatre and Performance in Toronto* (Playwrights Canada). She has published several essays on contemporary theatre and performance art, with a focus on performing gender and sexuality and site-specific and urban performance.

Michael McKinnie teaches at Queen Mary, University of London. His publications include *City Stages: Theatre and Urban Space in a Global City* (University of Toronto Press, awarded the Ann Saddlemyer Award by the Canadian Association for Theatre Research) and, as editor, *Space and the Geographies of Theatre* (Playwrights Canada).

M. NourbeSe Philip is an award-winning poet, essayist, novelist, and playwright who lives in the space-time of the city of Toronto. She has published five books of poetry, one novel, and three collections of essays. Her most recent work, *Zong!*, is a book-length poem which engages with ideas of the law, history, and memory.

Kim Solga is Associate Professor in the Department of English at the University of Western Ontario. She is the author of *Violence Against Women in Early Modern Performance* and co-editor of *Performance and the City*, both from Palgrave (2009).

After receiving an MA from the University of Toronto and working as a theatre reviewer and freelance writer, **Sandra Souchotte Ketchum** moved to Yellowknife where she worked for CBC North radio and served as a northern correspondent for *Maclean's Magazine*. She moved to Ottawa in 1986 and started a twenty-two-year career with the federal public service and was Director of Communications for several government departments.

Renate Usmiani was born in Vienna, and obtained her graduate degree from Harvard. She has taught at Dalhousie University and, Mount St. Vincent University, Halifax, where she is Professor Emeritus. Her publications include half a dozen books and innumerable articles on Canadian and European drama. She retired in 1996.

Robert Wallace is Professor Emeritus of English and Drama Studies at Glendon College, York University. He is author of *Staging a Nation: Evolutions in Contemporary Canadian Theatre* (2003), *Theatre and Transformation in Contemporary Canada* (1999), and *Producing Marginality: Theatre and Criticism in Canada* (1990); co-author of *The Work: Conversations with English-Canadian Playwrights* (1981); editor of *Quebec Voices* (1986) and *Making Out: Plays by Gay Men* (1992).

J. Chris Westgate is Assistant Professor of English at California State University, Fullerton. He is the author of *Urban Drama: The Metropolis in Contemporary North American Plays*, in-press with Palgrave Macmillan, and articles in *Modern Drama*, *Theatre Journal*, and *Comparative Drama*; and editor of *Brecht, Broadway, and United States Theatre*.